The Johnson Years, Volume One

The Johnson Years, Volume One

Foreign Policy, the Great Society, and the White House

Edited by Robert A. Divine

University Press of Kansas

First paperback edition published in 1987 by the University Press of Kansas
(Lawrence, Kansas 66045), which was organized by the Kansas Board of Re-
gents and is operated and funded by Emporia State University, Fort Hays
State University, Kansas State University, Pittsburg State University, the
University of Kansas, and Wichita State University

Originally published as *Exploring the Johnson Years*, this edition appears by
exclusive arrangement with the University of Texas Press.

Library of Congress Cataloging-in-Publication Data
The Johnson years.
   Contents: v. 1. Foreign policy, the Great Society, and
the White House.
   1. Lyndon Baines Johnson Library. 2. United States—
Politics and government—1963–1969—Sources—Bibliog-
raphy. 3. United States—Foreign relations—1963–1969—
Sources—Bibliography. I. Divine, Robert A.
E838.5.J644   1987   973.923   86-32443
ISBN 0-7006-0326-3 (pbk.: v. 1)

British Library Cataloging in Publication Data is available.

Printed in the United States of America
10 9 8 7 6 5 4 3 2

Preface to the Paperback Edition

"It is all here: the story of our time—with the bark off," Lyndon Johnson declared at the dedication of his library in Austin, Texas, in May 1971. "We have papers from forty years of public service in one place for friend or foe to judge, to approve or disapprove." At first, access to the papers was difficult, as archivists had to process and open the most important files. While he was still alive, President Johnson gave priority to education and civil rights; conferences on these topics accompanied the opening of the records in these areas in 1972 and early 1973. The President died a few weeks after the civil rights conference, and since then the great bulk of the more than 31 million pages of documents has been made available to researchers. And in addition to the traditional printed records, the LBJ Library has on deposit more than one thousand transcripts of oral history interviews, hundreds of thousands of still pictures, and miles of motion picture film and television videotapes.

Although biographers and historians made relatively little use of these materials in the first decade the library was open, the 1980s have witnessed a veritable explosion of books on Lyndon Johnson and the turbulent sixties. Three writers in particular have offered arresting interpretations of Johnson's political career—Robert Caro's critical view in the first of a planned trilogy on LBJ, Ronnie Dugger's skeptical analysis of Johnson as a political operator in Congress, and George Reedy's revealing personal glimpse of his experience as an aide to LBJ in both the Senate and the White House. The Great Society has been the subject of studies by political scientists and historians, notably Allen Matusow's provocative account of the failure of liberalism, *The Unraveling of America* (New York, 1984), while Vaughn Davis Bornet has surveyed the White House years in *The Presidency of Lyndon B. Johnson* (Lawrence, Kansas, 1982). The greatest outpouring has been on Vietnam, as historians, political scientists, journalists, and military commentators have tried to explain the tragic war in Southeast Asia to a bewildered American public.

Nearly all who sought to solve the puzzle of the sixties have found valuable clues, if not the final answers, in the voluminous files of the LBJ Library. This volume is the first, however, to attempt to survey the materials in the Johnson Library and relate them to the existing body of scholarly literature on the Johnson years. The idea grew out of the meetings of a committee consisting of faculty members from the history and government departments at the University of Texas and members of the staff of the library. With generous support from the Lyndon Baines Johnson Foundation, seven scholars visited the library to examine its holdings in their areas of special interest, wrote draft essays, and returned for a conference in January 1980. The revised essays form the substance of this volume.

As editor, I asked the contributors to combine a bibliographical survey with a sampling of the library's holdings. Each author has examined the pertinent published work in his field and then has related it to the material he has found in the library's files. It is our hope that the resulting volume will make scholars aware of the rich resources of the Johnson Library and stimulate new research on the Johnson years.

In the introductory essay, I have surveyed the general literature on Lyndon Johnson's political career. T. Harry Williams had originally agreed to take on this task; his death in the summer of 1979 cut short both his contribution to this volume and his projected biography of LBJ. The two essays on foreign policy reflect the areas in which the process of declassification of diplomatic records at the library is most advanced, although, as George Herring points out, the materials on Vietnam are scarce after mid-1965. The next three essays deal with major aspects of the Great Society and suggest the richness of the library's holdings on domestic issues, especially on education and civil rights. As Mark Gelfand notes, a full study of the War on Poverty would require extensive research in agency records at the National Archives. The last two essays focus on the White House. Political scientist Larry Berman probes the nature of Johnson's staff; David Culbert taps the wealth of audio and visual records to examine the relationship between Johnson and the media.

Harry Middleton, the director of the Lyndon B. Johnson Library, sponsored this study in the best sense of the word. He gave support and encouragement from the outset, but he allowed the participants free rein in their research and made no attempt to influence their interpretations. Charles Corkran, Tina Lawson, Michael Gillette, Martin Elzy, David Humphrey, Dorothy Territo, and other members of the library staff were extremely helpful throughout the project. As editor, I am particularly indebted to Gary Gallagher, who served as the library's coordinator. His cheerful cooperation and sensible suggestions made this a very pleasant experience for me.

Contents

About the Contributors

Larry Berman, professor of political science at the University of California at Davis, is the author of *Planning a Tragedy: The Americanization of the War in Vietnam* (New York, 1982).

David Culbert, professor of history at Louisiana State University, is the author of *News for Everyone: Radio and Foreign Affairs in Thirties America* (Westport, Conn., 1976).

Robert A. Divine, Littlefield Professor in American history, University of Texas at Austin, is the author of *Eisenhower and the Cold War* (New York, 1981).

Mark I. Gelfand, professor of history at Boston College, is the author of *A Nation of Cities: The Federal Government and Urban America, 1933–1965* (New York, 1975).

Hugh Davis Graham, professor of history at the University of Maryland, Baltimore County, is the author of *The Uncertain Triumph: Federal Education Policy in the Kennedy and Johnson Years* (Chapel Hill, N.C., 1984).

George C. Herring, professor of history at the University of Kentucky, is the author of *America's Longest War: The United States and Vietnam, 1950–1975* (2nd ed., New York, 1985).

Walter LaFeber, Noll Professor of history, Cornell University, is the author of *Inevitable Revolutions: The United States in Central America* (New York, 1983).

Steven F. Lawson, professor of history at the University of South Florida, is the author of *In Pursuit of Power: Southern Blacks and Electoral Politics, 1965–1982* (New York, 1985).

Introduction

The Johnson Literature

by Robert A. Divine

NEARLY A DECADE AFTER THE DEATH of Lyndon Johnson, the body of literature that focuses on his political career and presidency is surprisingly limited. Compared to the outpourings on Kennedy, there is but a meager trickle on Johnson, and nothing that would compare in influence, sales, or comprehensive coverage with books like Arthur Schlesinger's *Thousand Days* or Theodore Sorenson's *Kennedy*. By the 1950s, the Roosevelt bookshelf was already full, with Frank Freidel launching a multivolume biography, Arthur Schlesinger writing three long books on the New Deal, and James MacGregor Burns offering the first of his two incisive portraits of Franklin Roosevelt. There is as yet no comparable work on Johnson. The death of T. Harry Williams in 1979 cut short his planned biography; studies in progress by Robert Caro and Ronnie Dugger are still far from publication. Only the recent popular biography by Merle Miller, whose *Plain Speaking* did so much to rehabilitate Harry Truman, is likely to revive interest in the career and personality of Lyndon Johnson.

The literature on Johnson that does exist is predictably controversial. Composed largely of contemporary accounts by individuals either drawn to Johnson or repelled by him, the books reflect the strong emotions that the President evoked. On the one hand, his admirers focus on his political skill and legislative achievements, painting a flattering picture of a master craftsman at work in the Senate and the White House. His detractors, however, see only a cynical manipulator out for personal gain and self-advancement at the expense of the public welfare. Yet despite their dialectical nature, these books taken as a whole do give the careful reader a detailed portrait of one of the most fascinating and perplexing politicians of the twentieth century.

"You will never work for or with a more complicated man than Lyndon Johnson so long as you live," Robert McNamara told Joseph Califano in 1965. "I guarantee it."[1] Johnson was only simple on the surface. The easy stereotypes of a Texas wheeler-dealer or a mad bomber in Vietnam fade as one begins to probe into the complexity of Johnson's life and career. The equally misleading images of Johnson as the peerless Senate majority leader or as the progenitor of the Great Society also distort his curiously mixed political record. The man who first went to Congress with only 27 percent of the vote, the candidate who lost his first try for the Senate, won the second by eighty-seven votes seven days after the polls closed, and ran poorly against an unknown Republican college government teacher for his third term, the vice-presidential candidate who barely held Texas for Kennedy and failed to halt Nixon's inroads into the South in 1960, seems a far cry from the vaunted campaigner who surpassed Roosevelt's record landslide of 1936 to win reelection in 1964. Far from being a simple figure with transparent motives and predictable behavior, Lyndon Johnson emerges from the existing literature as a complex and often inscrutable man whose political contributions have yet to be properly understood and evaluated.

I

The earliest books on Lyndon Johnson are the most one-sided. Those written by friends and close associates portray Johnson as he wished to be viewed. The first biography, written by staff member Booth Mooney in 1956 when Johnson began to develop presidential fever, is purely and simply a campaign document. *The Lyndon Johnson Story*, updated and revised in 1964, tells the credulous reader that Johnson won handily in his race for Congress in 1937, receiving more than twice as many votes as his nearest competitor; describes the 1948 Senate race as ending in "a melodramatic finish" without any reference to the 202 late votes from Jim Wells County; and describes Johnson in the 1950s as a patriotic majority leader who placed country above party.[2] There is no mention of the way in which Johnson built his personal fortune while serving the public, nor any explanation of his postwar abandonment of the New Deal and support for the Taft-Hartley Act. In the 1964 edition, we are told that Johnson was above all "supremely an activist, a man who believed in getting things done," but at the same time he never acted on impulse, "never reached instinctively for the panic button in times of stress." Unlike his unnamed Republican opponent, Johnson "was a man of solid responsibility."[3]

While Mooney's book can be excused as a campaign tract, there can be no such defense for the unabashed flattery that *New York Times* journalist William S. White heaps on Johnson in *The Professional: Lyndon B. Johnson*. Writing soon after Johnson succeeded

Kennedy, White, a long-time friend and admirer of LBJ, apparently wanted to reassure the people that the reins of government were in good hands. As the title suggests, White focuses on Johnson's skills as majority leader and stresses his mastery of the art of politics. The new President was a man of liberal instincts, White claims, but one who also understood and respected conservatives. Those who had followed Johnson's Texas career must have been surprised to learn that he was personally "reticent," and that there was "not an ounce of demagogy in him."[4]

Even scholars were not immune to the Johnson influence. Three historians at his alma mater, William C. Pool, Emmie Craddock, and David E. Conrad, collaborated on *Lyndon Baines Johnson: The Formative Years*. Published in 1965, this book provides a detailed account of the President's boyhood and early life in Texas. Useful and reliable, with an especially informative chapter on Johnson's college years, this volume nevertheless suffers from local chauvinism. Johnson's father is described as "an agrarian progressive" and his mother as "a tower of strength to her young children"; under their tutelage LBJ grows to manhood infused with ideals based on the Constitution, the tenets of democracy, and political liberalism. The authors label his brief teaching career "distinguished," and conclude that the energetic and ambitious young man who began his public service in the 1930s was "the product of the people and the land from which he sprang."[5]

Johnson's political opponents quickly tried to set the record straight. Although their efforts were as biased and one-sided as those of his admirers, the books attacking Johnson at least have the virtue of a polemical appeal. Harsh and vengeful, they are never dull. In 1964, J. Evetts Haley, a popular historian of Texas and a far-right ideologue, wrote the classic account, *A Texan Looks at Lyndon: A Study in Illegitimate Power*. Outraged at the idea that LBJ could be viewed as a typical Texan, Haley tells his readers that Johnson is a product not of Texas but "of the strangely deranged times that have set the stage for his ambitious desires, his vanity and his evil genius."[6] In the pages that follow, Haley details the dark side of the Johnson story. He accuses Johnson of conspiring with George Parr to create the 202 additional votes that gave him the 1948 Senate victory; he traces the origins of the Johnson fortune to his acquisition of Austin radio station KTBC and his subsequent manipulation of the Federal Communications Commission to achieve a television monopoly in central Texas; and he repeats the familiar Texas rumors about Johnson's close ties to Brown and Root, the Houston-based construction firm whose rise to wealth and power paralleled that of Lyndon Johnson.[7]

Haley becomes most incensed over claims that Johnson was at heart a conservative. He belittles Johnson's 1958 statement, reprinted in Mooney's biography, that he was both a liberal and a conservative, and could not be pigeonholed or classified by a single label. For Haley, the only consistency in Johnson's career is a naked quest for power and wealth; he is a wheeler-dealer who tries to make "a public virtue of his denial of any abiding creed." A search of the record, Haley concludes, shows "no conclusive evidence of dedication to any eternal verity; no statement of basic spiritual belief; no yardstick based on moral principle."[8] Despite the intemperance of his attack, Haley does raise a critical question which must be faced by Johnson's biographers: What role did ideology play in Johnson's political career? Can he be viewed purely as a political manipulator or was there a set of beliefs that ran through his public life?

Robert Sherrill, a left-wing liberal writing at the height of the Vietnam War in 1967, is convinced that Johnson was totally without fixed principles. Disgusted at the thought of Johnson's being considered a liberal, Sherrill labels him "the Drugstore Populist" and then goes on to accuse him of practicing "welfare imperialism."[9] In the most effective part of his book, Sherrill belittles Johnson's political reputation. "Johnson had climbed by successes so small that the cumulative grand success," he writes, "seems an accident, as indeed in more than one way it was." He credits the President's early successes to what he calls "the cactus Mafia," men like John Connally and Jake Pickle who did Johnson's dirty work, and he points out how poorly Johnson did in all his campaigns except that of 1964, when the combination of Kennedy's memory and Goldwater's ineptitude created a landslide victory.[10]

By far the most sweeping critique of Johnson's career came in 1968 with the publication of Alfred Steinberg's 800-page biography, *Sam Johnson's Boy*.[11] A journalist who had earlier ghostwritten Tom Connally's Senate memoir and had published a flattering biography of Harry Truman, Steinberg set out to document and sustain the charges raised by Haley. The result is a curious mixture of fact and fancy, a book filled with many quite convincing episodes yet distorted by an adamant refusal to see Johnson as anything but the seeker after personal wealth and political power that Haley depicted. The author relies heavily on interviews with unnamed politicians; the book has the texture of detailed research and displays a solid working knowledge of both Texas and Washington politics in the 1940s and 1950s. The final sections on the presidency are much weaker than the earlier parts. Steinberg's antiwar sentiments preclude any rational discussion of Vietnam, and his heavy bias leads him to credit Senate Majority Leader Mike Mansfield rather than Johnson with the passage of the Great Society program. Despite these and other weaknesses, however, the book remains the most useful and reliable account of the *circumstances* surrounding Lyndon Johnson's emergence to national prominence.

Steinberg's most original and striking contribution is the concept of the "political daddy." He analyzes Johnson's technique of finding a patron, an established politician who could adopt him as his protégé. According to Steinberg, Johnson went through a series of such "daddies," ranging from the little known but influential Alvin Wirtz in Texas to such prominent national figures as Sam Rayburn and Franklin Roosevelt. Wirtz served as the prototype. A utility lawyer and liberal leader in Texas, Wirtz guided Johnson through the intricacies of state politics, serving as his mentor when he directed the Texas National Youth Administration and masterminding his successful campaign for Congress. It was Wirtz who introduced LBJ to George and Herman Brown of Brown and Root, and who helped him squeeze out his questionable victory in 1948. Yet Johnson later abandoned the Texas loyalists Wirtz had led, preferring to compromise with Allan Shivers to head off any possibility of a challenge to his Senate seat from the governor in 1954. Johnson followed the same pattern with his other "daddies," according to Steinberg. Thus his loyalty to Roosevelt and the New Deal quickly faded after the war, his long-standing relationship with Sam Rayburn was badly strained by his dealings with Shivers, and his obsequious behavior with Richard Russell, the man most responsible for his gaining power in the Senate, ended when he maneuvered Russell and the other southern die-hards into defeat on the 1957 civil rights bill.[12] One does not have to accept Steinberg's slanted view of Johnson to realize that he has offered a persuasive explanation for Johnson's rapid political rise.

Unlike other critics, Steinberg does not ignore foreign and defense policy in his discussion of Johnson's career. He points out that LBJ was a child of the 1930s, obsessed with the fear of appeasement and the supposed lesson of Munich. Above all, he portrays Johnson as a confirmed Cold Warrior, a hawk who consistently advocated heavy defense spending and wanted to turn the country into "a national armed camp." When Communist China intervened in the

Korean War in 1950, Johnson blamed the Truman administration for the resulting American retreat. "For the common defense we have thrown up a chicken-wire, not a wall of armed might," Steinberg reports Johnson telling the Senate. And after Sputnik, LBJ was in the forefront of those decrying the missile gap and calling for "a full, wartime mobilization schedule" in the race for the intercontinental ballistic missile. Thus Johnson's escalation of the war in Vietnam comes as no surprise to Steinberg: "Johnson's long-time militarism" flourished, destroying his "opportunity for greatness in the steaming jungles of far-off Asia." Rather than portraying LBJ as the captive of the prior decisions of Truman, Eisenhower, and Kennedy, Steinberg sees Vietnam as the natural consequence of Johnson's hawkish views.[13]

The rest of Steinberg's book fleshes out the Haley thesis: Johnson's career was simply "a lifetime of unceasing battle for personal wealth and political power."[14] The quests for money and power go hand in hand. Steinberg chronicles Johnson's close ties with Brown and Root, his use of political pressure to acquire special favors from the Federal Communications Commission for his radio and television stations, and his steady acquisition of land and banks through intermediaries in central Texas. Virtually every charge ever made against Johnson is repeated, and while many of the details may be accurate, the reader tends to react against the remorseless and one-sided prosecution. The political accusations are equally unbalanced. Steinberg quotes William White as saying that when Johnson first arrived in Washington, he asked only one question of the political system: "Who has the power and how is it exercised?"[15] According to Steinberg, Johnson's subsequent career was simply an elaboration on that theme. He turned against Truman and the Fair Deal to please Texas conservatives; he sponsored civil rights legislation only to weaken it fatally; his sole purpose as Senate majority leader was to advance his own presidential ambitions, not to unify his divided party. The result, Steinberg concludes, was tragedy both for Johnson and for the nation. "Unable to grow beyond his limited heritage and outlook, . . . he failed to emerge as a President of the United States."[16]

II

A more sympathetic portrait of Lyndon Johnson emerges from the extensive memoir literature. In 1971, Johnson published *The Vantage Point*, billed as a personal perspective on his presidential years. In fact, it was written largely by six former White House aides, including Walt Rostow and Doris Kearns. They did all the research and wrote the first drafts; Johnson then made the final revisions. At Johnson's insistence, the memoir focuses exclusively on public policy without any attempt to include the President's private views and thoughts. The result is a dry and juiceless official history, a sanitized account in which there is no trace of Johnson's flamboyant personality and earthy wisdom.

From the outset, Johnson is clearly intent on minimizing the theme of friction with the Kennedys. He insists that his focus on continuity in 1963 and 1964 was based on emotional commitment, not shrewd politics. "Rightly or wrongly," Johnson maintains, "I felt from the very first day in office that I had to carry on for President Kennedy." He views himself as "the trustee and the custodian of the Kennedy administration," and he says that on the flight back to Washington after the assassination, he made a vow to "devote every hour of every day during the remainder of John Kennedy's unfulfilled term to achieving the goals he had set." Throughout the book Johnson hews to this theme, playing down his growing feud with Robert Kennedy by describing their relationship as "cordial, though never overly warm."[17]

The reason for this stress on continuity becomes clear as the book unfolds: Johnson is as obsessed with Vietnam in his memoir as he was in the White House. The theme of continuity with John Kennedy, the idea that Johnson was simply carrying out the mandate of his popular predecessor, permeates the volume. Even though only five of the twenty-three chapters deal with Vietnam, they account for more than two hundred pages, over one-third of the book. In contrast, Johnson deals summarily with his legislative achievements and the Great Society in just over sixty pages. The imbalance is all the more striking in view of the unremitting defense of the Vietnam policy. There is no admission of possible error, no concession to antiwar critics. Failure to take a stand in South Vietnam, Johnson explains, would have meant the loss of all Southeast Asia to communism, a fearsome domestic debate that would have divided the nation, the loss of confidence in America by our allies, and above all, the global advance of Russia and China into the resulting vacuum of power. Such a development, Johnson believes, could only mean an eventual American struggle "to prevent their full takeover of Europe, Asia, and the Middle East."[18] Thus Johnson views his Vietnam policy as a determined effort to avert World War III.

Some of the personal qualities so notably absent in *The Vantage Point* come out clearly in Sam Houston Johnson's memoir, *My*

Brother Lyndon. The President's intense dislike of Robert Kennedy is apparent in Lyndon's statement to his brother in 1964, "I don't need that little runt to win." Moreover, Sam Johnson, perhaps reflecting Lyndon's true feelings, blames the Vietnam War on the advisers LBJ had inherited from Kennedy, especially McGeorge Bundy and Robert McNamara. Always protective of his brother, Sam Johnson sees Bill Moyers as a dangerous influence, "a kid who had his eye on the main chance" and who was always "bootlicking with the Kennedy crowd." Above all, Sam Johnson perceives his brother's insecurity about his own educational and intellectual attainments when in the company of polished and sophisticated Ivy Leaguers. Although Sam Houston clearly idolizes his brother, the book has many glimpses of the dark side of LBJ—his ruthless bullying of overworked aides and his inability ever to apologize for his excesses. And the author gives an insight into the President's monumental ego when he describes how LBJ began to organize his papers and clippings for posterity in 1957 by setting up a trained archivist in the Old Senate Office Building.[19]

None of these unpleasant but human qualities appears in Jack Valenti's memoir, despite its title, *A Very Human President.* Like Valenti's service as a presidential aide, the book is one long paean to the chief. Some useful material appears near the end, where Valenti describes the soul-searching Johnson went through while deciding to escalate the Vietnam War in 1965, yet even here Valenti concludes that this action was "inescapable." By far the most interesting passage is a letter from David Halberstam, author of *The Best and the Brightest,* replying to Valenti's critique of that book. Far from being a devil, wrote Halberstam, Johnson was "a very great man caught in a terrible turn of history." Valenti rushed this favorable estimate off to Johnson at his ranch, only to discover later that it arrived just a few minutes after the President had died.[20]

The most perceptive and eloquent of all the memoirs is Harry McPherson's *A Political Education,* which appeared in 1972. McPherson was a young Texan who went directly from law school to work as a legislative aide to Johnson in 1956; ten years later he served as White House counsel and speech writer. McPherson admired Johnson, who taught him the essence of politics, but he was always aware of the President's limitations, and his book is an honest and believable account which focuses more on the author's growing maturity than it does on Johnson.

The most revealing passages deal with Johnson's handling of Congress. As majority leader, he introduced his young assistant to the facts of life in the Senate, showing him how to win the support of the whales, such as Senators Richard Russell and Robert Kerr, and to avoid wasting time on the minnows. McPherson comes to understand, as Steinberg never did, why Johnson took such a hawkish stand on national defense: it was the price the Democrats had to pay during the Cold War to achieve their social welfare measures in Congress. He marvels at the way in which Johnson performed a highwire act in 1957 to keep "Dick Russell from walking across the aisle and embracing Everett Dirksen," thus killing the civil rights bill. Far more than William White, McPherson demonstrates that Johnson was indeed "a master craftsman of politics," someone who "knew where the power was, and how to use it." After the landslide victory in 1964, McPherson was puzzled by Johnson's haste in enacting the Great Society. "You've got to give it all you can, that first year," the President replied. "Doesn't matter what kind of majority you come in with. You've got just one year when they treat you right, and before they start worrying about themselves."[21]

Unlike Haley and Sherrill, McPherson believes that Johnson had a definite political ideology—he views LBJ as a southern populist with a distaste for large industrial corporations and a genuine sympathy for the poor. But it is a mistake, he thinks, to label Johnson a southerner. "His true province was not the South," McPherson explains. "It was Washington." He had both the strengths and weaknesses of a congressional politician, and his provincialism proved most damaging in 1960 when he thought he could win the Democratic nomination through his control of Congress, only to find that Kennedy had mastered the very different game of primary and caucus politics on the national level.[22]

Johnson's ultimate failing, according to McPherson, was his inability to communicate effectively to the northeastern media and to the middle class of the South and West. On the cool medium of television, he lacked Kennedy's calm composure; instead he came through like "a high-pressure salesman, always trying to get his foot in the door." Even more tragic was his total inability to relate to the new currents sweeping through the nation in the 1960s, and above all to disaffected youth. "He was a manipulator of men," McPherson writes, "when the young were calling for everyone to do his own thing." Thus his considerable political skills became useless as he lost touch with a rapidly changing nation.[23]

Two last memoirs, George E. Reedy's *The Twilight of the Presidency* and Joseph A. Califano's *A Presidential Nation*, were written as extended commentaries on the political system rather than as accounts of the authors' years spent as Johnson aides. Yet both give indirect evidence about the character of the Johnson presidency. Reedy, whose book received wide acclaim, focuses on the problem of presidential isolation. Without citing Johnson directly, Reedy claims that American presidents lose touch with reality when they surround themselves with sycophants and are treated with excessive deference. Califano, on the other hand, worries about the concentration of power in the presidency, claiming that it is not so much the result of executive tyranny as of the weakness of other institutions, notably Congress, the courts, and the political parties. The message of the two books is clear. Johnson's failure in the White House was the result of an imperfect political system, not a flaw in his character.

But despite their institutional focus, the two memoirs still give revealing glimpses of Johnson. Thus Reedy explains how Johnson "mistook the alert, taut, well-groomed young men around him for 'American youth' and could never comprehend the origins of the long-haired, slovenly attired youngsters who hooted at him so savagely when he traveled. . . . To him, they appeared to be extraterrestrial invaders—not only non-American but nonearthly." Califano includes several stories about Johnson's behavior, but none more revealing than Johnson's explanation of the difference between Hubert Humphrey and himself. According to LBJ, when Walter Reuther called on the Vice-President with his hand in his pocket asking for money for the Detroit ghettos, Humphrey would spend all his time considering how he could get the labor leader to take his hand out of his pocket so Humphrey could shake it. But when Reuther came to see the President, Johnson spent his time thinking: "How can I get him to take his hand out of his pocket so I can cut his balls off!"[24]

III

Some of the best insights on Lyndon Johnson come from the journalists who observed him at first hand from the time he emerged as a national figure in the 1950s. Relying both on their own conversations with Johnson and on interviews with his friends and enemies, reporters present a vivid portrait of the President. Their accounts, however, with one notable exception, tend to be long on description and short on analysis.

The most satisfying book on Johnson's involvement in national politics is *Lyndon B. Johnson: The Exercise of Power*, by two well-known Washington columnists, Rowland Evans and Robert Novak.

Writing in early 1966, they survey his career in the Senate, as Vice-President, and during the first two years of his presidency. They are at their best in describing his success as Senate majority leader, which they attribute to two factors—the Johnson "network" and the Johnson "treatment." The network was the group of Senators, both Democratic and Republican, liberal and conservative, whom Johnson could call on when he needed votes on the Senate floor. With the assistance of Senate Secretary Bobby Baker, Johnson built up his loyal following by using classic patronage techniques. He won the loyalty of some by giving them the committee assignments they desired; others received prize office assignments; still others got trips abroad at the taxpayers' expense or strategic campaign contributions. The result, Evans and Novak explain, was that "Johnson slowly built up a cadre of supporters who would vote for LBJ—even, on occasion, against their ideology, their conscience and their political self-interest."[25]

The key to the whole system was the "treatment," Johnson's personal technique of political persuasion. As described by Evans and Novak, Johnson would use the treatment whenever he had the opportunity for direct, one-on-one contact with a fellow Senator—"at the LBJ Ranch swimming pool, in one of LBJ's offices, in the Senate cloakroom, on the floor of the Senate itself." Sometimes Johnson relied on threats and accusations, sometimes on flattery and cajolery, sometimes even on tears. Above all, he used physical domination. "He moved in close, his face a scant millimeter from his target, his eyes widening and narrowing, his eyebrows rising and falling. From his pockets poured clippings, memos, statistics. Mimicry, humor, and the genius of analogy made the Treatment an almost hypnotic experience and rendered the target stunned and helpless." The accuracy of Evans and Novak's description is borne out by Steinberg, who reports that Texas Lieutenant Governor Ben Ramsey once explained why he agreed with Johnson on an issue: "Lyndon got me by the lapels and put his face on top of mine and he talked and talked and talked. I figured it was either getting drowned or joining."[26]

Two other journalists, Philip Geyelin and Tom Wicker, are less flattering but equally perceptive in describing Johnson's approach to foreign policy. Geyelin gives the fullest account in *Lyndon B. Johnson and the World*. Writing in 1966, Geyelin describes Johnson's foreign policy as President with growing apprehension over the Dominican Republic intervention and the escalation of the Vietnam War. He stresses basic uneasiness with international issues, citing

Johnson's classic complaint that foreigners were "not like the folks you were reared with." Yet he also credits Johnson with considerable expertise on defense matters and the instinctive ability to play power politics on a global scale. He was, Geyelin contends, in large measure "a self-taught statesman; he couldn't read the music, but he had come a long way on his ability to play by ear." His most distinctive quality as a diplomat, Geyelin believes, was his belief that action spoke louder than words. Convinced that previous American failures abroad had stemmed from foreign miscalculation of U.S. intentions, he was determined that under his leadership the United States would "communicate its purpose and make plain its awareness of its own self-interest loud and clear and over and over, and by deeds rather than words."[27] The eventual course of American policy in Vietnam is thus foreshadowed in Geyelin's shrewd observation.

Tom Wicker offers a more sympathetic view of Johnson's Vietnam decisions in *JFK and LBJ*. He claims that Johnson, handicapped by his southern background, wheeler-dealer reputation, and inexperience in foreign policy, had little choice but to implement the Vietnam policy he had inherited from John Kennedy. Kennedy might have been able to escape from the Vietnam quagmire, but Johnson could not. Once he had opted for a policy of continuity at home, he was trapped into continuing the American involvement in Southeast Asia. Wicker claims the decision came early, in November 1963, after a briefing from Ambassador Henry Cabot Lodge and reflected Johnson's intense concern with domestic politics. Recalling the impact of the fall of China on the Truman administration, Johnson told Lodge: "I am not going to lose Vietnam. I am not going to be the President who saw Southeast Asia go the way China went." "It *was* a political decision, made by a political man," Wicker concludes, "in political circumstances that left him no real choice."[28]

Most of the other reporters' books on Johnson fail to rise above the anecdotal level. Volumes such as Jack Bell's *The Johnson Treatment*, Charles Roberts's *LBJ's Inner Circle*, Frank Cormier's *LBJ: The Way He Was*, and Hugh Sidey's *A Very Personal Presidency* describe in great detail Johnson's vanity and pettiness as well as his gusto and exuberance. These men covered the White House for newspapers and magazines; all were fascinated by Johnson's personality. Cormier and Sidey in particular note Johnson's craving for approval. Cormier comments on Johnson's boasting after a well-received speech that he had been interrupted eighty times for applause. Sidey sees him as a loner desperately seeking approval to fill a "deep void within him." His search for consensus, according to

Sidey, was in reality his attempt to outdo his idol, Franklin Roosevelt, in achieving public favor. Booth Mooney notices the same craving in Johnson. Citing a campaign speech in which LBJ was interrupted time and again with applause and got a rousing ovation at the end, Mooney recalls a beaming Johnson chortling happily to an aide, "Oh, boy! Listen to that! It even beats screwing." [29]

The common failing of the journalists' accounts of Johnson's career is exemplified in the popular biography, *Lyndon*, by Richard Harwood and Haynes Johnson. The authors are experienced reporters who draw on their own observations as well as a series of off-the-record interviews with the President from the files of the *Washington Post*. Writing just after Johnson's death, they are unable to offer any broad explanation for his life and career. Johnson, they assert, was "an enigma," and they conclude their evaluation with the balanced but bland comment that he was "a man of massive talent, and equally massive insecurities." With some insight, they also note that he tried to carry out FDR's twin ideals of achieving the good society at home and protecting the nation from totalitarian danger abroad. He succeeded in the first but failed in the second. He was, they conclude, "one of our most tragic Presidents," and they regret that his failure "was a tragedy arising out of the best liberal impulses of his own generation." [30]

Louis Heren, a British journalist, takes this tragic President theme further in *No Hail, No Farewell*, by far the best reporter's account of the Johnson presidency. As a foreigner, Heren views Johnson dispassionately, noting both his coarse, sometimes grotesque personal behavior and his "superb" skills as a politician. Unlike Steinberg, Heren gives Johnson full credit for the passage of the stalled Kennedy legislative program in 1964 and 1965. But Heren also criticizes Johnson for attempting to rule rather than govern after his massive reelection victory in 1964. "With private wheeling and dealing, the control of most outlets of official information, and the occasional dishonesties," Heren asserts, "Johnson also avoided the further check of public oversight." He also notes, as does nearly every observer, that Johnson's personal insecurity kept him from engaging in a dialogue with the press and especially with influential Washington columnists like Walter Lippmann and James Reston. "For all his years in Washington, he was suspicious of ideas." [31]

Like Wicker, Harwood, and Johnson, Heren attributes LBJ's ultimate downfall to external events, not personal failings. "To a large extent he was a victim of circumstances beyond his control." The real tragedy, as Heren sees it, lay not in Johnson's character but in the bankruptcy of the liberal tradition that he inherited from Franklin Roosevelt and John Kennedy. Johnson tried to meet the problems of the 1960s with the outmoded solutions of the 1930s. "The old answers were often irrelevant," Heren claims, as the liberals proved to be "captives rather than heirs of the past." So the President who enacted long overdue civil rights legislation and prevailed on Congress to pass aid-to-education measures ended as the bewildered victim of black violence and campus protests. And in Vietnam Johnson took the Cold War liberalism of his predecessors and carried it to its logical conclusion. It was the liberal intellectuals who persuaded Johnson that "American national security depended upon the maintenance of a global nuclear, territorial and ideological balance of power." When Heren finally asked one of these pillars of the foreign policy establishment in 1969 what had gone wrong in Vietnam, the reply, given with "disarming candor," was simply, "We thought we would win."[32]

There were personal failings as well. The challenges Johnson faced were unprecedented—cultural revolution, a breakdown in law and order, massive racial unrest—but Heren feels that John Kennedy might have had the political sophistication, the appeal to restless youth, and the personal charisma to cope with the momentous upheavals of the mid-1960s. Johnson failed in part because he lacked "the power to persuade a majority to do something they might not want to do." His own very real political gifts worked very well in the Senate but not in the White House, where he had to lead 200 million Americans, not just 100 senators. "National leadership could not be exercised from a back room," Heren concludes, "with cajolery, fixing and the rest of his tricks, and Johnson knew no other way. . . . For all his years in public life, he could never treat people as people."[33]

It was Johnson's misfortune, Heren contends, to become President at the "beginning of what will surely be the most revolutionary period in history." Despite his enormous political skill, his great vitality and capacity for hard work, and his "deep and abiding love of country," Johnson failed to triumph over the economic and cultural revolutions of the 1960s. Cruel critics played up his personal flaws, but Heren dismisses them. "The northern ghettos did not erupt in flame because of his cornpone humor," he writes. "American society, and not Johnson, alienated the hippies and the flower children."[34] In the last analysis, Heren attributes the failure of Johnson's presidency to the magnitude of the problems he faced. The fact that the times overwhelmed the man thus says less about the nature of

Johnson's leadership than it does about the extraordinary decade of the 1960s.

IV

Scholarly analysis of Lyndon Johnson's career is still relatively meager. Only a handful of historians or political scientists have devoted themselves to an examination of LBJ's place among twentieth-century American Presidents. There have been a few pioneers, however, and they have concentrated on two themes—an explanation of Johnson's failure as President and an assessment of his ideological commitment to progressive reform.

Eric Goldman and Doris Kearns stand out as the two scholars who have studied Johnson most intensively, and both seek to explain why such a talented political leader met with frustration and rejection in the White House. Goldman combined his skill as a political historian with his experience as a presidential assistant from 1964 to 1966 to write the fullest and most reliable account of Johnson's presidency. In *The Tragedy of Lyndon Johnson*, Goldman describes the flowering of the Great Society in detail, perceiving it as the culmination of the reform movement that began with progressivism and continued with the New Deal, and yet acknowledging Johnson's own unique contributions. Goldman's book is less helpful on the Vietnam War, though he has a valuable chapter on the disaffection of American intellectuals. His account of the White House Festival of the Arts, which writers and artists used to denounce the Vietnam War, reveals how deep the alienation between Johnson and the liberal establishment had become by 1966.[35]

In his search for an explanation of Johnson's failure as President, Goldman divides the blame between LBJ and the urban middle class. Lyndon Johnson, he claims, was his own worst enemy. Plagued by a deep-seated sense of personal insecurity, he tried desperately as President to win the respect and love of the people but succeeded only in bringing out his own worst qualities. "Dubious whether people liked him," Goldman observes, "he pleaded, clawed and maneuvered to have them love him." He gave the people everything he had, Goldman contends, "except what they wanted and what his lurking suspicion of them held back, the gift of his genuine self." Compounding the problem in the 1960s was what Goldman calls the emergence of "the Metroamericans"—the rising middle-class citizens of the cities who prided themselves on their urbanity and

sophistication and viewed Johnson as a coarse and provincial pre-
tender. Influenced by a northeastern-dominated media, Metroamericans compared Johnson to a Kennedy they had idolized and found
him wanting.[36]

The result, according to Goldman, was tragedy. Even if he had
not become mired in Vietnam, Johnson was bound to face rejection
because of his own personal failings and the snobbish provincialism
of the urban middle class. Neither his genuine political skill nor his
devotion to progressive reform could earn him the love and respect
of the American people. Thus Goldman concludes that he became
"the tragic figure of an extraordinarily gifted President who was the
wrong man from the wrong place at the wrong time under the
wrong circumstances."[37]

Doris Kearns offers a very different explanation for Johnson's
failure in *Lyndon Johnson and the American Dream*. Like Goldman, she combines the insights of a trained scholar with personal
experience gained from service as a White House aide and ghost-
writer, but she widens the focus to cover Johnson's entire career.
Adopting the techniques of psychohistory and benefiting from a
close personal relationship with Johnson during the years of his re-
tirement, Kearns attempts to account for the contradictions in Johnson's behavior. The result is a striking and controversial portrait.

Kearns analyzes the relationship between Johnson and his par-
ents to explain the central contradiction in his life—the quest for
power and the desire for service. The quest for power came from his
father, Sam Johnson, who introduced Lyndon to the coarse but exciting world of politics during his brief stint in the Texas legislature.
His mother, Rebekah, on the other hand, was a genteel woman who
valued idealism and service. Relying on Johnson's personal reminiscences, Kearns claims that Rebekah withheld her love and affection
from her son as a way to force him to give up his father's crude ways
and accept her emphasis on culture and humanitarianism. Torn by
this domestic conflict, Johnson sought in public life the approval
and esteem he was denied at home. "From the world of work and the
conquest of ever-widening circles of men, Johnson hoped to obtain
the steady love he had lacked as a child," Kearns writes. "The problem was that each successful performance led only to the need for
more."[38]

Kearns uses her psychological theme to account for many aspects of Johnson's political career. Thus she claims that the wheeler-
dealer behavior followed his father's impulse toward power and manipulation, while the commitment to humanitarian reform was the

response to Rebekah's call to duty. Lyndon's insecurity is no longer a mystery—it stems from Rebekah's rejection, and it fuels Lyndon's restless ambition. Drawing heavily on Steinberg, Kearns plays up Johnson's reliance on patrons to advance his career, suggesting that he was always looking for a strong father figure to fill the place of the weak Sam Johnson. And she explains the curious fear of confrontation that haunted LBJ throughout his life, making him prefer behind-the-scenes negotiation to open debate and causing him to become ill on the eve of nearly every election. His boyhood fear of rejection became equated with political defeat, illustrating what Kearns calls "the connection of votes and love." It was this compulsion that drove Johnson to seek his landslide victory in 1964. When "millions upon millions" finally voted for him, he told Kearns, then "for the first time in all my life I truly felt loved by the American people."[39]

The problem with Kearns's analysis of Lyndon Johnson is that it is too pat. In one fell psychological swoop, she accounts for all the contradictions in his political career. Sam Johnson is responsible for his fondness for manipulation, Rebekah for his idealism as well as his insatiable desire for political success. The book is strongest on Johnson's service as Senate majority leader, and in these chapters Kearns relies on orthodox political interpretation, not psychological speculation. The most troubling aspect of her account is that it is virtually impossible to verify the information Johnson gave her in their early morning interviews. She admits to being puzzled about why Johnson was so open with her, dismissing his explanation that he confided in her because she reminded him of his mother. Kearns speculates that Johnson knew she planned to write a book about him and that in his last years he was preoccupied with "the final verdict of history."[40] One cannot help but wonder if the astute politician was not engaged in one last act of manipulation, using Kearns as his way of presenting an appealing image of himself to posterity.

Historians writing in the 1970s have shown greater interest in Johnson's political ideology than in his personal idiosyncrasies. Jim F. Heath stresses the theme of continuity with Kennedy in his book on the 1960s, *Decade of Disillusionment*. Despite the obvious differences in styles, the two Presidents, he contends, were very similar: both were activists, both were in the progressive tradition in domestic policy, and both were ardent Cold Warriors. In particular, Heath sees Johnson as a genuine liberal who "saw the Great Society as going well beyond the work of his great hero, Franklin Roosevelt." He gives LBJ the credit for "an amazing array of legislation," but

Heath concludes that Johnson simply brought about a culmination of the New Deal rather than initiating a new wave of reform.[41]

Two historians who have studied Johnson intensively arrive at equally positive evaluations of his place in the progressive tradition. Joe B. Frantz, writing in the *Journal of Southern History* in 1979, argues that Johnson's liberalism in the White House was not the result of political opportunism. Instead, relying on more than a thousand oral history interviews that he directed, Frantz asserts that Johnson was a lifelong liberal whose support for progressive causes dated back to his days as a National Youth Administration director and New Deal congressman in the 1930s. Frantz calls Johnson a populist at heart and in particular identifies him as "a compassionate man," a representative of the New South who never engaged in racism and who supported civil rights legislation out of personal conviction. He does admit that Johnson turned to the right after World War II, when he supported the Taft-Hartley Act and opposed poll tax repeal, but Frantz dismisses this retrogression as pragmatic politics necessary to secure Johnson's Texas political base. When the times changed, Johnson was then able to give his instinctive liberalism free rein. Thus Frantz concludes that in going from the New Deal to the Great Society, Johnson walked "a generally progressive line, with now and then an aberration."[42]

T. Harry Williams is more candid in admitting that Johnson trimmed his liberalism sharply in the 1950s in order to advance his political career. Yet Williams, writing in 1973 in the *Journal of American History*, agrees with Frantz that Johnson was a genuine progressive. He finds the source of Johnson's reform spirit in the populism of the rural South, and he sees LBJ as more the heir of Huey Long than of Franklin Roosevelt. Both men embodied the spirit of southern dissent and both spoke in the earthly rhetoric of the rural South. Johnson, however, was more pragmatic and less radical than Long; Williams asserts that "Lyndon did not want to master the system but to manipulate it." While Frantz thinks Johnson followed a straight line from the New Deal to the Great Society, Williams claims that LBJ "came to his rendezvous with reform over troubled and tortuous paths, advancing and then retreating but inexorably moving forward." Above all else, Williams sees the uniqueness of Johnson as stemming from his southern heritage, paying him a final tribute as "this tormented man from this tormented region who had such large visions of what his country might become."[43]

Williams agrees with Goldman that Johnson was out of place in the 1960s, but he blames the times more than LBJ, suggesting that he was "the right man . . . under the wrong circumstances." In that respect, Williams echoes Louis Heren's contention that Johnson's fundamental values—a belief in moderate reform shaped by the Depression and a conviction stemming from World War II that aggression was evil—doomed him to failure in the 1960s.[44]

V

A genuine consensus, to use LBJ's favorite word, seems to be emerging out of the Johnson literature a decade after his passing. The image of Johnson as a riverboat gambler, a manipulator of men and events, is too strong for even his most ardent admirers to dismiss. But at the same time, historians have established a solid ideological base for his Great Society programs and demonstrated that he acted out of conviction as well as expediency. His detractors have shown that he pursued power ruthlessly, but their efforts to portray him as an opportunist without any principles have fallen on barren ground.

The real challenge facing future historians is to explain why Johnson failed to meet the challenges of the 1960s. Simply to say that he was limited by the progressive and internationalist traditions of his generation is to deny him the capacity for growth and change, qualities he displayed in abundance throughout his career. Clearly the tumultuous domestic and foreign events he confronted while President required new and innovative solutions. Sidney Hyman is on the right track when he says the main problem with Johnson's presidency was his failure to create a new consensus to deal with "a whole order of domestic problems that cannot be resolved by conventional means in the progressive tradition" and "a whole order of external problems . . . in which Asia as much as Europe will be the focal point of American power."[45] It is not enough to speak of tragedy in the Greek sense that the outcome was foreordained, or to repeat the cliché that he was the wrong man for the wrong time. Scholars will have to dig deeper into the wealth of Johnson material to help us understand how such a dynamic and gifted political leader failed to transcend his own background—why he tried to solve the problems of the future with the answers of the past. Until they do, we are faced with the continuing enigma of Lyndon Johnson, the brilliant tactician who led the nation into strategic disaster.

Notes

1. Joseph A. Califano, *A Presidential Nation* (New York, 1975), p. 18.

2. Booth Mooney, *The Lyndon Johnson Story* (New York, 1964), pp. 63, 112–114.

3. Ibid., p. 6.

4. William S. White, *The Professional: Lyndon B. Johnson* (Boston, 1964), pp. 56, 63.

5. William C. Pool, Emmie Craddock, and David E. Conrad, *Lyndon Baines Johnson: The Formative Years* (San Marcos, Tex., 1965), pp. 48, 56, 59, 160, 180–181.

6. J. Evetts Haley, *A Texan Looks at Lyndon: A Study in Illegitimate Power* (Canyon, Tex., 1964), p. 7.

7. Ibid., pp. 27, 65, 83.

8. Ibid., pp. 15, 157.

9. Robert Sherrill, *Accidental President* (New York, 1967), pp. 16, 64–66.

10. Ibid., pp. 106, 121.

11. Alfred Steinberg, *Sam Johnson's Boy: A Close-up of the President from Texas* (New York, 1968).

12. Ibid., pp. 101, 132–134, 289, 330, 469–471.

13. Ibid., pp. 233, 312, 480, 696.

14. Ibid., p. 696.

15. Ibid., p. 71.

16. Ibid., p. 839.

17. Lyndon Baines Johnson, *The Vantage Point: Perspectives of the Presidency, 1963–1969* (New York, 1971), pp. 19, 42, 99.

18. Ibid., pp. 151–152.

19. Sam Houston Johnson, *My Brother Lyndon* (New York, 1969), pp. 155–156, 165, 191, 202, 207, 252, 269.

20. Jack Valenti, *A Very Human President* (New York, 1976), pp. 287, 308–309.

21. Harry McPherson, *A Political Education* (Boston, 1972), pp. 48–49, 109, 130, 263, 268.

22. Ibid., pp. 138–139, 177.

23. Ibid., pp. 249, 261, 444–445.

24. George E. Reedy, *The Twilight of the Presidency* (New York, 1970), pp. 96–97; Califano, *Presidential Nation*, p. 208.

25. Rowland Evans and Robert Novak, *Lyndon B. Johnson: The Exercise of Power* (New York, 1966), pp. 107–111.

26. Ibid., pp. 115–116; Steinberg, *Sam Johnson's Boy*, p. 425.

27. Philip Geyelin, *Lyndon B. Johnson and the World* (New York, 1966), pp. 13, 15, 31–32, 44–45.

28. Tom Wicker, *JFK and LBJ: The Influence of Personality upon Politics* (New York, 1968), pp. 179, 185, 205–206.

29. Jack Bell, *The Johnson Treatment: How Lyndon B. Johnson Took

Over the Presidency and Made It His Own (New York, 1965); Charles Roberts, *LBJ's Inner Circle* (New York, 1965); Frank Corimer, *LBJ: The Way He Was* (Garden City, New York, 1977); pp. 45, 79; Hugh Sidey, *A Very Personal Presidency: Lyndon Johnson in the White House* (New York, 1968), pp. 70–71; Booth Mooney, *LBJ: An Irreverent Chronicle* (New York, 1976), p. 10.

30. Richard Harwood and Haynes Johnson, *Lyndon* (New York, 1973), pp. 75, 177–178, 182.

31. Louis Heren, *No Hail, No Farewell* (New York, 1970), pp. 20, 67, 69.

32. Ibid., pp. 117, 118–119, 263, 266.

33. Ibid., pp. 248–249, 261–262.

34. Ibid., pp. 239 240, 251.

35. Eric F. Goldman, *The Tragedy of Lyndon Johnson* (New York, 1960), pp. 495–563.

36. Ibid., pp. 617–627.

37. Ibid., p. 628.

38. Doris Kearns, *Lyndon Johnson and the American Dream* (New York, 1976), pp. 21–48.

39. Ibid., pp. 58–59, 80, 97, 219.

40. Ibid., p. 18. In Fred Greenstein, et al., *Evolution of the Modern Presidency: A Bibliographical Survey* (Washington, 1977), Kearns's book is described as "a difficult if not impossible work to validate and hence evaluate."

41. Jim F. Heath, *Decade of Disillusionment: The Kennedy-Johnson Years* (Bloomington, Ind., 1975), pp. 10, 207, 292.

42. Joe B. Frantz, "Opening a Curtain: The Metamorphosis of Lyndon B. Johnson," *Journal of Southern History* 45 (February 1979): 3–26.

43. T. Harry Williams, "Huey, Lyndon and Southern Radicalism," *Journal of American History* 60 (September 1973): 267–293.

44. Ibid., p. 292.

45. Sidney Hyman, *The Politics of Consensus* (New York, 1968), pp. 262–263.

Part 1 | Foreign Policy

1 | The War in Vietnam

by George C. Herring

FOR LYNDON JOHNSON, the Vietnam War represented a personal as well as a national tragedy. Johnson had not created the commitment in Vietnam, and he would have preferred to shun what he once called "that bitch of a war" and concentrate on "the woman I really loved," his cherished Great Society.[1] But the war he took on so reluctantly and struggled unsuccessfully to conclude eventually destroyed the Great Society, tore the nation apart, and inflicted great pain on Johnson himself. "The only difference between the Kennedy assassination and mine," he lamented in 1968, is that "I am alive and it has been more torturous."[2] Johnson could console himself only with the hope that history would vindicate him for taking up the thankless burden of defending South Vietnam and for persevering in the face of a stalemated war and relentless pressures at home.[3]

This essay will examine the way in which history has dealt with Johnson and Vietnam. Comparing the official rationale and the "dove" and "hawk" rebuttals with subsequent interpretations, it will look first at Johnson's 1964–1965 decisions to escalate the war, then consider his management of the war, and conclude with a discussion of the Tet Offensive and the March 31, 1968, decision to withdraw from the presidential race. Like many nonhistorians, LBJ mistakenly assumed that history speaks with a single voice, but Vietnam, perhaps the most traumatic event experienced by the United States in this century, will never be free of controversy. Even at this early date, however, emotions have calmed and perspectives have sharpened. The availability of a vast amount of primary materials and the publication of a number of important scholarly studies have produced a partial reassessment of the war. The vindication Johnson craved has thus far eluded him, but he is being viewed with greater understanding and detachment.

I

The Johnson administration maintained that it had escalated the war in response to North Vietnamese aggression. Hanoi had instigated the insurgency in South Vietnam and had supported it with steadily increasing quantities of personnel and supplies. The United States had patiently endured North Vietnamese interference for years, responding only by sending aid and advisers to South Vietnam. But in 1964 and 1965, Hanoi had sharply stepped up its aggression, even dispatching regular units to the South. The United States had no choice but to carry the war to North Vietnam and to send its own combat forces to hold the line in South Vietnam.[4]

The administration justified each major step it took as a response to a specific enemy provocation. The first bombing raids against North Vietnam in August 1964 were in retaliation for "unprovoked attacks" by North Vietnamese gunboats on U.S. destroyers engaged in "routine patrols" in the Gulf of Tonkin. The President also used this Gulf of Tonkin incident to secure a congressional resolution authorizing him to "take all necessary measures" to "prevent further aggression." Rolling Thunder, the systematic bombing campaign initiated in February 1965, came in response to Vietcong raids on the United States air base at Pleiku. The commitment of major increments of American ground forces in July 1965 was necessary to counter North Vietnamese infiltration of regulars, specifically the 325th Infantry Division, a crack unit whose presence posed a mortal threat to South Vietnam.

Johnson and his advisers insisted that by intervening in Vietnam they were defending vital interests of the United States. The administration stressed that a noncommunist South Vietnam was necessary to contain an expansionist Communist China. It resurrected the "domino theory," first publicized by Eisenhower in 1954, warning that the fall of South Vietnam would cause the loss of all of Southeast Asia with disastrous economic, political, and strategic consequences for the United States. Johnson and Secretary of State Dean Rusk repeatedly emphasized that failure to stand firm in the face of aggression, as in the 1930s, would encourage further aggression, upsetting the international order the United States had established after World War II and perhaps provoking a third world war.

A group of so-called doves questioned the official explanation of the war from the outset. Included among them were prominent journalists, former government officials, and scholars—representatives of the most important segments of the nation's foreign policy elite. The doves ranged over the political spectrum. Liberals protested that the massive, indiscriminate use of military power in Vietnam was undermining America's moral position in the world. Conservatives deplored Johnson's neo-Wilsonian crusade and warned that by attempting to impose its will on the world the United States was "inviting a disaster beyond anything yet known to mankind."[5] The radical New Left proclaimed that Vietnam was but the most blatant manifestation of a reactionary America's commitment to destroy revolution in the third world. From 1965 to 1973, the doves subjected Johnson and his successor, Richard Nixon, to a steady barrage of sometimes vicious criticism.[6]

Doves differed among themselves in assessing American interests in Vietnam. Radicals agreed with the President's conclusion but reached it from a very different set of premises. Stressing the economic sources of American foreign policy, they argued that the survival of the capitalist system depended upon maintenance of the exploitative trade arrangements by which the United States had gained hegemony over the world economy. Conceding that U.S. economic interests in Vietnam were small, they nevertheless contended that the revolution there was symbolic of a larger, world-wide challenge to American dominance. The United States had gone to war in Vietnam, Gabriel Kolko concluded, to "stop every form of revolutionary movement which refuses to accept the predominant role of the United States. . . . On the outcome of this epic contest rests the future of peace and social progress in the world for the remainder of the twentieth century."[7]

Liberals and conservatives, on the other hand, vigorously challenged the administration's contention that Vietnam was vital to the United States. In the light of the Sino-Soviet split, they argued, the Cold War had ended or at least entered a new phase, rendering outmoded the assumptions of the policy of containment. Some doves questioned whether China in fact had expansionist aims; others insisted that Chinese influence was inevitable in Southeast Asia.[8] Most dismissed the domino theory as a sham and contended that, in any event, local nationalism rather than U.S. military power was the most effective barrier to any domino effect in a pluralistic world. In this context, they concluded, Vietnam was of no more than marginal importance to the United States.

All doves flatly rejected Johnson's explanation of the origins of the war. They conceded Ho Chi Minh's communist background but argued that he was primarily a nationalist whose fundamental goal was to complete the anticolonial revolution he had launched against the French in 1945. Radicals agreed that the insurgency in South Vietnam was an extension of Ho's revolution but accepted its legitimacy.[9] Liberals stressed that it had erupted spontaneously in the South in response to the corrupt and oppressive American-sponsored regime of Ngo Dinh Diem. Preoccupied with its own problems and fearful of provoking war with the United States, North Vietnam had ignored the southern insurgents' pleas for aid until American escalation of the conflict had forced it to respond. Even then, doves concluded, Hanoi's support was not crucial to the success of the Vietcong.[10]

The doves dismissed as blatant falsehoods the administration's accusations of North Vietnamese aggression. Following up on charges made by Senator Wayne Morse during the August 1964 congressional debate (later confirmed by *The Pentagon Papers*), they argued that the *U.S.S. Maddox* had been engaged in electronic espionage off the North Vietnamese coast and that its presence near an area where South Vietnam had launched commando raids the preceding night might have provoked the attacks. They questioned whether the second attack on August 4 had taken place and argued that even if it had, it was nothing more than a "casual naval skirmish" which by no means merited the retaliation ordered by Johnson.[11] The Pleiku incident was scarcely enough to justify the systematic bombing of North Vietnam; the speed with which the administration responded, doves speculated, suggested that it was poised and waiting for an appropriate pretext to act. Using statements issued by government officials, Theodore Draper questioned whether all or even part of the "mysterious 325th" was actually in South Vietnam at the time the United States committed large-scale combat forces to the war.[12]

Holding the United States primarily responsible for the escalation, doves charged that the bombing and the dispatch of ground troops were desperate attempts of the Johnson administration to stave off the collapse of South Vietnam from within. The succession of puppets following the overthrow of Diem in November 1963 had been unable to rally the fragmented population of South Vietnam, and vocal elements were demanding peace and reconciliation with the Vietcong. The Tonkin Gulf reprisals were designed to shore up the embattled government of Nguyen Khanh and to distract attention from the breakdown in the South. Some argued that Johnson also took advantage of the contrived crisis to secure passage of a resolution making possible an escalation to which he was already committed. Once the presidential election of 1964 was safely past, he initiated the bombing of North Vietnam and dispatched combat forces to head off the impending collapse of the South Vietnamese government. The theory of North Vietnamese aggression, Draper concluded, was used by the administration "to take flight from the intractable problems of the South and to seek comfort in the illusion that the solution to the whole war was located in the North."[13]

The doves thus accused Johnson of lying to get the nation to accept war. He misrepresented the situation in Vietnam and the reasons for escalation. While continually insisting that he was merely following the policies of his predecessors, he was in fact ordering drastic changes. He deliberately obscured the significance of these changes by portraying them as reprisals. He refused to take his case directly to Congress and the public, presumably because he perceived the weakness of his position. Johnson and his advisers "manipulated the public, the Congress, and the press from the start," David Halberstam concluded.[14]

Most doves agreed that intervention in Vietnam had been disastrous, but they differed among themselves about why it had occurred. Some argued that the administration had perceived war was not the answer to the "realities" in Vietnam but had acted to escalate conflict anyway. Conservatives stressed the "arrogance of power," the unwillingness of the policymakers to accept frustration and failure. "A weaker power might have suffered them in silence or angry self-recrimination," Draper observed. "But the United States is too rich and powerful to take a setback without seeking to impose its will."[15] Radicals emphasized the "operational code" of the "national security managers" for whom "toughness" was the "most prized virtue" and perseverance in Vietnam was essential to maintain an American-dominated world order.[16]

Most liberals were more charitable, stressing misperception as the basic cause of intervention. Despite the enormous changes that had taken place in the world, they argued, Johnson and his advisers continued to be guided by the Cold War certitudes of the 1950s: a rigid, militant, anticommunism and an unwavering faith that aggression, whatever its form, must be met forcibly. Any tendency to deviate from these views was countered by the lingering effects of McCarthyism. The "right wing of the Republican party tattooed on the skins of politicians and bureaucrats alike some vivid impressions of what could happen to a liberal administration that chanced to be in office the day a red flag rose over Saigon," Daniel Ellsberg observed.[17]

Liberal doves differed in assigning blame for the misperception. Some early writers advanced the "quagmire thesis" that overoptimistic advisers had misled unsuspecting Presidents step by step into the war in Vietnam. Others argued that Johnson's lack of experience in foreign affairs, the shallowness and rigidity of his intellect, and a temperament that could not stand the thought of anything resembling defeat were decisive factors in the escalation of the war.[18] Many of these same writers theorized, to Johnson's rage, that the more perceptive John F. Kennedy, who had become disenchanted with Vietnam at the time of his death, would have found a better solution.[19]

Liberals also focused on bureaucratic factors in explaining the commitment in Vietnam. The nation's leading Asian specialists had been purged from the government in the McCarthy era, they argued, and Vietnam policymaking suffered from a chronic lack of exper tise. Time-worn assumptions went unquestioned year after year because of the natural bureaucratic tendency toward conformity. Those who doubted or questioned either left government service; were "domesticated," that is, permitted to speak out but ignored when decisions were made; or dissented only in measured tones for fear of losing their effectiveness. Most writers agreed that conformity was common to all bureaucracies, but some argued that Lyndon Johnson was particularly intolerant of dissent and imposed a tightly closed system in which debate was always about means rather than ends or basic assumptions. "Through a variety of procedures, both institutional and personal, doubt, dissent and expertise were effectively neutralized in the making of policy," James Thomson concluded.[20]

The dove interpretation dominated writing on Vietnam through the early 1970s. As the war dragged on, seemingly without end, the volume and intensity of the attacks increased. Publication of *The Pentagon Papers* in 1971 added to the furor. Written by civilians in the Defense Department, many of whom had become disenchanted with the war, this collection of official histories seemed to confirm many of the dove charges, particularly those of deception and manipulation of public opinion. Moreover, the *New York Times* writers who compiled the best-selling, one-volume edition of the papers focused on the theme of government duplicity, leaving the distinct impression, as one critic has pointed out, that "US involvement was the product of a clique of willful men, who secretly led the nation into a full-scale war, even while denying this aim to the American public and Congress."[21] Most major works on Vietnam in the early 1970s reflected the influence of the doves. The high water mark was probably reached in 1972 with the near-simultaneous publication of David Halberstam's *The Best and the Brightest* and Frances Fitzgerald's *Fire in the Lake*, two best-sellers which approached the war from very different directions but bitterly indicted American involvement.

The climate of response to the war has changed significantly since the fall of South Vietnam in 1975. The immediate reaction was a collective amnesia, an overwhelming tendency to forget a painful experience. By the end of the decade, discussion of Vietnam had increased to a degree that would have seemed impossible just a few years before, but the debate continued in much more subdued tones. A huge majority of Americans have continued to regard the war as a mistake.[22] But the passage of time and the gradual subsiding of passions have enabled scholars to place the war in perspective and to view the policy makers with greater detachment. Vietnam's invasion of Cambodia in 1978 and the continued flight of thousands of refugees have made it increasingly difficult to view Hanoi as an innocent victim of American aggression. Indeed, in the summer of 1979 columnist George Will proclaimed that Lyndon Johnson had been "right about Hanoi before the boat people proved his point."[23] If most scholars have not gone this far, they are able to view Johnson with greater sympathy.

Simultaneously, the availability of extensive documentation on the Johnson era has considerably broadened the base of research on Vietnam. *The Pentagon Papers* have proved a veritable gold mine for scholars. Compiled under instructions from Secretary of Defense Robert McNamara, this invaluable collection contains historical analyses of a number of major topics along with supporting documents from Defense Department, State Department, and CIA files. The histories were done close to the event and in haste; they reflect the bias of the Pentagon civilians and must be used with caution. But they contain a wealth of important detail as well as excerpts from unpublished documents. These documents include such significant items as CIA intelligence estimates; position papers prepared by the Joint Chiefs of Staff, Pentagon officials, and the National Security Council staff; and cables exchanged between the State Department and the embassy in Saigon. *The Pentagon Papers* trace American involvement in Vietnam back to 1945, but they contain a particularly full discussion and documentation of Johnson's 1963–1965 decisions to escalate the war.[24]

The major gap in *The Pentagon Papers*—documents from White House files—has been partially filled in recent years. In his memoir, Johnson vigorously defends his major Vietnam decisions, often quoting at length from papers submitted to him by his leading advisers and from records of top-level conferences.[25] More important, a considerable volume of documents relating to escalation of the war is now available in the Lyndon B. Johnson Library. At this writing, only about 15 percent of the Vietnam material in the White House Central Files and in the National Security Files of McGeorge Bundy and Walt Rostow's office is open for research.[26] Nevertheless, a major portion of the Country File, Vietnam, in the National Security Files is open for the period November 1963 to July 1965. This important file contains much larger quantities of the sort of material published in *The Pentagon Papers* and also includes extensive White House documents. Among the most valuable items are covering memoranda submitted to the President by Bundy and his staff analyzing proposals emanating from the various departments and agencies, exploring options on major issues, or recommending a particular course of action. Unfortunately, most of the records of White House meetings are exempted from declassification, and very little of Johnson's point of view appears in the open material. Arranged chronologically, this file still provides an invaluable day-to-day record of the decisions which led to war in Vietnam.

In addition, apparently at Johnson's direction, the White House staff compiled a series of historical files on major policy decisions, two of which, "Gulf of Tonkin" and "Deployment of Major U.S. Forces to Vietnam, July, 1965," pertain directly to escalation of the war. Roughly three-fourths of the material in these two National Security Council Histories has been declassified. The documents duplicate to some extent those in the Country File, but they are supplemented by recollections of some of the major participants and by histories based in part on documents that remain classified. In short, the availability of a large quantity of materials in the Johnson Library now provides historians a reasonably firm basis for assessing the decisions leading to the war.

Several general studies on Vietnam have appeared in the past few years, each of which follows the broad outlines of the contemporary debate while modifying official and dove viewpoints in important ways. Characterized by one reviewer as the "first salvo in the refighting of the Vietnam war," Guenter Lewy's *America in Vietnam* focuses on U.S. military operations. In a background chapter, however, Lewy defends with only minor qualifications the administration's rationale for intervention.[27] Conceding that American policy makers exaggerated the importance of Vietnam in the early stages of involvement, he argues that the long-standing commitment there actually created a vital interest which Johnson had to uphold. America's fundamental mistake was not intervening in

Vietnam but fighting the war in a way that virtually ensured ultimate failure.

In *The Irony of Vietnam: The System Worked*, Leslie Gelb and Richard Betts accept the doves' contention that intervention was misguided but challenge their explanation of the reasons behind it.[28] Gelb was the supervisor of *The Pentagon Papers* project, and he uses this experience, along with newly declassified documents, to compile a richly detailed analysis of the decision-making process. Gelb and Betts flatly reject the quagmire thesis, arguing that Johnson (and his predecessors) clearly foresaw the consequences of their actions. Presidents from Truman to Nixon acted on the basis of two fundamental principles shared by the "attentive public": Vietnam must not be lost, but the United States must avoid a major war in Asia. The result was an incremental escalation intended to save South Vietnam but not to resolve the deeper problems, perpetuating a stalemate. Differing from those doves who located the source of American failure in bureaucratic error, Gelb and Betts maintain that "the system worked"—the United States preserved the independence of South Vietnam until domestic support evaporated. But, they conclude, the policy failed. Viewing Vietnam as an excessive commitment in a peripheral area, they locate the source of failure in the doctrine of containment which left policy makers little choice but to raise the level of involvement each step along the way.

My own study, *America's Longest War*, provides an overview of American involvement in Vietnam between 1950 and 1975, dealing with both the formulation and implementation of policy.[29] More dovish in tone and argument than the book by Gelb and Betts, it also rejects their contention that policy makers knowingly perpetuated a stalemate. In general, however, I concur with their emphasis on the long-term nature of the commitment and with their thesis that involvement stemmed logically from the containment policy and the American world view.

These works, along with other more specific studies, have initiated at least a partial assessment of Johnson's decisions in favor of war. Regarding the origins of the conflict, recent scholars generally support a position somewhere between those advanced by the administration and its critics. Relying on published and captured enemy documents, King C. Chen concurs with the doves that the insurgency began in the South in reaction to Diem's repression and apparently in violation of Hanoi's instructions. Chen also concludes, however, that North Vietnam committed itself to the revolution sooner and gave it greater support than most doves would have allowed. As early as

1960, he argues, Hanoi formally committed itself to the liberation of South Vietnam, and after an unsuccessful attempt to negotiate with Diem a settlement based on American withdrawal, it significantly stepped up its aid to the Vietcong in an attempt to topple the "puppet" Saigon government.[30] Although it remains impossible to get reliable figures on North Vietnamese infiltration, recent studies agree that it was substantial and more important to the success of the Vietcong than most doves were prepared to admit at the time.[31]

Most recent writers still reject, however, the administration's claim that it was responding primarily to North Vietnamese escalation. Even Lewy concedes (a point upheld by Herring and Gelb and Betts) that the doves were on "solid ground" in arguing that the main reason for the initiation of the bombing in 1965 was the "drastic deterioration of both the political and military posture of the Government of Vietnam, which threatened a complete South Vietnamese collapse."[32] Although the Johnson administration was alarmed by the apparent increase in infiltration, its major concern throughout 1964 was the chronic instability of the Saigon government, and as early as June it was considering taking the war to North Vietnam in an attempt to boost morale in Saigon and help an embattled government rally its people.

Some postwar studies also confirm the dove charges that the incidents cited by the administration to justify escalation were pretexts rather than causes. The Gulf of Tonkin affair remains a matter of controversy. In regard to the disputed second attack on August 4, Lewy unqualifiedly accepts the administration's position, arguing that intercepts of North Vietnamese radio messages leave "no doubt of the fact of an attack."[33] Recently declassified documents make clear that the administration regarded the intercepts as the clinching evidence needed to justify retaliation.[34] The intercepts themselves remain classified, however, and the earlier reports from the scene were sufficiently ambiguous and contradictory to provide ample reason for restraint had the administration been so inclined. Frustrated with the lack of progress in the South and enraged by Hanoi's apparent audacity, Johnson and his advisers were obviously in a mood to strike back, and they seem to have selected from the evidence available to them those parts that confirmed that an attack had actually taken place. The incidents also provided the occasion to secure passage of a congressional resolution authorizing escalation which had been drafted several months earlier but had been held back for fear that a debate on Vietnam might imperil passage of the civil rights legislation.[35] Whatever the facts of the incident, it is clear that the administration used it to implement plans which had been under consideration for some time.

Similarly, the Pleiku incident was the pretext for the decision to begin the systematic bombing of North Vietnam. The administration did not commit itself to escalation of the war in the immediate aftermath of the August incidents. The election campaign made such a step untimely. More important, persisting instability in Saigon raised fears that further attacks on North Vietnam might provoke reprisals the South Vietnamese government could not withstand. It would be rash, Johnson informed his advisers, to "enter the patient in a 10 round bout, when he was in no shape for one round."[36] Ironically, however, what had been the major reason for delay became the most compelling reason for action by early 1965. Despite frantic U.S. attempts to promote stability in South Vietnam, governments continued to come and go as through a revolving door, and the Buddhist leaders were in open revolt, demanding an American withdrawal and negotiations with the Vietcong. Although no formal decision was made, Johnson and his advisers agreed by late January that something must be done to avert disaster.[37] The Pleiku attacks provided the occasion to do what Washington felt could be delayed no longer. "Pleikus are like streetcars," McGeorge Bundy later conceded.[38]

The decision to deploy ground troops followed in short order and for similar reasons. The administration was unquestionably concerned about increased North Vietnamese infiltration and the intensification of Vietcong military operations. It was equally concerned about the persisting political chaos in Saigon, however. After an impossibly confusing series of coups and countercoups, a new government assumed power in May, the fifth since the death of Diem. The Ky-Thieu "directorate" would survive longer than any of its predecessors, but at the outset its future appeared singularly uncertain.[39] The commitment of significant numbers of U.S. combat forces seemed the only way to stave off imminent military and political collapse. Recent scholarship tends, therefore, to confirm the dove charge that the administration in 1964 and 1965 was responding as much to decay from within as aggression from without.

Johnson *was* less than candid in explaining the steps he took. His repeated insistence that he was not changing American policy was literally correct—the policy had always been to prevent a communist takeover of South Vietnam—but it deliberately obscured the significance of the changes that were being made. In the Gulf of Tonkin affair, the administration revealed considerably less than the

whole truth, and it never publicly admitted that the Pleiku "retalia-
tory" raids had quickly been converted into a sustained air offensive
against North Vietnam. The first U.S. combat forces were quietly
sent to Vietnam in March 1965 to guard American air bases, but
Johnson did not inform the public when he changed their mission
shortly afterward to offensive operations. The truth did not come
out until several months later—and then inadvertently.[40] Although
acutely aware of the importance of the July ground troop decisions,
the President did not take his case directly to the public or Congress. Instead, after consulting secretly with a small group of
congressional leaders, he ordered the decisions implemented in a
"low-keyed manner in order . . . to avoid undue excitement in the
Congress and in domestic public opinion."[41]

Recent writers are less concerned with building a case against
Johnson for duplicity than with explaining why he chose to take the
nation into war in this fashion. Both the Joint Chiefs of Staff and
Secretary of Defense Robert McNamara urged the President to mo-
bilize the reserves and declare a limited national emergency to persuade the nation that it was not embarking on some "two-penny
military adventure," and Johnson himself apparently toyed with
the idea of a congressional resolution explicitly endorsing his decisions.[42] He eventually rejected all such proposals, however. His attorney general assured him that he had the authority to send combat
forces to Vietnam without formal congressional approval.[43] As majority leader under Eisenhower, Johnson had operated on the principle that the President should be given the widest possible discretion
in foreign policy, and experience had taught him that Congress usually rallied around decisive presidential initiatives.[44] Johnson feared
that anything resembling a declaration of war might trigger a Soviet
or Chinese response, perhaps provoking a major war. He also expressed concern that it might unleash irresistible pressures from the
American right wing, which he once called the "great lurking monster," that could lead to all-out war.[45]

In her provocative biography of Johnson, Doris Kearns further
explains LBJ's decisions in terms of his personality. Throughout his
life, she argues, Johnson refused to make hard choices when faced
with conflicting demands, instead opting for compromise and consensus. A man of enormous ambitions, he was determined not to
"lose" Vietnam, but he was also determined to avoid a full-fledged
debate on the war lest it imperil the Great Society programs then
making their way through Congress. A man who accepted few limits, he was confident that he could do what no other President had

attempted: wage war and accomplish a major reform program simultaneously. The decision for war, Kearns concludes, "bore Johnson's own personal stamp to a unique degree."[46]

Scholars disagree sharply on Johnson's expectations about the war. Elaborating a theme developed earlier by Daniel Ellsberg, Gelb and Betts argue that Johnson was not deluded by the prospect of quick and painless success. Determined not to permit the fall of South Vietnam and yet unwilling to sanction a full-scale war, he and his advisers increased the American commitment incrementally in recognition that a stalemate would be the likely result. "At best they *hoped* they might be lucky, but they did not *expect* to be."[47] The argument rests on shaky evidence. White House files shed little light on the issue, and although intelligence estimates and Joint Chiefs of Staff projections often take a cautious line, this is common bureaucratic practice. The caution of the Joint Chiefs of Staff may have been calculated to pressure Johnson into making a larger commitment.[48] Gelb and Betts are certainly right in arguing that Johnson did not expect victory in the traditional sense—indeed, he did not seek it. As Bernard Brodie has observed, however, this interpretation falls into the "opposite error of implying that the President knew very well what he was getting into," which "on the face of it [is] an absurdity."[49] Accustomed to the precise calculations of the congressional cloakroom, Johnson was clearly frustrated by the unwillingness of his advisers to make firm predictions. "Why can't anybody tell me how it will turn out?" he complained repeatedly in 1965.[50] It is quite difficult to believe, however, that he would have taken such risks without the expectation that he could end the war in a reasonable period and on favorable terms.

While demonstrating conclusively Johnson's lack of candor and his deliberate, calculated decision to go to war in a "low-keyed manner," recent writers have nevertheless questioned the dove charge that he duped an unsuspecting public and Congress into an unwanted war. Examining the 1964–1965 views of journalists David Halberstam, Neil Sheehan, and Malcolm Browne, all of whom became leading doves, Ian Maitland finds that, like Johnson, they flatly rejected the idea of withdrawal from Vietnam and supported an enlarged commitment, even though recognizing that the cost might be great. Maitland thus surmises that Johnson's decisions may have "accurately reflected a broad consensus among the 'attentive public.'"[51] Gelb and Betts cite public opinion polls to demonstrate that Johnson's decisions had broad popular support and that his middle course between the extremes of withdrawal and all-out war reflected the mood of a nation that did not want to fight a major war in Asia but also did not want to be forced out of Vietnam.[52]

The role of Congress has also come under scrutiny. Some members of Congress have since conceded that the nation's plunge into war in Vietnam resulted as much from legislative failure as from executive manipulation. Polls taken as late as the end of 1966 indicated that Johnson enjoyed firm support in Congress.[53] Other evidence suggests that many congressional leaders, although skeptical of the wisdom of the President's 1965 decisions, quickly fell into line. Some, such as Senator Richard Russell, who had long questioned the strategic value of Vietnam and had opposed deeper commitment, simply concluded that "we are there now" and if "we were to scuttle and run, it would shake the confidence of the free world in any commitment we might make."[54] Others, accustomed to deferring to presidential leadership in foreign affairs, were more than willing to permit Johnson to make the tough decisions in full knowledge that he would have to bear the consequences.[55] "Numbed by the practice of its responsibilities and confirmed in the rightness of American intervention," Jack Sullivan and Alton Frye conclude, "Congress would have given the President whatever he said he needed, almost without regard for the circumstances."[56]

The issue of executive deception poses difficult problems. It seems clear that public opinion and Congress supported the President's policies until the costs were deemed excessive, and therefore they share responsibility for the war. It seems likely, moreover, that had Johnson been absolutely candid and taken his case directly to the people and Congress, the outcome would have been the same. The suggestion of some recent writers that public and congressional attitudes were so deeply entrenched that Johnson had little choice but to proceed as he did seems open to question, however. It is impossible to determine, for example, the extent to which these views were shaped by administration rhetoric, which at times consisted of distortion and half-truth. Opinion analysts have long recognized, moreover, the permissiveness of public opinion and its tendency to respond positively to decisive presidential moves. It can be argued, therefore, that the public and Congress would have responded with equal firmness to an attempt to extricate the United States from Vietnam.[57] In any event, there would seem to be some truth in LBJ's angry retort that this is "not Johnson's war, it's everybody's war."[58]

Recent writers have deemphasized Johnson's personal responsibility for the war in other ways. Arthur M. Schlesinger, Jr.'s revival of the argument that Kennedy would have avoided a large-scale war has not secured widespread acceptance.[59] Many writers simply contend that what Kennedy might have done can never be known and dismiss the issue as one that cannot be resolved. Kennedy himself has been the subject of considerable revisionism, moreover, and numerous scholars have assigned him a full measure of blame for Vietnam.[60] More important, while the doves tended to focus rather narrowly on the 1960s, recent emphasis has been increasingly on the long-range nature of the commitment in Vietnam. Research on the earlier years of American involvement has made clear that at various junctures between 1950 and 1965, Democratic and Republican administrations faced difficult choices of abstention or commitment. In each case, after carefully weighing the alternatives, they opted for expanded involvement that attached American prestige more deeply, bequeathed to their successors more dangerous and intractable problems, and significantly narrowed subsequent choices. Without minimizing the importance of Johnson's 1965 decisions, it seems fair to conclude that his predecessors must share responsibility with him for the eventual outcome.[61]

In searching for the larger sources of the commitment, recent critics of American involvement focus on the policy of containment. To be sure, American policy makers misperceived the nature of the conflict in Vietnam, and Johnson's world view was indeed unsophisticated. But another factor was the implicit assumption of the containment policy that no communist could be a genuine nationalist and that any gain for communism was a loss for the United States. Moreover, the doctrine of containment led to Vietnam's being defined as a vital interest. At the time Johnson made the crucial decisions on Vietnam, containment had few critics inside or outside of government. "As long as the general doctrine of containment of communism remained the consensus," Gelb and Betts conclude, "the specific military intervention in Vietnam followed logically. . . . Doctrine dictated commitment." The emphasis on containment is of more than academic importance. By perceiving Vietnam as a mistake or the misapplication of policy, some liberal doves assumed the continued viability and necessity of containment. Recent critics argue that the policy itself was flawed and urgently warn that the United States must adopt new policies to meet changing world conditions.[62]

Postwar debate on the war thus revolves around the central issue of America's proper role in the world. Conservatives such as Lewy defend intervention in Vietnam and argue that failure to pursue the war to a successful conclusion has had disastrous consequences at home and abroad. Gelb-Betts and others view intervention as the result of a policy which had already become outdated and warn that continued attempts to apply that policy in a more complex and pluralistic world where American power is increasingly limited can only lead to further frustration.

In each case, however, Johnson's role has come in for reconsideration. Conceding that he may have misperceived events in Vietnam and that he was less than candid, writers on both sides agree that by the time he inherited the problem his options were quite limited. More restrained in tone than the doves, they tend not to single him out for special criticism. From the vantage point of fifteen intervening years, LBJ appears less a fool or knave than a beleaguered executive attempting to maintain an established policy against an immediate threat in a situation where there was no attractive alternative.

II

Johnson's handling of the war has also provoked controversy, the debate closely following the positions staked out on the question of intervention. Those who defend American involvement as necessary or at least unavoidable criticize Johnson and his advisers for employing means that assured failure. Those who regard intervention as misguided question the morality of the means used and express doubts whether there was any acceptable way to preserve an independent, noncommunist South Vietnam.

Scholars studying these issues must work with very limited sources. The various military services have declassified some operational reports and have begun to produce official histories based partially on classified documents, but most major Joint Chiefs of Staff and Defense Department records remain under restriction.[63] The open materials in the White House Central Files in the Johnson Library reveal very little of the formulation and implementation of strategy. The Country File, Vietnam, contains an enormous amount of material on military operations, pacification, and relations with South Vietnam, but it is unavailable for the period after June 1965. Two National Security Council Histories, "Honolulu Conference (February 1966)" and "Manila Conference (October–November 1966)," are partially open and shed some light on American dealings with the Saigon government, but the most important documents remain classified. Scholars must rely on *The Pentagon Papers*, memoirs of participants, and a large but quite uneven secondary literature.

As with the decision to intervene, postwar controversy on the war itself closely parallels the contemporary debate. Determined to prevail in Vietnam without involving the United States in all-out war, Johnson deliberately chose a middle course of "enough, but not too much" military pressure, provoking fire from both sides.[64] Hawks urged the pursuit of victory and relentlessly pressed him to use the level of force required to end the war quickly and decisively. Doves bitterly protested the militarization of United States policy, denouncing the bombing of North Vietnam and of search-and-destroy operations in the South as at best ineffective, at worst immoral.

In their memoirs, General William Westmoreland and Admiral U. S. Grant Sharp reaffirm the hawk position, vigorously defending their conduct of the war and blaming American failure on the gradualist strategy pursued by Johnson and Secretary of Defense McNamara. Responding to critics of his strategy of attrition, Westmoreland argues that South Vietnam could not be stabilized or Hanoi compelled to negotiate until the North Vietnamese and Vietcong main units were eliminated. The search-and-destroy strategy was working, he contends, and could have succeeded if in 1967 he had been given the additional troops he requested, authority to strike enemy sanctuaries outside South Vietnam, and the means to close off Hanoi and Haiphong.[65] Sharp indicts the civilians in Washington for ignoring "sound, time vindicated principles of military strategy" in their direction of the air war. Instead of striking North Vietnam with devastating blows, they compelled the air force and navy to "peck away at seemingly random targets," always under "severe restrictions," nullifying America's "immensely superior firepower and technology" and resulting in a "strategy of defeat."[66] Had the military been permitted to use American power without restriction, Westmoreland and Sharp conclude, the United States could have won the war.

Most postwar commentators agree that American strategy was inherently unworkable. The search-and-destroy strategy was based on a gross miscalculation of North Vietnam's determination to resist and its capacity to replace its losses; as long as the United States would not attack the sanctuaries, it could not succeed. The strategy was counterproductive, moreover, causing enormous economic and social dislocation in South Vietnam, the country the United States was trying to save, and resulting in high draft rates and heavy U.S.

casualties which caused growing unrest at home. Whether the sort of air war advocated by Sharp would have achieved the desired result without even greater costs cannot be known, but scholars concur that the gradual escalation of the bombing produced minimal gains at a high price. North Vietnam was given time to disperse its population and resources, protect its infiltration routes, and develop an air defense system that took a large toll in American aircraft. Hanoi effectively exploited the bombing for propaganda advantage in world and even American opinion.

Many recent writers assign the civilian leadership a large share of responsibility for the military failure in Vietnam. Admitting a lack of expertise in military affairs, Johnson and McNamara provided the armed services no guidelines, leaving them free to develop strategy on their own. At the same time, Johnson and McNamara hemmed the services in with restrictions which rendered the chosen strategies unworkable. The various elements of U.S. policy were to a large degree improvised and compartmentalized and often conflicted with each other. Even after it was apparent that the strategy was not working, the contradictions and inconsistencies remained unresolved, causing pronounced civil-military tensions. The command system may have functioned less effectively in Vietnam than in any other American war.[67]

The military has also come in for extensive criticism, however. Robert Gallucci stresses the vital role of tradition, institutional pressures, and professionalism in shaping American strategy. The air force and navy pressed for the use of air power in Vietnam to prove the value of strategic bombing and to preserve their missions in the defense establishment. The search-and-destroy strategy accorded with the army's traditional strategic doctrine of massing large forces against the enemy's main units and also met professional needs, giving officers the "opportunity to perform well in ways that would not be guaranteed under a more conservative strategy."[68]

Although he defends American involvement in Vietnam and exonerates the United States from charges of war crimes and atrocities, Guenter Lewy concurs with Gallucci. The American military failed to understand the dynamics of revolutionary war, he argues, and fashioned a traditional strategy in a setting that "posed anything but traditional problems." Had U.S. military commanders been given everything they wanted, it would merely have compounded the difficulties without solving the basic problem—political instability in South Vietnam. What was needed was a strategy more attuned to the realities of the war, one that placed greatest emphasis on protecting and winning the support of the people of South Vietnam.[69]

While some postwar commentators focus on the misuse of American military power, others, echoing complaints heard at the time, argue that the United States erred in seeking a military solution to what was essentially a political problem. Had the Johnson administration concentrated on developing an effective pacification program to gain control of the countryside, former Ambassador Robert Komer has speculated, there "might have been a more satisfactory outcome. At the least, it would probably have resulted in less militarization and Americanization of the conflict."[70]

Such criticisms have an ironic ring, for improving the lot of the Vietnamese was the one area of involvement in Vietnam that struck a responsive chord in Johnson. He identified with the people of Asia and deeply sympathized with their presumed desire for political freedom and economic progress. Hope of bettering the lot of the people of South Vietnam enabled him to rationalize the use of military power. Like most of his colleagues, he felt that it was necessary to win the support of the people in order to defeat the Vietcong. He could wax eloquent about such enterprises as innoculation programs to increase life expectancy, educational reform, and using American expertise to teach the Vietnamese to raise larger hogs and grow more sweet potatoes.[71] "Dammit," he once exploded, "we need to exhibit more compassion for these Vietnamese plain people. . . . We've got to see that the South Vietnamese government wins the battle, not so much of arms, but of crops and hearts and caring."[72]

Pacification has received less attention than military operations, but available studies agree that despite Johnson's personal commitment and the expenditure of lavish funds, the campaign to win the "hearts and minds" of the people failed. A serious commitment to pacification came only after the Vietcong had become deeply entrenched in the countryside. At least until 1967, the programs were hastily improvised and poorly administered, and pacification and military operations were conducted in isolation from each other. It was not simply a matter of instituting programs and providing funds and technical know-how, as all too many Americans assumed, however. Profound cultural differences made it difficult for Americans to solve the problems of the Vietnamese countryside. More important, from beginning to end the South Vietnamese government was hampered by its own structural weaknesses, a lack of skilled personnel, and a marked inability to relate to its own people. The failure of pacification reflected not so much a lack of commitment, as Komer suggests, as the much larger problem of effective political action in an alien and often hostile environment.[73]

Would another approach have worked? Obviously no one can ever answer such a question definitively, and scholars are deeply divided in their judgments. Lewy argues that Johnson should have dealt with the American public and Congress more candidly, cultivating a solid base of support for his policies, and that he should have adopted a "population security" strategy combined with an intensive pacification program. "While one cannot be sure that these different strategies would have brought a different outcome," he concludes, "neither can one take their failure for granted."[74] My own conclusions, while equally tentative, are much more pessimistic. Stressing the fanatical determination of the North Vietnamese and Vietcong, the perilously weak basis for nationhood in South Vietnam, and the sharply defined limits on the use of American military and political power, I conclude that the American effort to "create a bastion of anti-Communism south of the seventeenth parallel was probably doomed from the start."[75]

While hawks attacked Johnson for not prosecuting the war with sufficient vigor, doves accused him of indifference and deviousness in the pursuit of peace. North Vietnam evinced a repeated willingness to talk, they argued, but the United States, in its stubborn determination to attain a military victory, "ruled out serious negotiations."[76] The Johnson administration's insistence on the withdrawal of all North Vietnamese troops from the South and the exclusion of the Vietcong from any political settlement was totally unrealistic and designed to stall negotiations until the United States could impose its terms. The much-publicized bombing pauses were meaningless gestures intended to appease domestic critics and lay the basis for future escalation. When several major peace initiatives failed in 1966 and 1967, some doves charged the administration with inexcusable blunders, the result of either a woeful lack of coordination within the government or disinterest in negotiations.[77] Others speculated that Johnson had deliberately sabotaged the initiatives for fear that he would be lured into negotiations when his bargaining position was still weak.[78]

Johnson responds angrily to such charges in his memoir. He claims to have followed up more than seventy peace overtures and insists that he significantly modified his terms to bring about negotiations. He concedes that he approved the bombing pauses reluctantly, but adds that he did so in a sincere attempt to get talks underway. All he got in return was a series of angry replies from Ho Chi

Minh and drastic increases in North Vietnamese infiltration. "The simple truth was that the North Vietnamese were not ready to talk with us," he concludes.[79]

The full story of the diplomacy of the war will not be known for many years. Little reliable evidence is available from the North Vietnamese side, and interpretations of Hanoi's position remain highly speculative. The voluminous White House and State Department files dealing with negotiations are still classified. The most important available source is that section of *The Pentagon Papers* dealing with diplomatic contacts, only recently released in "sanitized" form.[80] The historical analyses are not nearly as comprehensive or as penetrating as the other parts of the papers, and many documents have been deleted in whole or in part because of "national security" restrictions. Nevertheless, these documents, along with several of the oral histories in the Johnson Library and recent scholarly works, shed considerable light on American handling of the major peace initiatives.[81]

A brief survey cannot do justice to the impossibly complex diplomatic maneuvering, but several generalizations may be ventured. Johnson was unquestionably sincere in his desire for peace, and, in any event, domestic and international pressures required that he respond to initiatives from third parties and even the faintest signals from Hanoi. The administration dutifully pursued countless overtures and made determined efforts to open direct contacts with North Vietnam in Paris, Moscow, and Rangoon. The United States gradually backed away from its demand for the immediate withdrawal of all North Vietnamese troops, eventually agreeing to stop the bombing with the "understanding" that such action would lead to "prompt and productive" discussions and that Hanoi would not take military advantage of the American concession. In several vaguely worded proposals, the administration also modified at least slightly its opposition to Vietcong participation in a political settlement.[82]

Washington did handle several major peace initiatives badly. To cite but one example, the United States undercut British Prime Minister Harold Wilson's efforts to enlist the cooperation of Soviet Premier Alexei Kosygin in arranging talks with Hanoi by failing to communicate accurately to London a recent change in its conditions for a bombing halt. An enraged Wilson was left out on a limb when the new, harsher terms became apparent, and the initiative quickly collapsed. Johnson was essentially correct, however, when he later pointed out that the North Vietnamese had already privately rejected the earlier, more favorable American offer. The major result was to exacerbate Anglo-American relations and give critics an occasion to charge the United States with bad faith.[83]

In the final analysis, the administration's skepticism and its rigid bargaining position seem to have been more responsible for the failure of diplomacy than its ineptitude. Johnson's attitude toward the various peace initiatives was at best ambivalent. He dismissed many third-party overtures as "Nobel Prize fever."[84] Although desirous of peace and determined to show his willingness to negotiate, he suspected that Hanoi was using the prospect of talks to increase domestic and international pressures on the United States. He was reluctant to appear too conciliatory lest he play into Hanoi's hands or convey an impression of weakness. Most important, he was determined to secure a noncommunist South Vietnam, and he remained confident, at least until 1967, that he could achieve this goal by increasing military pressure. Thus, although he made concessions, they represented, as George Ball later conceded, "little more than rejuggling of words so as to make our own objectives seem more palatable without materially changing our basic position."[85]

It seems entirely likely, however, that the doves exaggerated the possibility of serious negotiations during this period. Johnson's assessment of the third-party initiatives may not have been off the mark. A former Hungarian diplomat has testified that at least one of them was based on a gross misrepresentation of Hanoi's position and was designed to enhance the prestige of its author, the Hungarian foreign minister. He has also speculated that the Soviet Union on several occasions may have misled the United States about the prospect of negotiations in order to do Hanoi a favor by getting the bombing stopped.[86] The firmness with which North Vietnam clung to its goals in the face of subsequent U.S. concessions and military punishment suggests that it was unlikely to enter serious negotiations unless convinced that it could get what it wanted by political means. Like Washington, Hanoi could not afford to ignore pleas for peace, and it probably appeared conciliatory on occasion to get the bombing stopped and to put the United States at a propaganda disadvantage. The North Vietnamese modified their bargaining position a bit over the years, but never to the extent that their basic goals would be jeopardized. They too seem to have remained certain that they could achieve their goals by military means and regarded major concessions as unnecessary and potentially dangerous. The diplomatic stalemate merely reflected the stalemate on the battlefield.[87]

III

Among the many issues raised by the Vietnam War, few have caused greater controversy than the Tet Offensive of 1968. Westmoreland and others have compared North Vietnam's strategy to that of Hitler in the Ardennes campaign. In a desperate, last-ditch effort to snatch victory from the jaws of defeat, a battered enemy hurled its best units against the cities of South Vietnam. The move failed disastrously. Although caught by surprise, the United States and South Vietnam quickly recovered, inflicting crippling losses on the attackers. Had the United States exploited its advantage, the war could have been ended. Westmoreland blames the media for the U.S. failure to do so. Ignoring massive evidence to the contrary, panicky and spiteful journalists portrayed Tet as an enemy victory, creating widespread disillusionment at home and forcing Johnson to seek a negotiated settlement. "It was like two boxers in a ring," Westmoreland concludes, "one having the other on the ropes, close to a knockout, when the apparent winner's second inexplicably throws in the towel."[88]

Doves have taken a very different view of the events of February 1968. Despite the huge losses suffered by the Vietcong, they question whether Tet significantly altered the balance of forces in South Vietnam. The offensive was designed primarily for its impact on public opinion in the United States, they contend, and in this it succeeded. Some doves hail Johnson's decisions to end the gradual escalation of the war as long overdue and give Clark Clifford the credit.[89] Others question the extent to which Johnson really changed his policy, arguing that he merely shifted tactics to preserve a position that was becoming untenable, permitting an unnecessary and destructive war to go on for four more years.[90]

A significant body of primary material for this period has recently been opened for research in the Johnson Library. The Country File, Vietnam, remains unprocessed, but approximately three-fourths of the National Security Council History, "March 31, 1968, Speech," has been made available. This file contains a brief, somewhat sketchy account of the events leading to Johnson's decisions, along with a substantial body of supporting documents. The latter includes extensive cable traffic between Washington and Saigon, CIA situation reports on developments in Vietnam, and memoranda to the President from his top civilian and military advisers and from such unofficial advisers as Dean Acheson, Henry Cabot Lodge, and Maxwell

Taylor. As with the other National Security Council Histories, the major items exempted from declassification appear to be records of White House meetings, and Johnson's views do not emerge at all. In addition to this important material, there are a few tantalizing items in Johnson's Diary Backup File and a larger body of documents in the files of speech writer Harry McPherson, particularly important because McPherson played a key role in the decision to cut back the bombing and press for negotiations.[91]

These primary materials may be supplemented by memoirs and by several major scholarly works published in the past few years. Lyndon Johnson, Clark Clifford, Harry McPherson, and Townsend Hoopes have each recounted their own roles during these crucial months in considerable detail. Peter Braestrup has compiled a massive assessment of the media's response to Tet. Using extensive interviews with participants, Herbert Schandler has produced a balanced and generally persuasive analysis of the decision-making process.[92]

Debate over the military significance of the campaigns of early 1968 will probably never be resolved definitively.[93] If the North Vietnamese sought to force the collapse of South Vietnam, they failed. The attackers were unable to secure firm positions in the urban areas and the South Vietnamese did not welcome them as liberators. Even if U.S. figures on enemy casualties are inflated, it is evident that the Vietcong, which bore the brunt of the fighting, suffered enormous losses from which it would never entirely recover. That victory was within grasp, as Westmoreland argues, is far from clear, however. Victory would have required a large-scale invasion of Laos, Cambodia, and North Vietnam, a move which would have brought heavy costs and considerable risk. If Tet represented a defeat for the enemy, moreover, it was still a costly victory for the United States and South Vietnam. They too suffered heavy losses. They were forced to withdraw troops to defend the cities, so that their position in the countryside, never strong, was further weakened. The heavy fighting created millions of new refugees, and the destruction in the cities heaped formidable new problems on a government which had shown only limited capacity to deal with the old ones. As with so much of the war, there was much suffering and destruction but no clear-cut winner or loser.

The role of the media has come in for scrutiny in the aftermath of the war. In his exhaustive study of television and newspaper reporting of Tet, Braestrup, himself a correspondent in Vietnam at the time, concludes that "rarely has contemporary crisis journalism turned out in retrospect to have veered so far from reality."[94] Shocked by the suddenness and magnitude of the attacks and under pressure to meet deadlines, reporters focused on the sensational, overlooking matters of real substance and making generalizations on the basis of isolated and unrepresentative incidents. Journalists who lacked expertise did not hesitate to offer authoritative judgments. According to Braestrup, the media created a totally misleading picture of Tet. From the first inaccurate reports that the Vietcong had taken over the U.S. embassy in Saigon, they depicted skillful and disciplined enemy forces inflicting devastating defeats on the unsuspecting Americans and South Vietnamese. In fact, Braestrup argues, the North Vietnamese offensive was poorly coordinated and indecisively executed, and the Americans and South Vietnamese fought extremely well. Tet was a defeat for the enemy, but the image of disaster portrayed by the media went uncorrected. Braestrup indicts the media, himself included, for a "major distortion of reality—through sins of omission and commission—on a scale that helped shape Tet's political repercussions in Washington and the administration's response."[95]

Tet had a profound impact on public attitudes toward the war, although, as Braestrup concedes, it is impossible to determine with precision the contribution of the media. Support for the war remained remarkably steady between November 1967 and March 1968, hovering around 45 percent. On the other hand, approval of Johnson's handling of it dipped to an all-time low of 26 percent, and by March an overwhelming majority of Americans were certain that the United States was not making any progress in Vietnam. Schandler concludes that the "shock and anger of the first days of Tet soon gave way to a sense of futility and despair. . . . The feeling grew that the cost of the war was no longer worth the goals for which it was being fought."[96]

Several other factors must be considered in assessing the impact of Tet on public opinion, however. The administration itself was at least partially responsible for the shock of the North Vietnamese offensive. Concerned by the steady erosion of public support for the war, Johnson in late 1967 had launched an intensive public relations campaign to demonstrate that significant progress was being made. In several major speeches, administration representatives had even hinted that the end was in sight.[97] The unduly optimistic reports of 1967, combined with the magnitude of the North

Vietnamese offensive, widened an already large credibility gap. Johnson and his advisers had "climbed way out on a limb, which the surprise attacks at Tet sawed off behind them," Don Oberdorfer has concluded.[98] Even then, the President had the means to counter the unfavorable images projected by the media, but his own public relations campaign after Tet was halting and ineffective, probably because his administration was sharply divided on what to do and because he himself was tired, confused, and dispirited.[99]

Public opinion does not appear to have been decisive in Johnson's rejection of Westmoreland's proposals to expand the war. The President had adamantly opposed extending the war into new areas from the outset. None of his civilian advisers supported Westmoreland's proposals, and Johnson seems to have rejected them in principle before the public reaction to Tet reached significant proportions. In the immediate aftermath of the enemy attacks, he was prepared to send additional troops to Vietnam if they were required to hold the line. Once it was clear that the American position in South Vietnam was secure, however, he saw no need to enlarge the force level.[100]

Public disillusionment does appear to have played a crucial role in Johnson's decisions to order a partial bombing halt, send out new overtures for negotiations, and withdraw from the presidential race. Pressed by the military to expand the war, by Rostow to "hang tough," and by Clifford and others to deescalate, Johnson wavered uncertainly for weeks. Whatever his inclinations—and they remain unclear—it was increasingly evident to him by late March that he must do something. His standing in the polls had dropped precipitously. Eugene McCarthy's showing in the New Hampshire primary and Robert Kennedy's announcement of his candidacy aroused grave concern among Johnson's political advisers. His famous meeting with the "Wise Men" on March 26 and 27 was probably decisive. After listening to briefings on the military and political situation in Vietnam, this distinguished panel of private citizens concluded that there was no military solution and that the President should deescalate. "The establishment bastards have bailed out," a dispirited Johnson is said to have remarked after the meeting.[101]

The significance of the March 31 decisions is still subject to debate. Schandler concedes that the President's agreement to limit the bombing and freeze the force level was both reluctant and tentative, but he demonstrates that Clifford, through a series of public statements, gradually converted these steps into firm, if not irrevocable, commitments. The policy of gradual escalation quietly ended in

1968, he concludes, and the United States started "down a new road in Vietnam."[102]

That conclusion is certainly true, but it overlooks several critical points. First, although Johnson abandoned the strategy he had pursued since 1965, he did not discard his original goals. His commitment to an independent, noncommunist South Vietnam remained firm, and his March 31 decisions represented less a change of policy than a shift of tactics to maintain a policy that had come under fire at home. Despite the uproar over Tet, the President clung stubbornly to his original objectives in the certainty that history would praise him for his courage and perseverance.

Second, the tactics Johnson fashioned in 1968 were even less well calculated to achieve the illusive objectives than those of 1965. As before, he improvised, splitting the difference between those who wanted to escalate in pursuit of victory and those, including Clifford, who wanted to scale down American military involvement and political objectives and seek the most graceful withdrawal possible. Most of Johnson's civilian advisers agreed that the search-and-destroy strategy should be abandoned in favor of a strategy of "population control," and the President did recall Westmoreland to Washington. But he gave no strategic guidance to Westmoreland's successor, General Creighton Abrams, and Lewy has shown that the ground strategy in fact changed very little.[103] Anticipating Nixon's Vietnamization policy, the administration, largely on the basis of domestic political expediency, agreed to shift a greater part of the military burden to the Vietnamese. There was little in the past record of the various South Vietnamese governments to suggest, however, that Thieu and his cohorts could conciliate their noncommunist opponents and pacify the countryside while effectively waging war against a weakened but still formidable enemy. The President made new overtures for negotiations on March 31, but he did so apparently in the expectation that Hanoi would reject them and primarily to appease public opinion.[104] When, to his surprise, the North Vietnamese accepted his offer, he went into the negotiations unprepared to give in on the major points and insistent that he would not agree to a "cheap peace," a "giveaway peace," a "peace at any price."[105] In the absence of basic political concessions, however, negotiations could achieve nothing, and their failure in time intensified the domestic pressures they were designed to alleviate. Johnson's 1968 tactics therefore perpetuated the inconsistencies, ambiguities, and contradictions that had vexed American policy from the start. The military and diplomatic stalemate persisted after Tet, and it would take four more years of "fighting while negotiating" before the United States extricated itself from Vietnam.

Historical writing on Johnson's management of the Vietnam War is obviously still in an embryonic stage. Little material is open in the Johnson files for the period after 1965. State Department and Defense Department records remain closed. Scholars must therefore rely on *The Pentagon Papers*, memoirs of participants, such material as can be gleaned from interviews, and older accounts by journalists. Despite the extensive secondary literature, many important topics remain virtually uninvestigated. Most of the work done thus far has been by participants, journalists, and international relations specialists, many of whom have had a particular axe to grind, lesson to proclaim, or doctrine to promote.

In fairness to Johnson, it must be stressed that the situation he inherited in Vietnam lent itself to no easy solution—perhaps to no solution at all. Those who argue that a more decisive use of military power, a deeper commitment to negotiations, or greater stress on pacification would have brought the desired results conveniently overlook what appear from this perspective the harsh realities of the conflict. Those realities included (1) a determined, indeed fanatical foe, willing to sacrifice everything for its cause and driven by the centuries-old impulses of Vietnamese nationalism; (2) the threat of Soviet and Chinese intervention, heightened during the Johnson era by the fierce rivalry between the two communist giants; (3) a weak ally, lacking most of the basic ingredients for nationhood, eager for the United States to assume the burden of its defense but resentful of American domination; and (4) a domestic consensus which wanted success in Vietnam without paying a high price. The President was poorly served by his advisers, none of whom displayed exceptional imagination in perceiving, much less coping with, these admittedly intractable problems. Moreover, as Johnson himself repeatedly pointed out, his critics offered no viable solutions.

This much being said, it is still clear that the vindication Johnson hoped for has not come. Historical judgments to a large degree rest on perceptions of success or failure or commitment to a cause regarded as worthy. The events of April 1975 leave little room for debate on the outcome of the war. Although Hanoi's subsequent actions have led some writers to reaffirm the essential morality of the commitment in Vietnam, this view has not gained wide acceptance. Johnson was wise to avoid a larger war, a policy for which he should be given full credit, especially in view of the pressures he withstood and the disastrous actions of his successor. Yet he miscalculated drastically in assuming that his goals could be attained by limited means. He imposed restrictions on the military, but he provided little direction to American military strategy. Even after it was evident that the chosen instruments were not working, he refused to resolve the contradictions or clear up the ambiguities, continuing instead to pursue an improvised consensus approach that could not work. Johnson once observed of Vietnam that if "I have to turn back I want to make sure I am not in too deep to do so."[106] Yet this is precisely the position he found himself in by 1967. Indeed, the longer the war went on and the more unlikely a favorable solution became, the more resistant he became to turning back. What he saw as courage and perseverance now seem more like rigidity and stubbornness. Lyndon Johnson no longer appears an evil or sinister figure, the warmonger of the rhetoric of protest, but rather a tragic figure, trapped in a dilemma not entirely of his own making and stubbornly persisting despite the enormous pain he was inflicting on the nation and himself.

Notes

1. Doris Kearns, *Lyndon Johnson and the American Dream* (New York, 1976), p. 251.

2. Chalmers M. Roberts, *First Rough Draft: A Journalist's Journal of Our Times* (New York, 1973), p. 252.

3. See especially Jack Valenti, *A Very Human President* (New York, 1973), pp. 313, 363.

4. The official point of view is in U.S. Department of State white paper, *Aggression from the North* (Washington, 1965), and in Johnson's Johns Hopkins speech of April 7, 1965, in *The Viet-Nam Reader*, ed. Marcus Raskin and Bernard Fall, Vintage ed. (New York, 1965), pp. 343–350.

5. Theodore Draper, *Abuse of Power*, Viking ed. (New York, 1967), p. 219.

6. The dove literature is voluminous and I make no attempt to be exhaustive here. Among the best statements of the conservative position are Draper, *Abuse of Power*, and Hans Morgenthau, *A New Foreign Policy for the United States* (New York, 1969), especially pp. 110–156. Gabriel Kolko expresses the radical point of view in *The Roots of American Foreign Policy* (Boston, 1969). The liberal position is developed in Arthur M. Schlesinger, Jr., *The Bitter Heritage* (Greenwich, Conn., 1968), and in Franz Schurmann, Peter Dale Scott, and Reginald Zelnik, *The Politics of Escalation in Vietnam* (Greenwich, Conn., 1966). Among the best later syntheses are Chester L. Cooper, *The Lost Crusade* (New York, 1970), and David Halberstam, *The Best and the Brightest* (New York, 1972), each highly critical in tone but

emphasizing the responsibility of the policy makers rather than the system. Richard Barnet, *Roots of War* (Baltimore, 1973), and Richard Barnet, Ralph Stavins, and Marcus Raskin, *Washington Plans an Aggressive War* (New York, 1971) incorporate many of the liberal and moderate criticisms but, like the radicals, focus on the system rather than on personalities.

7. Kolko, *Roots of American Foreign Policy*, p. 132.

8. Hans Morgenthau, "We are Deluding Ourselves in Vietnam," in *Viet-Nam Reader*, ed. Raskin and Fall, pp. 37–45.

9. Kolko, *Roots of American Foreign Policy*, p. 117. Kolko nevertheless argues that the insurgency began in the South rather than at the initiative of Hanoi.

10. George M. Kahin and John W. Lewis, *The United States in Vietnam* (New York, 1969), pp. 119–120.

11. Schurmann, Scott, and Zelnik, *Politics of Escalation*, p. 41. The literature on the Tonkin Gulf incident is extensive and quite similar in sources used, tone, and interpretation. The major works are: Joseph C. Goulden, *Truth is the First Casualty: The Gulf of Tonkin Affair* (New York, 1969); John Galloway, *The Gulf of Tonkin Resolution* (Rutherford, N.J., 1970); Anthony Austin, *The President's War* (Philadelphia, 1971); and Eugene C. Windchy, *Tonkin Gulf* (Garden City, N.Y., 1971). All rely heavily on the congressional hearings of 1967 and 1968 and on personal interviews, question whether the second attack actually occurred, and charge the administration with deceit and manipulation of public opinion.

12. Draper, *Abuse of Power*, p. 11.

13. Ibid., p. 98.

14. Halberstam, *Best and the Brightest*, p. 655.

15. Draper, *Abuse of Power*, p. 4.

16. Barnet, *Roots of War*, pp. 95–133.

17. Daniel Ellsberg, *Papers on the War* (New York, 1972), p. 101.

18. Schlesinger, *Bitter Heritage*, develops the quagmire thesis. Johnson's personality is emphasized in Philip Geyelin, *Lyndon B. Johnson and the World* (New York, 1966); Eric Goldman, *The Tragedy of Lyndon Johnson* (New York, 1968); and Robert W. Sellen, "Old Assumptions versus New Realities: Lyndon Johnson and Foreign Policy," *International Journal* 28 (Spring 1973): 205–229.

19. Roger Hilsman, *To Move a Nation* (New York, 1967), pp. 536–537; and Bernard Brodie, *War and Politics* (New York, 1973), pp. 135–138, cautiously advance this argument.

20. James C. Thomson, Jr., "How Could Vietnam Happen? An Autopsy," *The Atlantic* 221 (April 1968): 47–53.

21. Edward Jay Epstein, *Between Fact and Fiction* (New York, 1975), p. 80.

22. John E. Rielly, "The American Mood: A Foreign Policy of Self-Interest," *Foreign Policy* 34 (Spring 1979): 79.

23. George Will, *Newsweek* (July 5, 1979), p. 89.

24. There are three editions of *The Pentagon Papers*: Neil Sheehan et

al., *The Pentagon Papers as Published by the New York Times* (New York, 1971); U.S., Senate, Subcommittee on Buildings and Grounds, *The Pentagon Papers (Senator Gravel Edition)*, 4 vols. (Boston, 1971); and U.S., House of Representatives, Committee on Armed Services, *United States-Vietnam Relations, 1945–1967: A Study Prepared by the Department of Defense*, 12 vols. (Washington, 1971). For a comparison and an excellent assessment of these editions as historical sources, see George M. Kahin, "The Pentagon Papers: A Critical Evaluation," *American Political Science Review* 69 (June 1975): 675–684.

25. Lyndon B. Johnson, *The Vantage Point: Perspectives on the Presidency* (New York, 1971). Two valuable essays comparing the Johnson memoir and *The Pentagon Papers* are Paul K. Conkin, "The Johnson Years: An Essay Review," *Wisconsin Magazine of History* (Autumn 1972), pp. 59–64, and Leslie H. Gelb, "*The Pentagon Papers* and *The Vantage Point*," *Foreign Policy* 6 (Spring 1972): 25–41.

26. For a description of the major files dealing with foreign relations, see Martin I. Elzy, "Researching American Diplomatic History in the Johnson Library," *Society for Historians of American Foreign Relations Newsletter* 8 (December 1977): 17–22.

27. Guenter Lewy, *America in Vietnam* (New York, 1978). Larry Van Dyke, "Getting the Facts on Vietnam," *Chronicle of Higher Education* (December 11, 1978), pp. R3–R5, contains an interview with Lewy as well as excerpts from some early reviews. Useful summaries of recent writings on Vietnam may be found in Peter Braestrup, "Vietnam as History," *The Wilson Quarterly* 2 (Spring 1978): 178–187, and in Joe P. Dunn, "In Search of Lessons," *Parameters* 9 (December 1979): 28–40. For a harsh critique of Vietnam revisionism, see Marilyn B. Young, "Revisionists Revised: The Case of Vietnam," *Society for Historians of American Foreign Relations Newsletter* 10 (June 1979): 1–10.

28. Leslie Gelb and Richard Betts, *The Irony of Vietnam: The System Worked* (Washington, 1979).

29. George C. Herring, *America's Longest War* (New York, 1979).

30. King C. Chen, "Hanoi's Three Decisions and the Escalation of the Vietnam War," *Political Science Quarterly* 90 (Summer 1975): 239–259.

31. Lewy cites official figures indicating that 5,800 North Vietnamese regulars were in the South by March 1965 and goes on to argue that these may err on the low side (*America in Vietnam*, p. 40).

32. Ibid., p. 41.

33. Ibid., p. 35.

34. See especially "Chronology of Events, Tuesday, August 4 and Wednesday, August 5, 1964, Tonkin Gulf Strike," Vietnam, Country File, National Security Files, Lyndon B. Johnson Library, Austin, Texas, literally a minute-by-minute account compiled shortly after the incident by members of the White House staff on the basis of documents and interviews.

35. Robert McNamara to Dean Rusk, June 11, 1964, Vietnam, Country File, National Security Files, Johnson Library.

36. McGeorge Bundy memorandum for the record, September 4, 1964, Ibid.

37. U.S. Senate, *Pentagon Papers (Gravel)*, 3: 685.

38. Anthony Lake, ed., *The Vietnam Legacy* (New York, 1976), p. 183.

39. It "seemed to all of us the bottom of the barrel, absolutely the bottom of the barrel," William Bundy later recalled (William Bundy Oral History Interview, Johnson Library).

40. U.S. Senate, *Pentagon Papers (Gravel)*, 3: 447.

41. Benjamin Read to (unknown), July 23, 1945, Vietnam, Country File, National Security Files, Johnson Library.

42. Earle Wheeler Oral History Interview, Johnson Library.

43. Nicholas Katzenbach to Johnson, June 10, 1965, Vietnam, Country File, National Security Files, Johnson Library.

44. Harry McPherson, *A Political Education* (Boston, 1972), pp. 107–108, 111.

45. Janos Radvanyi, *Delusion and Reality: Gambits, Hoaxes, and Diplomatic One-Upmanship in Vietnam* (South Bend, Ind., 1978), p. xiii.

46. Kearns, *Johnson*, pp. 282–285.

47. Gelb and Betts, *Irony of Vietnam*, p. 3.

48. The only available record of the internal discussions leading up to the ground troop decision is in Valenti, *Very Human President*, pp. 318–363. Valenti's account indicates that the President repeatedly raised the question of expectations and that his military advisers were optimistic, much too optimistic as it turned out. General Wheeler advised the President that North Vietnam would not try to match U.S. escalation and even if it did, the dispatch of large enemy forces to South Vietnam would "allow us to cream them." The North Vietnamese, he concluded, would probably decide that they could not "win by putting in forces they can't afford." The caution of the Joint Chiefs of Staff related more to the number of U.S. forces required than to the ultimate outcome. McNamara was more pessimistic, arguing that the chances of a "military solution" were slim, but he, Johnson, and others seem to have felt that steadily increasing military pressures would in time force Hanoi to accept a settlement pretty much on American terms.

49. Brodie, *War and Politics*, p. 129.

50. Roberts, *First Rough Draft*, pp. 249–250.

51. Ian Maitland, "Only the Best and the Brightest?" *Asian Affairs* 3 (1976): 263–272.

52. Gelb and Betts, *Irony of Vietnam*, pp. 129–130, 292–293. The most recent analysis, Peter W. Sperlich and William L. Lunch, "American Public Opinion and the War in Vietnam," *Western Political Quarterly* 32 (March 1979): 21–24, confirms Gelb's and Betts's findings and goes a step beyond, arguing that from early 1966 until late 1967, a majority of the American public favored escalation of the war. I know of no study of the response of the press to the 1965 decisions, but Richard N. Pfeiffer, "The Popular Periodical Press and the Vietnam War, 1954–1968," (M.A. thesis, University of

Louisville, 1978), provides a full analysis of the views of *Newsweek, Time,* and *U.S. News and World Report* and shows that all three clearly understood the direction the President was heading. *Newsweek* expressed deep skepticism and *Time* and *U.S. News* firmly supported the administration's policies.

53. See, for example, the poll in the *New York Times,* October 29, 1966.

54. Russell to Mrs. David Belcher, June 30, 1965, Vietnam, Subject File, International File, Richard B. Russell Papers, Richard B. Russell Library, Athens, Georgia.

55. Mike Mansfield to Johnson, July 27, 1965, Deployment of Major U.S. Forces to Vietnam, July 1965, National Security Council History, National Security Files, Johnson Library. Mansfield emphasized that many of his colleagues supported the President not because they approved his policies but because he was President.

56. Alton Frye and Jack Sullivan, "Congress and Vietnam: The Fruits of Anguish," in *The Vietnam Legacy,* ed. Anthony Lake (New York, 1976), pp. 198–199.

57. Sidney Verba et al. make this point in "Public Opinion and the War in Vietnam," *American Political Science Review* 61 (June 1967): 317–333, a study based on independent polling data.

58. Roberts, *First Rough Draft,* p. 251.

59. Arthur M. Schlesinger, Jr., *Robert Kennedy and His Times,* Ballantine ed. (New York, 1979), pp. 779–783, cites new evidence of Kennedy's disenchantment with Vietnam but rests his case on personality. "He was a prudent executive, not inclined to make heavy investments in lost causes." Two scholarly works which continue to emphasize the decisive importance of Johnson's personality are John G. Stoessinger, *Crusaders and Pragmatists: Movers of Modern American Foreign Policy* (New York, 1979), and James D. Barber, *The Presidential Character* (Englewood Cliffs, N.J., 1977).

60. See, for example, Richard J. Walton, *Cold War and Counterrevolution: The Foreign Policy of John F. Kennedy* (Baltimore, 1973), especially pp. 166–201; Thomas G. Paterson, "Bearing the Burden: A Critical Look at JFK's Foreign Policy," *Virginia Quarterly Review* 54 (Spring 1978): 193–212; and, from a different point of view, Henry Fairlie, *The Kennedy Promise* (New York, 1973).

61. Gelb and Betts, *Irony of Vietnam;* Herring, *America's Longest War;* and Lewy, *America in Vietnam* all agree on this point.

62. Gelb and Betts, *Irony of Vietnam,* pp. 361, 366; Herring, *America's Longest War,* pp. 270–271. For extended comment on this point, see Earl C. Ravenal, *Never Again: Learning from America's Foreign Policy Failures* (Philadelphia, 1978).

63. The annual volumes in the *Declassified Documents Reference System* provide a handy guide to recently declassified documents. One important Joint Chiefs of Staff document recently declassified is "Concept for Vietnam," August 27, 1965, Deployment of Major Forces, National Security

Council History, National Security Files, Johnson Library. This strategic plan for the war accepts the administration's concept of applying sufficient military pressure to force North Vietnam to stop its support of the war in the South, but it envisions a much larger military commitment than Johnson was prepared to undertake at this stage. The document also speaks repeatedly and without apparent fear of the possibility of a war with China, suggesting that Johnson's concerns on this score may have stemmed as much from the Joint Chiefs of Staff as from Chinese threats or actions.

64. Henry Graff, *The Tuesday Cabinet* (Englewood Cliffs, N.J., 1970), p. 54.

65. William C. Westmoreland, *A Soldier Reports* (Garden City, N.Y., 1976), pp. 149–150, 410. Dave Richard Palmer, *Summons of the Trumpet* (San Rafael, Calif., 1978), a concise, readable military history, generally supports Westmoreland's arguments.

66. U. S. Grant Sharp, *Strategy for Defeat: Vietnam in Retrospect* (San Rafael, Calif., 1978), pp. 96, 268.

67. Herring, *America's Longest War*, pp. 146–147.

68. Robert L. Gallucci, *Neither Peace nor Honor: The Politics of American Military Policy in Viet-Nam* (Baltimore, 1975), pp. 74, 86, 126–128.

69. Lewy, *America in Vietnam*, pp. 46, 438.

70. W. Scott Thompson and Donaldson D. Frizzell, *The Lessons of Vietnam* (New York, 1977), p. 223.

71. Lady Bird Johnson, *A White House Diary* (New York, 1970), pp. 370–371.

72. Valenti, *Very Human President*, p. 133. After a whirlwind tour of the Far East in late 1966, Johnson reported to Richard Russell with almost breathless enthusiasm his discovery of a "vital and exciting Asia" where people were making "sometimes amazing progress." Johnson to Russell, November 3, 1966, Red Line File, Richard B. Russell Papers, Russell Library, Athens, Georgia.

73. Thompson and Frizzell, *The Lessons of Vietnam*, p. 223. The best scholarly appraisals of pacification are Douglas S. Blaufarb, *The Counterinsurgency Era: U.S. Doctrines and Performance* (New York, 1977), and Lawrence E. Grinter, "South Vietnam: Pacification Denied," *Southeast Asian Spectrum* 3 (July 1975): 49–78. Both conclude that the failure of various South Vietnamese governments to develop a sense of community with the rural population of the country was ultimately fatal. For extended and eloquent comment on this point, see Frances Fitzgerald, *Fire in the Lake* (Boston, 1972).

74. Lewy, *America in Vietnam*, p. 439.

75. Herring, *America's Longest War*, p. 262.

76. Gareth Porter, *A Peace Denied: The United States, Vietnam, and the Paris Agreements* (Bloomington, Ind., 1975), p. 59.

77. David Kraslow and Stuart H. Loory, *The Secret Search for Peace in Vietnam* (New York, 1968). Regarding one such incident, the authors on p.

54 quote a U.S. official as saying: "You will never get the inside story because it makes our government look so bad."

78. Porter, *Peace Denied*, pp. 56–57.

79. Johnson, *Vantage Point*, pp. 250–252.

80. "United States-Vietnam Relations: History of Contacts and Negotiations," is available in the Johnson Library and on microfiche in the Declassified Documents Reference System, (75)60-B.

81. The most valuable oral history interviews are those of William Bundy, which is especially detailed, Chester Cooper, Benjamin Read, Averell Harriman, and Nicholas Katzenbach. All are in the Johnson Library. Dean Rusk's massive oral history memoir, which should be most helpful on this subject, is still under restriction. Among the major works recently published on negotiations are Allan E. Goodman, *The Lost Peace: America's Search for a Negotiated Settlement of the Vietnam War* (Stanford, 1978), and Radvanyi, *Delusion and Reality*.

82. "United States-Vietnam Relations, VI.C.4., 1967–1968, Settlement Terms," Johnson Library, sums up the changes in bargaining positions on both sides.

83. The Wilson-Kosygin initiative is discussed in "United States-Vietnam Relations, VI.C.3., Sunflower," Johnson Library. See also Harold Wilson, *The Labour Government: A Personal Record* (London, 1971), and the Benjamin Read Oral History Interview, Johnson Library.

84. Goodman, *Lost Peace*, p. 44.

85. George Ball in introduction to Radvanyi, *Delusions and Reality*, p. xvi.

86. Ibid., pp. 141–142.

87. Goodman, *Lost Peace*, p. 24.

88. Westmoreland, *Soldier Reports*, p. 410.

89. Townsend Hoopes, *The Limits of Intervention* (New York, 1970), p. 224.

90. Porter, *Peace Denied*, pp. 71–72.

91. The March 26, 1968 folder, Appointment File, Diary Backup, Johnson Library, contains some intriguing notes on the "Wise Men's" reaction to the official briefings and Johnson's reactions to the Wise Men's conclusions.

92. Johnson, *Vantage Point*, pp. 380–437; McPherson, *Political Education*, pp. 420–439; Hoopes, *Limits of Intervention*, pp. 139–224; Clark Clifford, "A Viet Nam Reappraisal," *Foreign Affairs* 47 (July 1969): 601–622; Peter Braestrup, *Big Story*, 2 vols. (Westview, Colo., 1977); Herbert Y. Schandler, *The Unmaking of a President: Lyndon B. Johnson and Vietnam* (Princeton, 1977). See also John B. Henry, "February 1968," *Foreign Policy* 4 (Fall 1971): 3–33, an early account based on personal interviews with participants, and Don Oberdorfer, *Tet* (Garden City, N.Y., 1971), a readable study by a journalist.

93. The best brief appraisal is Bernard Brodie, "The Tet Offensive," in *Decisive Battles of the Twentieth Century*, ed. Noble Frankland and

Christopher Dowling (London, 1976), pp. 321–334. Palmer, *Summons of the Trumpet*, pp. 189–210, is good on the military events but uncritically accepts Westmoreland's assessment of the results. The most balanced and probably most accurate contemporary appraisal was made by Philip Habib, then deputy assistant secretary of state, on February 26, 1968 ("March 31, 1968, Speech," National Security Council History, National Security Files, Johnson Library). Habib concluded that there was still too much confusion and uncertainty to know exactly where the United States and South Vietnam stood. He argued that the United States had not won a victory despite the losses inflicted on the enemy and that indeed in many areas it had suffered serious setbacks.

94. Braestrup, *Big Story*, p. 608 (this and subsequent quotations are taken from the one-volume, paperback edition).

95. Ibid., p. xi.

96. Schandler, *Unmaking of a President*, p. 101.

97. For the 1967 campaign, see Oberdorfer, *Tet*, pp. 98–106, and the extensive correspondence in box 32, Marvin Watson Files, and box 53, Harry McPherson Files, Johnson Library.

98. Don Oberdorfer, *Courier-Journal* (Louisville), February 5, 1978.

99. There is some evidence to suggest that the administration's low-key approach was calculated. In a cable to the Saigon Embassy on February 5, 1968 ("March 31, 1968, Speech," National Security Council History, National Security Files, Johnson Library), the State Department warned against "overplaying our 'successes' at this stage" and "making excessive claims prematurely." Although most published accounts stress the pressures on Johnson to deescalate, the documents in the National Security Council History file make clear the substantial counterpressures to stand firm. Throughout February and March, advisers in and out of government pleaded with Johnson to take the lead in rallying public opinion behind the war, and Walt Rostow even proposed a new congressional resolution reaffirming the commitment of 1964. Aside from several speeches tending in this direction, the President made no sustained effort.

100. Johnson, *Vantage Point*, pp. 396–397.

101. Roger Morris, *An Uncertain Greatness: Henry Kissinger and American Foreign Policy* (New York, 1977), p. 44; Schandler, *Unmaking of a President*, pp. 256–265.

102. Schandler, *Unmaking of a President*, p. 318.

103. Lewy, *America in Vietnam*, p. 134.

104. "March 31, 1968, Speech," National Security Council History, National Security Files, Johnson Library.

105. Johnson, *Vantage Point*, pp. 505–506.

106. Valenti, *Very Human President*, p. 134.

2 | Latin American Policy
by Walter LaFeber

WHEN PRESIDENT JOHN F. KENNEDY launched the Alliance for Progress in 1961, the plan called for a mammoth joint effort between both private and public capital and North and South Americans to increase the economic growth rate in Latin America to an annual rate of at least 2.5 percent per capita. That growth was to enable the middle classes to grow, become more stable, and perhaps form a base for the development of democratic governments. United States officials hoped the governments would become stable and anticommunist. The alliance got off to a stumbling start. In 1963 the change in the per capita gross national product amounted to −0.4 percent.[1] The worst performances were turned in by the two giants, Brazil and Argentina. As Jerome Levinson and Juan de Onis observe in *The Alliance That Lost Its Way*, when Lyndon Johnson became President in November 1963, the plan seemed on the brink of failure. United States business leaders, who were supposed to provide much of the development capital, were particularly alienated.[2] Coups in Peru, Ecuador, and Santo Domingo brought military officers to power. Meanwhile Fidel Castro, whose shadow haunted United States policy makers throughout the decade and whose existence had indeed spawned the alliance in 1961, remained firmly in power in Cuba.

Lyndon Johnson had not devoted himself to a deep study of foreign policy before becoming President, but because of his Texas background, his early experience teaching Mexican-American students, his travels in Mexico, and his concern for noncommunist stability in the North American backyard, Johnson did consider himself something of an expert on Latin American affairs. Early observers of the new President expressed some doubts about that expertise. Philip Geyelin, whose *Lyndon B. Johnson and the World* remains the best overall analysis of the President's foreign policies, implies that Johnson supposed other Latin Americans could easily achieve Mexico's level of stability. As a frame of reference, however, Mexico could be a misleading model.[3] Lincoln Gordon, Johnson's ambassador to Brazil and later his assistant secretary of state for inter-American affairs, has told the Johnson Library Oral History Project that it seemed Johnson's "emotional concern was concentrated mainly on the Mexican relationship," apparently at the expense of other hemispheric interests. In his oral history interview, Ralph Dungan, who came into government during the Kennedy years before serving as Johnson's ambassador to Chile, claims that the President's "romantic, Tex-Mex view of Latin America" actually "distorted his view" of the entire southern continent.[4]

There were few romantic overtones, however, when Johnson made his first major appointment in the area. Thomas C. Mann was a conservative Texan who had served in Eisenhower's State Department and who was ambassador to Mexico under Kennedy. Considered a close friend of Johnson, Mann was apparently not so much a presidential intimate as a proponent of the President's view of Latin American strategy. The Kennedy style, for example, was to be shunned. (Mann "not only didn't have charisma," Geyelin wrote, "he didn't believe in it.") A more businesslike approach was adopted. To ensure that the administration spoke with one voice, Johnson appointed Mann to be both assistant secretary for inter-American affairs and coordinator of the Alliance for Progress. The President probably also hoped to stabilize a State Department job that had virtually become a revolving door: between 1960 and 1964 the Latin American desk had changed hands four times. If such was Johnson's hope, it was in vain. Four men served as his top Latin American official during his five years in office: Mann, Jack Hood Vaughn between early 1965 and January 1966, Lincoln Gordon from 1966 to early 1967, and Covey Oliver. Nor were other key Latin American posts any more stable. Within a year after the United States intervened in the Dominican Republic in 1965, nearly all important State Department officials who had been involved as Latin American experts no longer held their 1965 jobs.[5] Some critics naturally approved, but the frequent changes were not the best way of ensuring stability and consistency even in the policies aimed at nonintervention and alliance building.

Eric Goldman's critical insider's account and Samuel Baily's scholarly analysis represent a strong consensus view that in early 1964 both Johnson and Mann thought the alliance was "a thoroughgoing mess" (Goldman's term).[6] A 1963 United Nations study revealed not only that growth was stagnant, but that middle class citizens, on which the alliance's hopes were fastened, had "been among the most frequent and militant participants in strikes in recent years."[7] The President and his new adviser wanted to increase the role of private capital and get tougher with Latin Americans who refused to create a congenial climate for investment. Johnson was particularly interested in the military aspects of handling guerrilla movements. As Walt W. Rostow emphasizes in his account of the 1960s, Johnson and Secretary of State Dean Rusk also wanted to give the initiative in the alliance to the Latin Americans.[8] In 1963 the hemispheric nations established the Inter-American Committee on the Alliance for Progress (CIAP) to dramatize the new relationship. Each nation had one representative on CIAP, and the group was to oversee the alliance. CIAP's existence also allowed the United States to monitor Latin American planning less noticeably.

These new policy emphases stand out in the Johnson Library's records, particularly in the oral histories, White House Central Files, and National Security Files. From the outset, Mann and Johnson worked to find an increased role for private capital and cooperated with David Rockefeller's Business Group for Latin America (BGLA), formed in October 1963 to help rescue the alliance. Comprised of senior executives of thirty-eight companies with "major interests in Latin America" as well as the officials of seven national organizations, the BGLA was to form a link between the U.S. government and corporate interests in Latin America. When Johnson prepared to meet the group, Mann suggested the President announce that "in no other sector of foreign policy is understanding and cooperation so important between business communities and the U.S. Government."[9] At the same time, according to the oral history interview of Felipe Herrera, who served as head of the Inter-American Development Bank (IADB) during the 1960s, the United States began in 1964 to restrict the use of its governmental funds to the bank. The monies were permitted to purchase goods only in the United States and Latin America. Even access to American capital markets seemed to become more difficult when balance-of-payments difficulties began to plague Washington officials in the mid-1960s. Johnson and Mann worked with the Rockefeller group, but the Treasury Department, with its devotion to resolving the growing balance-of-payments problems, placed obstacles before Latin American lending operations on both private and public levels.[10]

In a briefing to U.S. ambassadors to Latin America whom he had summoned to Washington in March 1964, Mann spelled out the new policy, which became known as the Mann Doctrine. In addition to protecting the nearly $10 billion U.S. private investment in the area, the Johnson administration would stress economic growth, take no strong position on wide-ranging social reforms, and—stating a contradiction that would continually plague officials—avoid intervention in other nations' internal affairs but allow no communist faction to take power. The Mann Doctrine was leaked to Tad Szulc of the *New York Times* and the assistant secretary's hard-line image was enhanced. When Mann prepared an address to spell out the doctrine, Bill Moyers in the White House labored to moderate the speech, which had "already been interpreted as Tom's 'hard line.'"[11] Meanwhile White House speech writer Harry McPherson developed concern over the President's determination to go in the opposite direction: "He [LBJ] spoke about the Alliance . . . in passionate terms that seemed to welcome revolution, and at the same time we were dealing on behalf of our businessmen in Latin America; we were dealing with the governments that existed, and here we were up here talking a wild semi-revolutionary liberalism or radicalism. It just seemed a lot of crap to me to do it that way and I think it hurt us."[12] At least Mann's rhetoric matched the new policies.

As John Strasma has pointed out in an important essay, the alliance's charter did not commit any government to undertake land reform, and the President pressured none to do it. When one alliance official indicated interest in agrarian reform in a 1968 speech, his superior, Assistant Secretary of State Covey Oliver, added a statement clearly indicating that the United States would tolerate but not encourage policies that might actually change existing structures. In the end, only in Chile, where President Eduardo Frei took the initiative and U.S. Ambassador Ralph Dungan cooperated, was any significant land reform program carried out.[13] More important, as Oliver indicated, was the need to preserve stability.

In his outspoken oral history, Mann comments, "We're living in an age, I think, of revolution." The United States, however, "should favor orderly evolution."[14] In a recent comprehensive study of North American reactions to South American revolutions, Cole Blasier notes that the 1960s revolutionaries differed from their predecessors: they sought to overthrow, not create, reformist democratic governments, and they were "openly anti-American and espoused radical Marxist programs." These differences and Castro's presence led the administration to place increased emphasis on U.S. military assistance, special training for Latin American military officers in the Panama Canal Zone or the United States, and courses in crowd control taught by agents of the Federal Bureau of Investigation. Most of the guerrilla groups, Blasier concludes, were gradually rendered harmless until by 1967, when Bolivian units trained by U.S. Green Berets killed Ernesto "Che" Guevara and his group, the major rebel organizations were largely neutralized or eliminated.[15]

The focus on **military assistance** helped simplify Johnson's and

Mann's perception of hemispheric affairs. Over and over, particularly in the early crises that occurred in Panama and Brazil, the two men interpreted the problem as one of communists versus anticommunists. Except in unusual cases, such as Chile, where Salvador Allende's more radical programs made Frei's agrarian reforms tolerable, top administration officials saw little middle ground between the alternatives of good and evil. One source of evil, Cuba, was to be isolated. After an Organization of American States (OAS) investigating committee determined that Castro had dispatched arms to Venezuelan terrorists, in mid-1964 the hemisphere's foreign ministers voted 15–4 to sever all diplomatic ties and suspend trade and sea transportation with Cuba. By the end of the year all nations but Mexico complied.

While the United States was leading the effort to quarantine Cuba, the British government suddenly announced it was selling 450 buses to Castro with London-based credit. Johnson became so furious that a new White House phrase appeared: when an aide made a stupid mistake it became known as "selling buses on the White House steps." The President sent Undersecretary of State George Ball to tell the Europeans they were not to help Castro. French President Charles De Gaulle, who was trying to shred Johnson's European policies, predictably reacted by selling locomotives to Castro.[16]

The triangular relationship among the European, North American, and Latin American governments needs study, but it is apparent that Western European dealings with Castro intensified the administration's efforts to quarantine him and to strengthen bilateral and OAS attempts to develop antiguerrilla forces. By 1966 even the efforts within the OAS were running into strong opposition, however. When the United States proposed in March 1966 that the OAS increase its peace-keeping powers, the measure was opposed by Argentina, Brazil, Chile, and Peru. They feared not only Washington's use of any OAS force for U.S. purposes, but also the injection of such a unit into historical Latin American disputes, such as border troubles between Argentina and Chile. They preferred to settle those arguments among themselves.[17]

A Central Intelligence Agency study sent by Ray S. Cline to National Security Adviser McGeorge Bundy in April 1964 summarized the problems which were threatening the alliance and changing Johnson's and Mann's policies. "Journalists and some Latin American politicians" expected too much of the alliance, the CIA believed. When these expectations were not met, the United States was blamed for a "violation" of the program. Some small victories had been won, but "one of the principal difficulties" was the failure of private investment to participate: the "climate for private enterprise has taken a sharply adverse turn." Unilateral governmental attacks in Argentina, Peru, Colombia, and Brazil had led to a "concomitant sharp drop in business confidence in many countries." The resulting economic vacuum was being filled by "statism" (state socialism), despite "the pronouncedly adverse experience of most countries with state economic enterprises."

One culprit was visible to the CIA. Latins were watching Castro's "almost total state socialism." If at all successful it could "have an extensive impact . . . elsewhere in the area." The analysis observed that "sharp divisions among the member states" prevented effective action against Cuba. Latin Americans not only argued with each other, but even carried OAS disputes to the United Nations, as Cuba had done in 1960–1961 and an angry Panama threatened to do in 1964. These actions set "harmful precedents to OAS authority." Also threatening were the "ostensible adjustments in relations between the West and the Soviet bloc" watched closely by the Latin Americans, particularly as they prepared to increase trade with the bloc. Some nations even indicated they would follow De Gaulle's example and recognize China. Those events added up to an "emergence in some countries of a special brand of non-alignment, usually styled 'independent' by most leaders, which in translation often means taking a position opposite to, or at odds with the United States. Brazil and Mexico are exponents of this policy, although their motivation differs considerably."[18]

It was a sad picture. State socialism threatened the private enterprise on which the Johnson-Mann plans increasingly depended, European allies set bad precedents for the Latin Americans, and North American power in the OAS was diluted by OAS members who appealed to the United Nations. Castro continued to infect the hemisphere with his example (an ironic and corrupted version of earlier North American views about examples set by "cities on a hill"), and Latin American independence seemed to mean opposition to United States policies. The CIA report noted that this opposition had been led by Brazil and Mexico, but that the most recent challenge was posed by Panama, one of the smallest nations.

Panama was also the Latin nation most dominated by the United States. The Canal Zone dividing the country and the continued integration of the U.S. and Panamanian economies created a relationship that went beyond dependency into what could be called informal colonialism.[19] For two decades student-led nationalists had demanded more control over the Canal Zone. John Kennedy held talks on the problem but did little of substance. On January 9, 1964, riots erupted in and around the zone that over the course of four days killed four U.S. soldiers and twenty-four Panamanians. Ralph Dungan, who sometimes handled Panamanian problems for the White House during the early 1960s, believed that the 1964 crisis was "not all that attributable to Johnson and . . . can be laid at the feet of the Kennedy administration" because it had not earlier moved to resolve the problems.[20]

The Johnson administration's policy can now be detailed from the National Security Council History of the affair. Some important papers remain classified or sanitized, but most of the material has become available since 1977. The history verifies Johnson's comment in *The Vantage Point* that he viewed the explosion as dangerous because "Castro, working closely with the Panamanian Communist party, had been sending guns, money, and agents into Panama."[21] Immediately after the riots began, Mann flew to Panama City and informed President Roberto Chiari that communists were deeply involved in the riots. Chiari agreed, although he seemed to accept the view held in both Panama and the United States (at least outside White House and State Department circles) that the communists could not effectively start the fire but, when they heard the bell, would rush into the streets to take the credit. The Panamanian Communist Party was weak, and the amount of Castro aid that had entered the country was in dispute. But Washington officials immediately divided the opposition into pro- and anticommunists. They did so despite a CIA report that could only find "some 100 Cuban-trained Panamanian would-be revolutionaries" and an OAS Peace Team's conclusion on January 11 that the rioting was "not Communist prompted," but "a typical example of 19th century nationalism." (When another OAS team appeared in February, Mann ordered that it be prevented from "an investigation of the facts or . . . other important action.")[22]

Despite the CIA and OAS findings, Mann insisted to Chiari on June 14 that "Castroites, the Communists, have penetrated high positions" in the Panamanian government, including Chiari's personal circle, and that "Castro would soon be trying to introduce arms into Panama." Neither allegation was ever proven, and in the meantime the weary Chiari "only nodded. He made no comment." That same day, Johnson ordered the U.S. commander in the Canal Zone to cooperate with Panamanian police to prevent "a Communist coup." The documents available do not indicate that such a coup was ever threatened. Convinced that "pro-Castro" groups were sneaking into the country, authorities boarded forty-three vessels in Colon, including "five suspect vessels," and found nothing.

Johnson's and Mann's views should have been but were not complicated by a report from the President's personal emissary in Panama, Edward Martin. Although the middle and upper classes were very tense, Martin reported, they were not pressing for an accommodation with the United States, but for concessions to the "Panamanian hard line." (At that point in the document, an apparently surprised Washington official put an exclamation point in the margin.) Martin nevertheless concluded that the communists were "better prepared to seize control in this type of situation" than other groups. Nearly a month after the rioting ended, the administration had not discarded its belief that Panama was threatened by a communist takeover.[23]

That view was at least arguable, but another was not: Chiari and Panamanians of all classes wanted to use the rioting to force the United States into negotiating a new treaty. Johnson and Mann were convinced of this at the time. The President immediately warned Chiari "that we cannot negotiate under pressure of violence."[24] After the rioting stopped, however, mistrust between the two governments prevented continued negotiations on a new pact. Domestic pressures on both sides created formidable obstacles. The National Security Council History provides a clear view of the cautious way in which Johnson conducted negotiations until after the November 1964 elections.[25] On November 6 the Panama Review Committee recommended that a solution be quickly reached, and in December the President instructed the State Department to seek an entirely new treaty to replace the 1903 agreement, particularly in the matter of recognizing Panama's sovereignty in the Canal Zone. As Thomas M. Franck and Edward Weisband comment, it was "a landmark concession: that opened a new era in U.S.-Panama relations, for it led directly to the historic 1978 treaty.[26]

Johnson Library files reveal that the President's decision was encouraged, if not shaped, by three developments: Dwight D. Eisenhower's approval, the administration's conclusion that the United States "never had sovereignty" in the Canal Zone, and the State Department's success in formulating a trade policy that would help quiet congressional opposition and make the Panamanians more dependent on the United States. Panama, the State Department believed, "would beseech the United States to remain in partnership in canal operations in order to retain the trade preference that would be made dependent upon the canal partnership."[27] The negotiations dragged on for another twelve years, but Johnson made the decision that marked the turn.

Justifiably pleased with this accomplishment, the President was also proud of his response in early 1964 when Castro shut off the water supply to the U.S. base at Guantanamo just as the presidential primary campaigns began. His excuse was the American capture of Cuban fishing boats that had strayed, apparently according to plan, into U.S. territorial waters. Johnson spoke softly and put contingency plans into effect that created an independent water supply for the base. The fishermen were released after the captains paid fines. Castro offered to turn the faucet back on, but Johnson told him not to bother. It had been a superb performance. The moral drawn by the President, however, was somber: the Panama crisis and the water shut-off were part of Castro's "plans for testing the United States and its new President."[28]

As the Panamanian and Guantanamo crises simmered down, Mann made the widely publicized remarks that became known as the Mann Doctrine. It was reported that at no point in his presentation did he mention the Alliance for Progress and its emphasis on building democratic governments. On the contrary, Robert Packenham, as well as other scholars, concluded that Mann's comments meant that the United States "would no longer seek to punish military juntas for overthrowing democratic regimes."[29] Two days after Mann's announcement, Packenham notes, the administration approved a $2.5 million loan by the IADB to François Duvalier's dictatorship in Haiti. Two weeks later Joao Goulart's constitutional government in Brazil was overthrown by a military coup. The United States recognized the new regime in twelve hours.[30]

Pre-1979 literature on the Brazilian coup is not clear about the U.S. role. Johnson's memoir contains little on Brazil. Rostow's *Diffusion of Power* argues that the President followed a "minimum intervention" policy as Goulart, "with communist support and advice, brought Brazil to the brink of dictatorship." According to their earlier account, however, Levinson and Onis believed the CIA, Ambassador Lincoln Gordon, and some North American business executives were involved in the overthrow. Geyelin had also mentioned a U.S. role.[31]

According to the Johnson Library's National Security Files, Agency File, the Agency for International Development (AID) urged in early 1964 that Washington officials not spend large amounts of economic aid funds. Goulart's "incompetence" was not to be rewarded, and the "democratic forces," including "the Church, business and farm leaders, and certain elements of the military," were to be encouraged to restrain Goulart's "extreme leftist or ultranational supporters" from "excesses."[32] The National Security File, Country File on Brazil, is more revealing, particularly since much of its material was declassified before the Carter administration's retrogressive executive order on the handling of classified documents.

Using these files, along with other records and interviews with many of the key U.S. officials involved, Phyllis Parker demonstrates conclusively that "U.S. actions ranged from political and economic sanctions and manipulations to military support for ridding Brazil of its president."[33] Her well-researched, understated, and sometimes cryptic account traces the Kennedy and Johnson administrations' growing bitterness toward Goulart's economic and political policies. She demonstrates how the Mann-Gordon policies led to a close U.S. relationship with the Brazilian military while they squeezed the Brazilian economy. The Brazilian press gave heavy coverage to Mann's statement, supposedly made privately to U.S. ambassadors, that "military and right-wing dictatorships will no longer be punished by non-recognition when they overthrow democratic regimes."

On the eve of the coup, the U.S. Embassy in Rio devised a plan to provide petroleum supplies to the military quickly if Goulart supporters destroyed the refineries. Gordon also urged that a U.S. carrier task force be stationed off the coast of Brazil. The ships were to protect North Americans and their property, but they would also give considerable encouragement to the Brazilian military. Johnson dispatched the task force in an operation known as "Brother Sam." The task force was not needed, however, for the military rapidly overthrew Goulart's regime. Ambassador Gordon reported that the "only unfortunate note was [the] obviously limited participation in [a public march of support for the military] of lower classes." Important documents remain to be opened, but Parker's conclusion seems sound: although the United States did not directly cause Goulart's downfall, it contributed indirectly by cutting off most economic aid to his government and giving aid instead to "those elements of Brazilian society that eventually overthrew" him. As for the military side, "There is no evidence that the United States instigated, planned, directed, or participated in the execution of the 1964 coup," but it did approve of the plan from the start and "reinforced its support by developing military contingency plans that could be useful to the conspirators should the need have arisen."[34]

In May 1964 Ambassador Gordon told Brazilian military officers that the "revolution" could "indeed be included along with the Marshall Plan proposal, the Berlin Blockade, the defeat of Communist aggression in Korea, and the resolution of the missile crisis in Cuba as one of the major turning points in world history in the middle of the twentieth century."[35] By 1968, as the regime imposed an oppressive authoritarian rule on Brazil, Gordon expressed second thoughts. It cannot be doubted, however, that as the Castelo Branco government forcefully created stability, undertook drastic deflationary programs, opened the country anew to foreign capital, and smashed left-wing opposition, the rapid funneling of U.S. economic and political support to Brazil seemed justified to administration officials.[36] Nor can it be denied that if the alliance's ideals—or what remained of them—included the encouragement of open, representative governments, the Brazilian coup delivered a body blow to the Alliance for Progress.

The effect was softened only slightly in late 1964 when Bolivian President Paz Estenssoro became the victim of another military coup. This time the United States waited five weeks before extending recognition, then granted it on the grounds that the military regime had promised national elections, retained sound economic advisers, respected trade-union rights, and uttered the right words about communism and especially Cuba.[37]

Overall the Johnson administration was optimistic about Latin American affairs as the November election approached. Walt Rostow reported on November 2 that economic developments could be better, but the "trends look reasonably good." McGeorge Bundy, writing to Hubert Humphrey in late August, suggested that the vice-presidential nominee brag about hemispheric affairs: "After all, the OAS has recently squeezed Castro some more; Branco [in Brazil] does seem to be turning into quite a fine fellow; Venezuela is marching vigorously ahead; . . . and relations with Panama have picked up." Gordon Chase, Bundy's assistant on the National Security Council, wanted to get the story to the electorate: "Latinos like [Tad] Szulc [of the *New York Times*] and [Dan] Kurzman [of the *Washington Post*] are not likely to write what we would like them to write." Chase thought "Joe Kraft might be a possibility," especially after Frei won the Chilean election held a week later.[38]

After the U.S. election, Thomas L. Hughes of the State Department's Intelligence and Research desk informed Rusk that "No government in Latin America is seriously threatened by the current level of terrorist and guerrilla activity." Attacks had "ceased, for the moment at least, in the Dominican Republic and Haiti," and had greatly diminished elsewhere.[39] Within only a year, the administration's quest for stability and its fixation on eliminating Castroite rebels were apparently paying off.

But five months later Johnson responded to civil war in the Dominican Republic by sending 22,000 U.S. troops to restore order and, according to his public announcement, to prevent Castroite elements from seizing power. The reasons for this invasion are among the most hotly argued problems in post-1945 U.S.-Latin American historiography. The first important account was written by Theodore Draper in articles in 1965–1966 and then in book form in 1968. He argued that after dictator Rafael Trujillo was gunned down in 1961 and, after a short period of confusion, the liberal government of Juan Bosch was voted into power, the Kennedy administration handled the situation well. The President, however, did little to save Bosch (whom the Kennedyites quickly perceived to be a scholarly bumbler) when military groups overthrew him in 1963. Johnson and Mann were angry, Draper believed, when a Boschist-constitutionalist uprising against the government occurred on April 24, 1965. They viewed it as an intolerable, disorderly revolt that could fall into communist hands. Consequently Johnson sent in troops on April 28 to smash not only the communists but also the liberal Boschist left. The President released lists of communists involved in the uprising. Draper described these documents as "hastily put together to justify an already adopted policy."[40]

In 1970 Jerome Slater gained privileged access to U.S. governmental records and wrote another account. He argued that Johnson invaded the Dominican Republic not to put down the Boschists, but because he truly believed the Communists were threatening to seize power. The threat of a "Communist takeover" was not "a figment of the Johnson administration's paranoiac imagination," Slater wrote, for by April 28 there was "some risk" that "Castroite forces" could emerge victorious. Slater's major criticism centered on the administration's refusal to purge the Dominican military of powerful pro-Trujillo elements after the United States had helped restore the army to power, albeit under civilian rule. Abraham Lowenthal also wrote an influential account of the crisis. He argued—through what he termed a "bureaucratic" perspective—that it is difficult to define exactly how Johnson and his advisers viewed the situation. Their problem was magnified, Lowenthal added, by the shifting, confused nature of Dominican politics. Those politics were nonideological and centered around individuals, thus presenting a complex, rapidly changing picture to Washington officials. In 1978 Slater repeated his earlier thesis in large part. He emphasized that the tragedy of the intervention was that it dealt "a death blow to the Alliance for Progress and the policy of nonrevolutionary democratic change that underlay it." Nearly everyone who has examined the affair, with the notable exception of former administration officials, agrees with Slater's final point.[41]

In 1978 Piero Gleijeses published what is now the standard account of the events that led to the intervention.[42] (He says little about Dominican affairs after May 1965.) His book, *The Dominican Crisis*, is based on research conducted during visits to the Dominican Republic over a six-year period after 1969, including interviews with nearly all the leading figures. Gleijeses differs from Draper by claiming that Kennedy bore considerable responsibility. Instead of purging the Dominican military when it was possible to do so after 1961, Kennedy gave the military virtually free rein. Johnson carried on this policy. Finally in 1965 the military fought over the spoils and allowed the constitutionalist uprising to occur. The problem, therefore, was not created by the Johnson administration. In the opinion of Gleijeses, the incompetence of the entire U.S. policy-making process during the 1960s and before led to a preference for military stability over the openness of constitutional government.

In his most important contribution, Gleijeses dismisses Slater's argument that Johnson's only target was the communist element. Gleijeses also transforms Lowenthal's view of Dominican politics, demonstrating that they were heavily ideological and split both the military and the political left. Most important, he marshals evidence to show that the radical-left communist groups were disorganized, confused, and ineffectual; when the constitutionalists nearly seized power in the early hours of the revolt, the radical-left communist leaders thought the whole rebellion must be a CIA plot. In truth, Gleijeses concludes, the constitutionalist movement was the great hope for a real liberal reform government. When Johnson intervened to prevent the victory, he committed a historic mistake. "The Dominican far left—Washington's nightmare—was strong only in the mind of its enemies." The U.S. Embassy's plea to Johnson to send troops on the grounds that the communists were taking control of the revolution was a "pathetically absurd" view, given the reality of the far left's weakness.[43]

Quite surprisingly, Gleijeses's work is based on little or no material in the Johnson Library. He obtained access to some official documents through friends, but otherwise depended on earlier publications, Dominican sources, and interviews. The lack of Johnson Library materials may be due in part to the book's being based on a doctoral dissertation written before important documents were made available in the library. Papers examined at the library support Gleijeses's arguments, although it should be emphasized that there was time to read only a few of the available materials.

An example of library documentary support for Gleijeses's account is the material covering a pivotal meeting on Sunday, April 25, 1965, between moderate-left leaders and U.S. Embassy officials. Gleijeses emphasizes that the embassy misperceived the leaders as communist inclined and thereby lost a critical opportunity to stop the revolt, allow the constitutionalists to come to power, block reactionary army elements, and thus make further U.S. intervention unnecessary. "Ignorance allied with paranoia and fear can be very dangerous," he says, and all combined in the embassy's decision to dismiss the visitors. The State Department Historical Studies Division's analysis of the crisis reveals that on April 25 the embassy official whom the constitutionalists encountered cabled that the communist presence was apparent, the constitutionalist movement had fallen into the hands of "its most extremist element," and hope had to be placed in the military—a conclusion with which the State Department warmly agreed.[44]

State Department views went beyond ignorance, paranoia, and fear to catastrophic thinking. Jack Valenti, one of the President's closest assistants, warned Johnson on April 30 that "the choice is: Castro in the Dominican Republic or U.S. intervention." Valenti emphasized that "*One fact is sure*: If the Castro-types take over the Dominican Republic, it will be the worst domestic political disaster any Administration could suffer." Those words were especially alarming because Johnson was beginning to fight for historic civil rights legislation and medicare measures on Capitol Hill, and had begun his major buildup of conventional forces in Vietnam. The President reportedly wondered aloud how anyone could believe his determination in Indochina if he appeared weak in the Caribbean. His resolve was further strengthened, if it needed such support, by old Latin American hand Adolf Berle. A former ambassador to Brazil and adviser to Franklin D. Roosevelt, Berle had retired from government service after his involvement in the Bay of Pigs operation. Berle called the Dominican Republic intervention "an early skirmish in the projected Cold War attack on the Caribbean Basin, possibly timed to help the upcoming North Vietnam operation. Our Latin American friends are clear the Chinese and the Soviet Communists cooperate in Latin America—despite their quarrels else-where." Berle was convinced that the U.S. invasion only tem-porarily postponed "wars of liberation" by communists in Haiti, Guatemala, Venezuela, and Colombia.[45]

From personal inclination as well as bureaucratic arrangement, Johnson no doubt believed the warnings of Valenti, State Depart-ment officials, and perhaps even Berle. By doing so he plunged his administration into its first "credibility crisis." North American cor-respondents on the scene refused to believe that the communists posed any threat. They picked to pieces lists of supposed commu-nists released by embassy officials in Santo Domingo. On May 3, 1965, after Johnson had already announced he was sending troops to prevent a Castroite victory, Rusk demanded that the U.S. Embassy produce some evidence regarding "Communists or suspected Com-munists now in or close to rebel seat of power. To what degree are these people now running rebel show. . . ? What specific incidents and other evidence reflect Communist influence?"[46] Despite such orders, the State Department was never able to make a convincing case. As early as mid-May, the *New York Times* reported the belief of observers, including foreign diplomats, that "while the U.S. exag-gerated the Communist influence at the outset of the revolution, it may have pushed a great many people into the arms of the Com-munists because it gave the rebels no alternatives. Right now the Communists are grinning like Cheshire cats, watching the rebellion become increasingly nationalistic and anti-American."[47]

Helped by the U.S. forces, special emissary Ellsworth Bunker did not have to worry about the communists as negotiations dragged on through the summer. Indeed, one of Bunker's and Johnson's im-mediate problems was to prevent U.S. military commanders from attacking the constitutionalists. It took all of Bunker's considerable skill to prevent such a confrontation. After Bunker's hand-picked nominee, Hector García Godoy, took over the government in late summer, U.S. officials had to intervene twice during the first eight weeks of his regime to prevent his overthrow by Dominican mili-tary units.[48] It says much for Bunker's diplomacy and the U.S. mili-tary and economic presence that in mid-1966 open elections were held in which Bosch came in second to Joaquín Balaguer.

The credibility crisis and the obvious role of the American mili-tary in determining Dominican affairs led to an ominous division between Johnson and Senator J. William Fulbright, chairman of the Senate Foreign Relations Committee. Before 1965 the two men trusted each other, even though they were not close friends. After the Dominican crisis and the unveiling of Johnson's Vietnam policy, they became bitter enemies. This enmity prevented key parts of Johnson's Latin American policies from being passed on Capitol Hill. It should be added here that cynicism about the administration's policies grew after Mann made a series of contradictory statements about the Dominican Republic intervention. In May he remarked that Washington's action "was not for the purpose of intervening in the internal affairs of the Dominican Republic." On October 12 he indirectly attacked Fulbright's criticisms of the policy, then piously defended the OAS charter, whose anti-intervention pledge the United States had solemnly signed and then violated, by declaring that "nonintervention is a keystone of the structure of the inter-American system."[49]

Johnson's and Mann's credibility was at stake not only on Capitol Hill, but also in parts of Latin America. The President had sent the U.S. troops and then had gone to the OAS with a fait accompli. The new Brazilian military regime took the lead in organizing an inter-American force to help the U.S. troops occupy the country. Liberal governments in Mexico, Chile, and Peru voted against the OAS policy of sharing occupation of the Dominican Republic. Venezuela at first hoped the organization would take action, but refused to participate after the United States insisted that the OAS expressly approve the intervention of April 28. In the words of Sheldon Liss, Venezuela's "faith in the OAS had diminished considerably."[50]

Gleijeses's account should be supplemented by a study using the large number of documents available at the Johnson Library, particularly those in the National Security Files. This can be done despite continued State Department insistence that many papers be partly "sanitized." It is doubtful, however, whether such a study will change the central parts of his argument, for these rest on a careful reconstruction of Dominican politics, particularly among the left-wing and military groups. Unless that reconstruction can be proved wrong, the tragic fixation of U.S. officials on the supposed power of the radical left and the Castroites will only be confirmed by the library's sources.

The direct use of U.S. military power and the pressure applied on the OAS gravely injured what remained of the alliance's ideals. Those ideals had not been helped by the policy toward Brazil in 1964, nor were they enhanced when the Argentine military—directly encouraged by the Brazilian experience—overthrew a weak, constitutionally elected government and set up General Juan Carlos Onganía as virtual dictator.[51] Assistant Secretary of State Lincoln

Gordon and Ambassador Edwin Martin tried to stop the coup. As early as 1964 AID had not been happy with the elected government's economic policies, but in June 1966, when the military told Martin it wanted to follow the Brazilian example—and sweetened the message by saying it would encourage U.S. investment—he tried to dissuade the army from rebelling. Rusk had U.S. military officials try to discourage their Argentinian counterparts. The Argentinians replied that only they could resolve their problems and that any "interruption" of U.S. aid "would not be a great disaster." The overthrow occurred on July 27.

At first the administration refused to recognize Onganía, but it gave in when he promised to respect international obligations and his regime was recognized by Chile and seven other Latin American nations. Rusk told Johnson, "We cannot exercise any significant influence in Argentina unless we maintain relations with the authorities."[52] The National Security Files and White House Central Files at the Johnson Library outline the story and its immediate results in some detail. A cabinet crisis in December 1966 allowed new, more sound economic advisers to enter the Argentine government. By mid-1967 foreign companies were moving into Argentine oil fields and taxes were being collected. In the words of one journalist, these changes were occurring "without the slightest interference with citizens' constitutional rights—except, of course, the right to choose a governing party."[53]

From Washington's viewpoint the story in Peru followed much the same lines but with less happy results. In that nation not only did the Johnson administration lose an elected and staunchly democratic government to a 1968 military coup, but the new rulers proceeded to nationalize the International Petroleum Company (IPC), owned by Standard Oil of New Jersey. Two primary alliance objectives—a representative, reform-minded government and incentive to private investments—were simultaneously defeated.

Recently published studies have traced the IPC controversy in some detail.[54] Since the 1920s the company had dominated oil and refinery production in Peru. IPC had not been reluctant to pressure Peruvian governments, even by cutting off operations, until they gave in to the company's demands. To use David Werlich's phrase, IPC was "a very vulnerable target, a highly visible example of 'Yankee economic imperialism.'" The company was also the largest private employer in the country. In 1963 a military regime that had claimed power the year before held elections. Fernando Belaunde, who won the presidency, embarked upon a program of agrarian and educational reform while remaining friendly to the United States.

Belaunde's friendship was soon undermined, however, by the crisis involving IPC, which claimed rights to a rich oil field. Belaunde tried to take a moderate position, but he was outflanked. The Peruvian Congress, which his party did not control, claimed the subsoil rights as Peru's, not IPC's. Peru demanded back taxes and IPC's pledge to give preferential purchase of the oil once the fields were nationalized. The Johnson administration faced a dilemma. Too much pressure on Peru could lead to further victories by anti-American nationalists. Too little pressure would fail to protect a vital foreign investment and would open Johnson to the charge that he did not enforce the Hickenlooper amendment. This amendment, passed over State Department objections in 1962, required suspension of foreign aid to any government that seized U.S. property and did not take "appropriate steps" within six months to make "equitable and speedy compensation." In the view of State Department and White House officials, the amendment was a sure method for turning reform-minded nationalist governments into radical regimes that could not afford to recognize international obligations, particularly those to foreign investors.

The Johnson administration did not want to impose the amendment's terms, but neither would it tolerate Peru's treatment of IPC. The White House Central Files reveal that as early as February 1964, the President's advisers, including Mann, Gordon, and Rostow, recommended that no more program loans be given until Belaunde instituted "a realistic self-help program" and guaranteed that no "confiscatory action" would be taken against IPC.[55] No pressure was apparently placed on IPC to moderate its own demands, but loan commitments to Peru fell drastically in fiscal year 1965. Anti-American sentiment increased in Peru. In late summer 1966, however, Rostow reported that Belaunde was trying to work out a deal acceptable to IPC.[56]

In the following months two crises interrupted the progress of negotiations. Claiming a 200-mile territorial limit off its coasts, Peru seized two U.S. tuna boats. After heated exchanges, including one in which Belaunde threatened not to go to the Punta del Este presidential summit to meet with Johnson, the State Department softened its position and negotiations got underway. Johnson's "talking paper" for the meeting of the two presidents read in part: "We hope [Peru] will continue to [support private enterprise] and not take any actions which would destroy investors' confidence." U.S. loans would be given, moreover, only if Capitol Hill was convinced that

Peru was "not wasting resources"—a direct reference to Belaunde's plans to buy new jet fighters.[57] In May 1968 he announced his intention to buy Mirage V jets from France. The U.S. Congress again threatened to cut off aid in the amount spent by Peru on the aircraft. Credits were virtually stopped and grants curtailed. Belaunde went ahead with the purchases, but—now enmeshed in a reelection campaign—he also tried to resolve the IPC controversy.

Washington's role in the next series of events is not clear from the library records presently open. On August 13, 1968, Belaunde triumphantly announced that the dispute was over. When the terms became public, however, Peruvians were shocked. IPC surrendered title to subsoil minerals and surface installations, but it retained certain vital refineries. All tax claims, estimated officially at $144 million, were canceled. The Peruvian national oil company promised to sell 80 percent of its crude oil to IPC, thereby turning over to IPC the most profitable part of the process, the refining of crude oil. At the announcement of the settlement, Belaunde's cabinet and political party fell apart. On October 3 a military coup overthrew him. The generals promptly seized the oil fields and repudiated the agreement with IPC.[58]

The story of U.S.-Chilean relations ended more happily. Indeed, the Johnson administration's later policy in Panama and its cooperation with Eduardo Frei's Chilean government may be the most constructive accomplishments of its Latin American programs. A primary reason for U.S. cooperation in Chile was the alternative that existed to Frei's policies. Salvador Allende, whose leftist supporters and economic plans frightened Washington officials throughout the 1960s and early 1970s, waited in the wings to ride into power if Frei's reform program failed. As the 1964 Chilean election approached, administration officials carefully shaped policies and planned economic aid to help Frei in every possible way. The aid program was even designed to permit "timely reassessment . . . should the candidate of the Communist-Socialist front [Allende] win."[59] Such coordinated planning was perhaps one reason why Johnson wanted both AID and political policy consolidated under the direction of Thomas Mann. The assistant secretary told other Latin American experts in the administration that the United States had to do everything possible to ensure Frei's election. If Allende nevertheless won, no hostile action would be taken "unless and until he takes decisive steps against U.S. interests" and "Chilean opinion has crystallized" against him.[60] An economic squeeze could obviously help crystallize such "opinion."

The election results delayed that strategy for another six years. As Paul Sigmund and Cole Blasier have observed, Frei moved to nationalize Chilean copper mines and carry out agrarian reform programs, but he carefully compensated owners and took pains not to be at cross-purposes with U.S. interests.[61] Johnson reciprocated by granting more per-capita economic aid to Chile than any other country. The assistance, however, consisted mainly of long-term loans that sharply increased Chile's foreign debt and placed an intolerable burden on Allende's government in the early 1970s. Despite overall success, crises did appear. The most notable occurred in mid-1965, when word leaked out in Chile that American University in Washington, D.C., and the U.S. Department of the Army were conducting studies in Chile to design a system that would give "early warning of internal unrest and insurgency." A political explosion occurred around Frei, but it turned out that the State Department and U.S. Ambassador Ralph Dungan in particular knew nothing about the so-called Camelot project. Joseph Califano tried to defend the Defense Department's support of the project, but the brief was not persuasive. The State Department, with considerable sensitivity to the vulnerable positions of Frei and Dungan, obtained cancelation of Camelot in 1965.[62]

Besides the successful approaches in Panama and Chile, the administration could also claim by 1967 that it had accomplished perhaps its primary goal: containing or eliminating guerrilla groups that threatened Latin American nations. Some of this success, as Sheldon Liss has observed in the case of Venezuela, was due to the guerrillas' making tactical errors that split their movement.[63] The U.S. Joint Chiefs of Staff also claimed credit, however, because the military had cooperated closely with Latin American units. When Secretary of Defense Robert McNamara attempted to reduce military assistance to Latin America in 1965, he was opposed not only by the Joint Chiefs but also by an outspoken State Department paper. It warned that any cutbacks could cause Latin Americans to turn to third parties for vital equipment and "adversely affect the civic action objective" of providing such assistance. The paper emphasized that U.S. policy rested heavily on the friendship of Latin American military officers.[64] The aid program continued at previous levels, and by 1967 National Security Adviser Walt Rostow could announce that aggressive "romantic revolutionaries" were finally being replaced by "pragmatists" throughout the third world.[65] On the other hand, the buildup of the Latin American military helped create what Rostow later called "the most profound" of the alliance's problems: the inability of some nations to maintain constitutional government in the face of military demands and coups.[66]

Along with continued military assistance, the alliance's aid programs reached an all-time high in 1968. Official lending jumped from $981 million in 1963 to $1.7 billion in 1968. Yet growth in Latin America remained uneven. The economic growth rate per capita reached only 1.8 percent, and the external debt doubled during the 1960s to $20 billion. In 1959, 25 percent of Latin American export income was paid out to foreign investors and lenders in profits and interest; in 1968 the amount reached 36 percent. This increase was largely due to an export trade growth rate of only 3 percent annually between 1950 and 1968, while the rest of the world averaged 7 percent.[67] Latin Americans blamed these figures in part on the refusal of the United States to trade on equitable terms. Their share of the U.S. market during the 1960s dropped from 21 percent to 13 percent. At the Punte del Este summit meeting in 1967, Colombian officials told Johnson that through tariffs and the "restricted access by establishment of quotas," the United States systematically excluded cheaper Latin American goods. At the same time, they had to use Washington's aid to buy only American goods, which were not necessarily the cheapest. Assistant Secretary of State Covey Oliver believed, moreover, that U.S. export industries were coming suspiciously close to price rigging in selling goods to that protected market.[68]

By the mid-1960s, however, one important part of Washington's economic leverage was disintegrating. When Venezuela moved to raise its price of residual oil, the administration vigorously protested and tried to hold prices in line. Mann understood, however, that the United States had little bargaining power, given military demand in Vietnam and consumer demand at home. Nor could officials stop Venezuela in 1968 from using Russian tankers to haul its oil.[69]

As U.S. economic and political power in Latin America slipped, Johnson also found his own popularity sliding. During a visit to Mexico City in 1966, the press reported a warm welcome and huge crowds—perhaps partly because of Bill Moyers's efforts. He asked two police motorcyclists to estimate the crowd. When they guessed over one million, Moyers suggested two million. He then talked the police chief into signing a statement that more than two million lined the presidential route.[70] However, when Johnson prepared to attend the 1967 summit meeting, he received a "Dear Chief" letter from columnist Drew Pearson, who had just returned from the southern continent. The letter regretfully announced, "You are not popular in Latin America" and urged him "not to get out and mingle with the crowds."[71]

Johnson's ability to negotiate successfully at the summit was also undercut by his declining popularity on Capitol Hill. Since the Dominican intervention and the intensified Vietnam involvement in 1965, influential Democrats led by Senator Fulbright had split the party on foreign policy issues. Some opposition also came from the right wing. The Selden resolution of 1965, for example, proposed to give any OAS member the right to use forceful intervention to prevent communist domination in any hemispheric nation. The White House and the State Department fought the resolution on the grounds that "We do not regard the estimate of a mere threat of communist intervention as sufficient grounds for acting unilaterally."[72] Most of Johnson's trouble, however, came from Democrats who were considerably more liberal.

The Johnson Library's White House Central Files, Confidential File, and oral histories are important sources for understanding this growing opposition. In its early stages, the opposition arose as much from disagreement with Latin American policy as with the Vietnam involvement. After the Dominican landings, Fulbright publicly attacked the administration's policy. Lincoln Gordon replied with a long private letter that tried to instruct the senator on the realities of the "true social revolution" needed by the Latins.[73] Fulbright's criticism nevertheless continued to build until early 1967, when he threatened to prevent congressional passage of a resolution, requested by the White House, that would commit Congress to help the Latin Americans develop a South American Common Market. David Rockefeller's business group and the U.S. Chamber of Commerce tried to help Johnson, but without success.[74] Rusk's attempt to testify on behalf of the resolution "was a very unhappy affair," in Lincoln Gordon's words. "Rusk sat at one end of a long table and Fulbright at the other, and the two men glared at each other like mortal enemies. It was really almost biblical."[75] Johnson flew off to the summit meeting without the resolution and, not by coincidence, without any members of Congress in the delegation.

He nevertheless pressed hard to have some kind of Latin American Common Market in operation by the 1970s. In a long background briefing, Rostow provided a fascinating analysis of Latin American industry. In his view, it was at the point where it needed investment in steel, metal working, chemicals, and heavy engineering. All these industries required the promise of continental, not merely regional, markets. Rostow compared Latin America's position to that of Western Europe in the mid-1950s.[76] That analogy may have frightened some of the officials at the summit. United States business leaders had seized upon the European Common Market as a tremendous investment opportunity after 1957. Abraham Lowenthal has observed that the Latin Americans suspected "that LAFTA [the Latin American Free Trade Association] was really a stratagem for favoring U.S. businesses . . . and that therefore regional integration should be resisted."[77] It is also true, however, that key nations like Argentina and Brazil resisted for more nationalistic reasons.[78]

Johnson never fully forgot the vision of a Latin American Common Market. In 1966 he had begun to understand that regional development offered a middle way, one that avoided narrow national approaches on the one hand and cumbersome international efforts on the other. He was also coming to believe that the United States, faced with Cold War obligations and declining economic leverage, had to become a junior rather than senior partner in hemispheric development. Rostow had long espoused these views.[79] The State Department's Latin American experts were less enthusiastic. They doubted that either sufficient capital or efficient planning was available.[80] But Johnson persisted at Punta del Este. "They were days of work as intensive as any I had experienced, except during a major crisis," he recalled in his memoir.[81] The Latin American leaders nevertheless remained cool; the State Department was skeptical; and key congressional figures opposed the administration's resolution.

Despite the President's efforts at the summit, his Latin American policy, with the notable exception of the counterinsurgency program, had not functioned well. Counterinsurgency aid and the simplistic anticommunist view that too often shaped official perceptions had played a part in helping Latin American military officers replace thirteen governments during the decade. A second Castro never ascended to power, but the Alliance for Progress—both Kennedy's and Johnson's versions of it—had failed.

Notes

1. An excellent if at times overly optimistic view of the alliance between 1960 and 1968 is U.S. Congress, House, *A Review of Alliance for Progress Goals . . . March 1969*, 91st Cong., 1st sess., 1969.

2. The first important independent survey and still a most useful source is Jerome Levinson and Juan de Onis, *The Alliance That Lost Its Way* (Chicago, 1970).

3. Philip L. Geyelin, *Lyndon B. Johnson and the World* (New York, 1966), p. 25.

4. Lincoln Gordon Oral History Interview, 1:30, Lyndon B. Johnson Library, Austin, Texas; Ralph Dungan Oral History Interview, pp. 23–24, Johnson Library.

5. *New York Times*, April 24, 1966, p. 27.

6. Eric Goldman, *The Tragedy of Lyndon Johnson* (New York, 1968), p. 89; Samuel Baily, *The United States and the Development of South America, 1945–1975* (New York, 1976), pp. 105–106.

7. *New York Times*, April 7, 1963, p. 24.

8. Walt W. Rostow, *The Diffusion of Power* (New York, 1972), pp. 216–217, 424.

9. Thomas Mann to Lyndon Johnson, March 15, 1965, Co 1-8, Executive File, White House Central Files, Johnson Library.

10. Felipe Herrera Oral History Interview, Johnson Library.

11. Bill Moyers to McGeorge Bundy, June 5, 1964, vol. 1, Latin America, Country File, National Security Files, Johnson Library.

12. Harry McPherson Oral History Interview, tape 4, p. 13, Johnson Library.

13. John Strasma, "Agrarian Reform in Peru," in *U.S. Foreign Policy and Peru*, ed. Daniel A. Sharp (Austin, 1972), pp. 164–166.

14. Thomas Mann Oral History Interview, p. 13, Johnson Library.

15. Cole Blasier, *The Hovering Giant* (Pittsburgh, 1976), pp. 243–246; see also Mann's definition of this problem in the *New York Times*, May 9, 1965, p. 3.

16. Geyelin, *Johnson and the World*, pp. 90–93.

17. *New York Times*, March 13, 1966, p. 28.

18. Ray S. Cline to McGeorge Bundy, April 17, 1964, attached to Central Intelligence Agency, "Survey of Latin America," April 1, 1964, vol. 1, CIA Survey of Latin America, Latin America, Country File, National Security Files, Johnson Library.

19. This point is argued in Walter LaFeber, *The Panama Canal: The Crisis in Historical Perspective*, expanded ed. (New York, 1979), pp. 66–68.

20. Ralph Dungan Oral History Interview, Johnson Library.

21. Lyndon Johnson, *The Vantage Point: Perspectives of the Presidency, 1963–1969* (New York, 1971), p. 180.

22. John McCone to McGeorge Bundy, January 6, 1964, Central Intelligence Agency, vol. 1, Agency File, National Security Files, Johnson Library; "Meeting with OAS Peace Commission," January 11, 1964, Panama Crisis, National Security Council History, National Security Files, Johnson Library; Thomas Mann to Edward Martin, February 8, 1964, Ibid.; Sheldon Liss, *The Canal* (Notre Dame, 1967), p. 110.

23. Thomas Mann to Dean Rusk, January 11, 1964, Panama Crisis, National Security Council History, National Security Files, Johnson Library; Chronology, January 9–29, 1964, Ibid.; Thomas Mann to Dean Rusk, January 12, 1964, Ibid.; Thomas Mann to Edward Martin, January 14, 1964, Ibid.; Johnson to General O'Meara, January 14, 1964, Ibid.; Intelligence Summary to Joint Chiefs of Staff for 7:00 a.m. to 7:00 p.m., January 16, 1964, Ibid.;

Edward Martin to Ralph Dungan, January 29, 1964, Ibid.; Thomas Mann to Edward Martin, February 8, 1964, Ibid.; Chronology, January 30 to March 19, Ibid.; Cottrell to Thomas Mann, February 19, 1964, Ibid.

24. Memorandum for the Secretary, February 1, 1964, Ibid.; Johnson to Thomas Mann, January 11, 1964, Ibid.; Thomas Mann Oral History Interview, p. 16, Johnson Library.

25. See Richard Scammon to Ralph A. Dungan, January 17, 1964, and Dungan to Scammon, January 21, 1964, Co 232, Executive File, White House Central Files, Johnson Library.

26. U.S. Embassy in Panama to Department of State, November 6, 1964, Chronology, March 20–April 3, 1964, Panama Crisis, National Security Council History, National Security Files, Johnson Library; Thomas M. Franck and Edward Weisband, "Panama Paralysis," Foreign Policy no. 21 (Winter 1975–76), pp. 185–186.

27. John A. McCone to Johnson, December 17, 1964, Co 232, Executive File, White House Central Files, Johnson Library; James R. Jones to W. Marvin Watson, January 17, 1967, Ibid.; Ambassadors Anderson and Irwin to Johnson, September 2, 1965, Chronology, March 20–April 3, 1964, Panama Crisis, National Security Council History, National Security Files, Johnson Library.

28. Johnson, Vantage Point, p. 184.

29. Robert A. Packenham, Liberal America and the Third World (Princeton, New Jersey, 1973), pp. 95–96; Baily, United States and South America, p. 106.

30. Packenham, Liberal America and the Third World, p. 30.

31. Rostow, Diffusion of Power, p. 411; Levinson and Onis, Alliance That Lost Its Way, p. 89; Baily, United States and South America, p. 108; Geyelin, Johnson and the World, p. 121.

32. AID and Alliance for Progress, "Program and Project Data, FY 1965," Agency for International Development, Agency File, National Security Files, Johnson Library; also see Gordon Chase to McGeorge Bundy, March 19, 1964, Latin America, Country File, National Security Files, Johnson Library.

33. Phyllis Parker, Brazil and the Quiet Intervention, 1964 (Austin, 1979), p. xi.

34. Ibid., pp. 58, 63, 68–70, 81, 92–93, 102–103.

35. Packenham, Liberal America and the Third World, p. 171.

36. Levinson and Onis, Alliance That Lost Its Way, p. 96; New York Times, December 14, 1965, p. 62. For Gordon's later thoughts, see Parker, Brazil, p. 111; New York Times, December 28, 1965, p. 44.

37. Donald Marquand Dozer, "Recognition in Contemporary Inter-American Relations," Journal of Inter-American Studies 8 (April 1966): 335.

38. McGeorge Bundy to Hubert Humphrey, August 31, 1964, vol. 1, Latin America, Country File, National Security Files, Johnson Library; Robert M. Sayre to Bundy, November 3, 1964, attached to Walt Rostow to Thomas Mann, November 2, 1964, Alliance for Progress vol. 2, Agency File,

National Security Files, Johnson Library; Gordon Chase to McGeorge Bundy, August 27, 1964, vol. 2, Latin America, Country File, National Security Files, Johnson Library.

39. Thomas L. Hughes to Dean Rusk, November 18, 1964, vol. 2, Latin America, Country File, National Security Files, Johnson Library.

40. Theodore Draper, *The Dominican Revolt* (New York, 1968), pp. 6–7, 17–19, 138–141.

41. Jerome Slater, *Intervention and Negotiation* (New York, 1970), p. 194; Abraham Lowenthal, *The Dominican Intervention* (Cambridge, Mass., 1972); Jerome Slater, "The Dominican Republic, 1961–1966," in *Force Without War; U.S. Armed Forces as a Political Instrument*, by Barry M. Brechman and Stephen S. Kaplan (Washington, D.C., 1978), pp. 310, 312, 317, 328–329, 336. See also Melvin Gurtov, *The United States against the Third World* (New York, 1974), pp. 118, 122 for a pro-Draper position. Blasier, *Hovering Giant*, p. 246; and Rostow, *Diffusion of Power*, pp. 412–414 represent an exception to the consensus.

42. Piero Gleijeses, *The Dominican Crisis: The 1965 Constitutionalist Revolt and American Intervention*, trans. Lawrence Lipson (Baltimore, 1978).

43. Ibid., pp. 196–197, 217–218, 282.

44. Ibid., pp. 217–218; Blasier, *Hovering Giant*, p. 247; "The Response of the Department of State to the Dominican Crisis of April–May, 1965," July 1968, pp. 6–8, State-DOD-OAS Chronologies and Summaries, Dominican Crisis, National Security Council History, National Security Files, Johnson Library.

45. Jack Valenti, "Report for the President," April 30, 1965, Co 1-8, Executive File, White House Central Files, Johnson Library; Adolf A. Berle to Johnson, June 3, 1965, Ibid.

46. Dean Rusk to American Embassy, Santo Domingo, May 3, 1965, Outgoing State Cables April 25–May 14, 1965 [A], Dominican Crisis, National Security Council History, National Security Files, Johnson Library; *Newsweek*, May 17, 1965, p. 52 has the attack of the journalists on the lists.

47. *New York Times*, May 16, 1965, p. E1.

48. Sherman Kent to Director of Central Intelligence Agency, October 26, 1965, Dominican Republic, 1964–1965, Co 62, Confidential File, White House Central Files, Johnson Library.

49. *New York Times*, May 9, 1965, p. E3; and October 14, 1965, p. 6.

50. Sheldon Liss, *Diplomacy and Dependency: Venezuela, the United States, and the Americas* (Salisbury, N.C., 1978), pp. 204–205; *Newsweek*, May 17, 1965, p. 44; *New York Times*, May 20, 1965, p. 1. Johnson, *Vantage Point*, p. 204 gives the President's different view of the results.

51. Levinson and Onis, *Alliance That Lost Its Way*, pp. 96–97.

52. AID and Alliance for Progress, "Program and Project Data, FY 1965," Agency for International Development, Agency File, National Security Files, Johnson Library; Edward Martin to Lincoln Gordon, June 9,

1966, vol. 2, Argentina, Latin America, Country File, National Security Files, Johnson Library; Dean Rusk to Buenos Aires Embassy, June 15, 1966, Ibid.; Dean Rusk to Johnson, July 12, 1966, Ibid.

53. Walt Rostow to Johnson, December 29, 1966, vol. 2, Argentina, Latin America, Country File, National Security Files, Johnson Library; American Embassy in Buenos Aires to Dean Rusk, January 5, 1967, Ibid.; Forster-Economy teletype script of Hearst Headline Service story, July 4, 1967, Co 17, Executive File, White House Central Files, Johnson Library.

54. Much of the material that follows is from David P. Werlich, *Peru: A Short History* (Carbondale, Ill., 1978), pp. 291–292; Charles T. Goodsell, "Diplomatic Protection of U.S. Business in Peru," in *U.S. Foreign Policy and Peru*, ed. Daniel Sharp, pp. 247–251; and Blasier, *Hovering Giant*, pp. 253–254.

55. Robert W. Komer to Johnson, February 21, 1964, Co 234, Confidential File, White House Central Files, Johnson Library.

56. Walt Rostow to Johnson, August 10, 1966, vol. 4, Latin America, Country File, National Security Files, Johnson Library; Bruce Blomstrom and W. Bowman Cutter, "The Foreign Private Sector in Peru," in *U.S. Foreign Policy and Peru*, ed. Daniel Sharp, p. 263; Goodsell, "Diplomatic Protection," p. 248.

57. "Peru—President Fernando Belaunde Terry," April 12, 1967, Appointment File, Diary Backup, Johnson Library.

58. Werlich, *Peru*, pp. 26, 294–296; Sharp, *U.S. Foreign Policy and Peru*, pp. 3–4.

59. AID and Alliance for Progress, "Program and Project Data, FY 1965," Agency for International Development, Agency File, National Security Files, Johnson Library; James M. Frey to Latin American Policy Committee, May 5, 1964, vol. 1, Latin America, Country File, National Security Files, Johnson Library.

60. Latin American Policy Committee, Action Minutes, Meeting 90, July 9, 1964, vol. 2, Latin America, Country File, National Security Files, Johnson Library; Gordon Chase to McGeorge Bundy, March 19, 1964, Ibid.

61. Paul E. Sigmund, *The Overthrow of Allende and the Politics of Chile, 1964–1976* (Pittsburgh, 1977), p. 10; Blasier, *Hovering Giant*, p. 256.

62. The Camelot story can be found in Llewellyn E. Thompson to Stephen Ailes, June 19, 1965, Defense Project Camelot, Agency File, National Security Files, Johnson Library; Dean Rusk to Johnson, June 30, 1965 and attachments, Ibid.; Sigmund, *Overthrow of Allende*, pp. 40–42.

63. Liss, *Diplomacy and Dependency*, pp. 222–224.

64. Robert McNamara to McGeorge Bundy, June 11, 1965, vol. 3, Latin America, Country File, National Security Files, Johnson Library.

65. *New York Times*, February 24, 1967, p. 2.

66. Rostow, *Diffusion of Power*, p. 425.

67. E. Bradford Burns, *Latin America*, 2nd ed. (Englewood Cliffs, N.J., 1977), pp. 260–262.

68. Covey Oliver Oral History Interview, tape 2, p. 36, Johnson Library; Notes of Conversations at OAS Summit, April 1967, George Christian Papers, Johnson Library.

69. Thomas Mann to Joseph Califano, January 6, 1966, in "Memorandum for Mr. Marvin Watson," February 1, 1966, TA/6, Confidential File, White House Central Files, Johnson Library; W. G. Bowdler to DeVier Pierson, July 24, 1968, Ibid.; Liss, *Diplomacy and Dependence*, pp. 207–208.

70. Memorandum for the President, April 16, 1966, Appointment File, Diary Backup, Johnson Library.

71. Drew Pearson to Johnson, March 13, 1967, OAS Summit, George Christian Papers, Johnson Library.

72. W. G. Bowdler to Bill Moyers, September 20, 1965, vol. 4, Latin America, Country File, National Security Files, Johnson Library.

73. Lincoln Gordon to McGeorge Bundy, October 4, 1965, Ibid.

74. David Rockefeller to Clifford Case, March 27, 1967, filed Sol Linowitz to Johnson, March 31, 1967, Organization of American States, Subject File, White House Central Files, Johnson Library.

75. Lincoln Gordon Oral History Interview, 1:84–86, Johnson Library.

76. "Background Briefing," April 6, 1967, OAS Summit, George Christian Papers, Johnson Library.

77. Abraham F. Lowenthal, "Alliance Rhetoric versus Latin American Reality," *Foreign Affairs* 48 (April 1970): 504–505.

78. Covey Oliver Oral History Interview, tape 1, pp. 35–36, Johnson Library. For a good analysis of the Latin American movement toward integration, see Joseph Grunwald et al., *Latin American Economic Integration and U.S. Policy* (Washington, 1972), especially pp. 77 to 83 on the Johnson administration's policies.

79. Johnson, *Vantage Point*, pp. 348–349; Rostow, *Diffusion of Power*, pp. 426–427, 687–688; W. G. Bowdler to Walt Rostow, August 2, 1966, attached to Dean Rusk to Johnson, August 2, 1966 (?), Alliance for Progress, Agency File, National Security Files, Johnson Library.

80. Milton Barall to Walt Rostow, July 8, 1966, Ibid.

81. Johnson, *Vantage Point*, pp. 350–351.

Part 2 | The Great Society

3 | Civil Rights

by Steven F. Lawson

LYNDON JOHNSON SPENT THE final months of his life filled with memories of the civil rights struggle that had greatly influenced his political career. In December 1972, at a symposium held at the Johnson Library, the former President heard an array of notable civil rights leaders commemorate his achievements in promoting racial justice. Several weeks later, during his last televised interview, Johnson spoke about civil rights. With the sound of explosions in Southeast Asia fading and in the relaxed one-to-one format in which he clearly excelled, the retired chief executive passionately recalled for Walter Cronkite the way it was in demolishing Jim Crow. These farewell appearances, unlike so many other presentations during his presidential years, did not generate charges of a credibility gap. Indeed, Johnson's remarkable performance in the area of civil rights commanded overwhelming praise during his lifetime, and the accolades have continued seven years after his death. The Texas politician who so zealously courted consensus would be pleased with the widespread acclaim for his civil rights record.

Most commentators have agreed that the passage of three pieces of civil rights legislation in 1964, 1965, and 1968 provided ample testimony of the President's political skills and humanitarian instincts. Even those who found Johnson offensive personally or philosophically have commended his actions in behalf of black Americans. The list of admirers contains the names of members of both races and representatives of both ends of the American political spectrum. Bayard Rustin, a leading theorist in the civil rights movement, remembers "that the Johnson Administration . . . had done more . . . than any other group, any other administration. . . . I think Johnson was the best we've ever had."[1] Doris Kearns, whose psychoportrait of Johnson does not flatter the man, best states the white liberal point of view: "His position on racial issues was more advanced than that of any other American President: had he done nothing else in his entire life, his contributions to civil rights would have earned him a lasting place in the annals of history."[2] From the conservative side, which has preferred to move cautiously in expanding federal jurisdiction over race relations, George F. Will approvingly calls

Johnson "the man who was more right than anyone since Lincoln on the permanent American problem, race."[3] Seconding these judgments of Johnson on the left, Bruce Miroff, a radical critic of Kennedy-Johnson liberalism, concludes that "no other administration accomplished so much in the way of civil rights legislation; no other President undertook such a rhetorical commitment to the black cause."[4]

This historical consensus, however, has not guaranteed unanimity. Detractors of Johnson's civil rights efforts generally have attacked from the left. Some dissenters have attributed the failure to eradicate racial inequality to the liberal capitalist system and its most successful practitioner of reform. Ronald Radosh discerns an "Administration plan for keeping the Negro movement tied to the corporate system" and deplores "politicians of the Democratic Party [who] have co-opted the Negroes and used sentiment and the vote to reinforce the predominance of the Washington consensus."[5] Others have condemned President Johnson for not pursuing stronger measures than he did within the prevailing politico-economic system. According to this view, Johnson could have wielded presidential authority to protect civil rights workers in the South, to realign the Democratic party in Dixie, and to enforce more vigorously the powerful civil rights legislation he had helped place on the books. "To overcome the tendency of states' rights to hurt the cause of civil rights for black people," James C. Harvey contends, "strong presidential leadership was needed. It never was forthcoming."[6] These critics ascribe Johnson's weakness to a traditional conception of the limits of national power in a federal system, a failure to develop and support effective enforcement machinery within the executive bureaucracy, a cautious response to the political backlash of disgruntled white voters, and a preoccupation with the Vietnam War. For these reasons, John Herbers, a perceptive journalist for the *New York Times,* charges that once civil rights laws were enacted "it was the Johnson Administration that instituted, in 1965, a gradualism of its own and passed along the whole process to its successor."[7]

Most appraisals of the Johnson presidency and civil rights have been written without benefit of research at the Lyndon B. Johnson Library. Contemporary accounts relied extensively on data gleaned from the public record and from personal interviews with individuals who played leading roles in shaping administration policy. The civil rights revolution of the 1960s attracted intensive and high-caliber media coverage; reporters sketched the broad outlines of Johnsonian strategy and its execution. The first-rate quality of investigative journalism provided inside accounts of public policy making that in the past were seldom available until historians invaded dusty archives years after the events. In scooping stories from historians, journalists fortunately dug up raw materials that might never have found their way into manuscript collections. Considering Johnson's fondness for conducting business over the telephone, the enterprising reporter who pieced together unrecorded conversations based on interviews with a network of informants blazed an important historical trail. Information leaked by unnamed sources must be evaluated carefully, but scholars looking for valuable leads ignore such evidence only at their peril.

Today researchers do not have to rely exclusively on the columns appearing in newspapers and journals. In addition to periodical literature, the Government Printing Office has cranked out reams of paper documenting activities within each branch of government. Efforts to extend to blacks constitutional guarantees of equality required extraordinary exertions from Presidents, members of Congress and judges. Civil rights advocates demanded from Washington an exercise of national power that would assist Afro-Americans in reversing centuries of discrimination. Thus, writing a history of the racial struggle during the Johnson years demands a substantial expenditure of energy just to collect and read through accessible published works. The President's public papers, transcripts of congressional proceedings, agency reports, particularly the volumes put out by the United States Commission on Civil Rights, and the opinions of the Supreme Court abundantly mark the course for historians to follow. The problem for current researchers stems from abundance rather than shortage.

Those interested in probing beyond the massive public record will also encounter a huge collection of documents deposited at the Johnson Library. Open since 1973, the library has swiftly processed manuscripts related to civil rights. The rapid availability of these papers attests to Johnson's deep personal faith in the cause of civil rights and, perhaps, to his confidence that the documentary evidence would demonstrate that no other chief executive had exceeded him in furthering racial equality. Over the past seven years, researchers have not rushed to dispute the glittering evaluation offered by Clarence Mitchell, an NAACP official whose oral memoir is stored at the library. Johnson "made a greater contribution to giving a dignified and hopeful status to Negroes in the United States than any President including Lincoln, Roosevelt, and Kennedy," Mitchell rhapsodized.[8]

The general agreement on Johnson's sponsorship of the civil rights cause has not closed off considerable opportunities for original research. The holdings of the Johnson Library have lured an increasing number of investigators in recent years; however, only a few monographs on race relations have appeared in print. Historians seem reluctant to enter a field which has received so much prior attention from journalists, participant-observers, and analysts in such sister disciplines as sociology and political science. Nevertheless, many aspects of Johnsonian policy toward Afro-Americans await careful study based on a fresh reading of the large quantity of archival sources. The task involves an exploration of the fields of education, employment, housing, voting, military service, criminal justice, and public accommodations. While examining the political arena in Washington, investigators must also keep track of forces at the grass roots level—demonstrations, riots, backlash—beyond the direct control of the federal government. Writers who manage to thread together the diverse strands of the civil rights mosaic will weave a rich design surpassing previous compositions.

An accurate assessment of President Johnson's role in civil rights must take into account the distance traveled by the Texan since the beginning of his political career. Johnson developed gradually into a forceful advocate of racial emancipation. He was not a Negrophobe, but until 1957 he faithfully followed the southern congressional coalition in opposition to civil rights legislation. In 1957 and 1960, however, he used his position as Senate majority leader to maneuver passage of the first civil rights bills enacted since Reconstruction. At the time, commentators speculated that Johnson had changed his mind, hoping to enlarge his appeal nationally and to increase his availability as a Democratic presidential candidate.[9]

On the basis of a review of Johnson's congressional papers dealing with civil rights, historians have deemphasized personal ambition and have stressed that Johnson showed a capacity for growth as he represented broader constituencies than those in the Lone Star State. Monroe Billington has authored the most complimentary appraisal of Johnson's early years as a director of the National Youth Administration and a congressman from the tenth district in Texas. Although Johnson "did not support civil rights legislation in the 1930's and 1940's," Billington concludes, "there is no reason to believe that he did not sincerely desire to help blacks. The practical situation tempered his private attitudes."[10] This account does not focus on the period when Johnson served as majority leader and his public stand shifted. Examining his performance during that era,

Steven Lawson and Mark Gelfand contend that Johnson desired to preserve peace between the warring factions of the Democratic party. He attempted to accomplish this aim by molding a civil rights bill acceptable to northern moderates and southern conservatives.[11] In contrast, Joe B. Frantz pays less attention to the political considerations influencing Johnson's decisions. Drawing upon interviews from the Johnson Library Oral History Project, Frantz argues that Johnson advanced "in a remarkably straight line, a generally progressive line, with now and then an aberration that might be inexcusable but no more damnable than the aberrations that most of the remainder of us sometimes perpetrate."[12] The availability of Johnson's congressional papers on civil rights should encourage a continuation of the inquiry into how he balanced regional loyalties and national aspirations to move beyond the parochialism of his southern colleagues.

The support Johnson gave to civil rights legislation paralleled his climb up the political ladder. Having shed some of the stigma that frustrated the presidential ambitions of other Dixie politicians, this grandson of a Confederate soldier teamed with John F. Kennedy, a senator from Yankee New England, to capture the White House in 1960. As Vice-President, Johnson continued to mature as a proponent of equal rights, but this process has received scant attention. His thousand days in the number two spot were not happy times, because, as T. Harry Williams points out, "Johnson, who knew about power and had exulted in its use, now had none and could only watch others use it, most of them younger men, the courtiers of Camelot who ignored or patronized him and out of his hearing called him Uncle Cornpone."[13] Nevertheless, life in the Kennedy administration offered him new opportunities to expand his understanding of the moral dimensions of the quickening black struggle.

During those years, Johnson headed the President's Committee on Equal Employment Opportunity (PCEEO). Charged with this responsibility, he worked closely with Plans for Progress, a project designed by the administration to persuade government contractors to correct racially biased employment practices. Journalist Leonard Baker and historian Carl Brauer have commented upon the Vice-President's role in civil rights. Both acknowledge the limited effectiveness of the job programs which depended upon voluntarism and conciliation. Whereas Baker observed Johnson assuming a more activist position on civil rights by the middle of 1963, Brauer did not hear the Vice-President raise his voice within Kennedy councils in defense of strong legislative measures. He pictures Johnson as a cautious adviser urging the President to avoid the prospects of a disastrous fight over the civil rights bill introduced in June.[14]

An extraordinary document contained in the prepresidential files of the Johnson Library reveals LBJ's reservations about Kennedy's civil rights strategy. On June 3, 1963, the Vice-President and Theodore Sorenson, a top White House aide, held a lengthy telephone conversation which Johnson recorded on a dictaphone machine. The tape and transcript of the talk offer fascinating insights into Johnson's views of racial politics. Almost uninterrupted for over thirty minutes, Johnson criticized the Kennedy people for failing to do their legislative homework in paving the way for legislation. "I think it can be more constructive," he lectured, "and I think it can be better . . . I don't know who drafted it; I've never seen it. Hell, if the Vice President doesn't know what's in it how do you expect the others to know what's in it? I got it from the *New York Times*." According to the former majority leader, the question centered on timing. A poorly planned congressional fight would sacrifice the rest of the New Frontier measures. If Kennedy sent up his civil rights proposals immediately, Johnson warned, "Howard Smith is going to be in the lead in one place and Dick Russell in the other place, and they're going to sit quietly in these appropriation committees and they're going to cut his outfit off and put it in their pocket and never mention civil rights. So I'd move my children on through the line and get them down in the storm cellar and get it locked and key, and then I'd make my attack. I'd tell the Negroes what I'm doing."[15]

Johnson's approach to racial problems was clearly evolving. This native son of Dixie believed that white southerners could be persuaded to listen to reason, and he recommended that President Kennedy travel to a southern city, look its residents "in the eye," and articulate "the moral issue and the Christian issue." At the same time, the Vice-President maintained that blacks felt uncertain that the federal government stood behind their struggle. Thus, Johnson urged a strong presidential expression of the morality of racial equality to show blacks that "we're on their side . . . and . . . until they receive that assurance, unless it's stated dramatically and convincingly, they're not going to pay much attention to executive orders and legislative recommendations."[16] Eight days after the Johnson-Sorenson discussion, President Kennedy delivered his most fervent civil rights address on national television; however, it is unknown whether this message reflected Johnson's advice.

Vice-President Johnson's thinking on this subject needs further study. The Johnson Library's prepresidential files contain records of the PCEEO and the files of George Reedy and Hobart Taylor, Johnson's closest advisers on racial matters at the time. A review of these papers will help illuminate the Vice-President's performance in carrying out his major civil rights assignments, his role in fashioning administration responses to racial confrontations, and his outlook toward the escalating pace of those conflicts. Given the former majority leader's successes in shepherding two civil rights acts through Congress and his ongoing contacts on Capitol Hill, investigators should look for clues to explain why Kennedy refrained from utilizing him to push strong legislative measures before a wave of terrorism rolled through the South in the summer of 1963.[17]

Several months after a long, hot season of demonstrations culminating in a mammoth march on Washington, D.C., tragedy presented Lyndon Johnson with the opportunity and power to prove how deep his concern for racial equality had grown. The murder of President Kennedy gave Johnson a chance to fulfill what he had come to recognize as his "moral obligation to every person of every skin color" and also to help his native South cast aside the oppressive race issue.[18] The extension of freedom to blacks carried the potential of liberating white southerners from a caste system which economically and socially impoverished both races in the region. Tom Wicker, a native-born North Carolinian and an astute columnist for the *New York Times*, observes that Johnson "*as a Southerner* . . . was better placed than any man to recognize that full national unity and sweeping national progress . . . was not possible until the South had somehow been brought back into the Union."[19] Building on this journalistic analysis, Professor T. Harry Williams remarks, "It has been insufficiently appreciated that Johnson believed the elimination of segregation would lift an onus from his section, would enable southern whites to stand as equals with that majority that had looked down on them for their racial practices."[20]

Over the next five years, President Johnson signed into law three civil rights measures aimed at crushing the barriers of racial separation in public accommodations, education, and housing; extending equal employment opportunities; and expanding the right to vote. Their passage tested the President's ability to construct a consensus around controversial proposals and to patch up the coalition when it showed signs of cracking. President by virtue of assassination, Johnson had much to prove. Doris Kearns recalls his saying, "I knew that if I didn't get out in front on this issue, [the liberals] would get me. . . . I had to produce a civil rights bill that was even stronger than the one they'd have gotten if Kennedy had lived. Without this, I'd be dead before I could even begin."[21] At the outset, the martyrdom of John Kennedy and vivid memories of southern blacks suffering "Bull" Connor's racist brutality in Birmingham created the right political atmosphere for Johnson to work his miracles in Congress. However, the chief executive had to exercise his formidable skills in a hostile climate once the feeling of national bereavement wore off and liberals attacked the administration's escalation of the war in Vietnam. Thus, passage of a series of monumental civil rights bills occurred under varying circumstances within a short span of years.

When Johnson took office on November 22, 1963, his predecessor's civil rights bill lay stalled in the Rules Committee of the House of Representatives. The Kennedy administration had conducted intensive negotiations with members of Congress in order to write legislation with sufficient clout and favorable chances for enactment. Such a proposal had emerged from the House Judiciary Committee, which was dominated by civil rights proponents. Committed to its passage as a memorial to the slain Kennedy, on November 27 President Johnson delivered a stirring civil-rights-as-redemption message to a grieving Congress. However, neither the preliminary work done in the preceding months nor the sorrow gripping the nation ensured swift approval of the administration-backed Judiciary Committee bill. Before Johnson signed the measure into law on July 2, 1964, civil rights advocates had painstakingly broken fifty-seven days of filibustering in the Senate. At the same time, they had kept momentum for the bill rolling over the presidential primary bandwagon of George Wallace, the Alabama governor whose bigoted appeals found increasing acceptance in the North.

The Johnson administration finally overcame traditional congressional roadblocks and an incipient white backlash, but its achievement has attracted little interest from scholars. A few brief accounts of the parliamentary maneuvering leading to passage of the act have appeared, but they are limited in scope. The most detailed treatment to date, Daniel Berman's *A Bill Becomes A Law*, follows the legislative routes taken by the Civil Rights Act of 1960 and, to a lesser extent, the 1964 statute. The author describes proceedings on Capitol Hill, largely ignoring events outside the halls of Congress.[22] For some specialists of the Kennedy years, neglecting the Johnson White House has not constituted much of a loss. They have implied that Johnson's presence as chief executive made little difference in obtaining the ultimate victory. "What might have happened had Kennedy not been assassinated is of course impossible to establish," Carl Brauer asserts, "but many of those closest to the legislative process later reflected that essentially the same goal would have been reached."[23]

Johnson has minimized his own efforts in battling for the bill. Writing in *The Vantage Point*, he remembers, "I deliberately tried to tone down my personal involvement in the daily struggle so that my colleagues on the Hill could take tactical responsibility and credit."[24] This strategy has partially obscured the diligence with which the President commanded the congressional offensive. Whether courting the indispensable Everett Dirksen, the Senate Republican leader, or making public speeches, Johnson never ceased guiding the long legislative fight. One of the most crucial reasons for success was Johnson's refusal, uncharacteristic of his style as a legislator, to accept compromise. Indeed, he insisted that Congress postpone other business until it had favorably disposed of the omnibus civil rights bill. Patience paid off as liberal senators outlasted their loquacious southern adversaries and Dirksen lined up his followers behind the measure.[25]

The Johnson Library offers documentation of some of the activities initiated by the executive branch to clear passage of the bill. Administrative histories furnish a good place to start. Compiled by departmental officials in the waning months of the Johnson term, these accounts consist of a narrative appended with selected material from bureau files. Although these annals exude self-congratulation, they shift attention away from the pervasive White House and refocus it on the routine work of the federal bureaucracy. These chronicles trace internal policy deliberations which preceded a final recommendation conveyed to the President by the top agency chief.

According to the *Administrative History* of the Justice Department, major policy decisions concerning the bill had been made during the Kennedy regime. After November 1963, the Justice Department concentrated on "Congressional liaison and preparation of materials in support of the Administration bill."[26] Civil Rights Division lawyers helped lawmakers to understand and defend critical provisions of the proposal, while the White House rounded up support in its behalf. Lee White, who advised both Kennedy and Johnson on racial affairs, reported that there "have been countless meetings, discussions, phone calls to Congressional leaders, minority group representatives, and Administration personnel." Some of those conversations involved attempts to obtain enough votes to impose cloture in the Senate. To win over Carl Hayden of Arizona, "who [would] carry several other votes with him—such as the two Nevada Senators," the administration promised to negotiate a favorable solution to a controversial water project in Hayden's home state, "contingent upon the promise of a cloture vote by Hayden on civil rights."[27] One oral history interview indicates that Johnson also exerted pressure on his reform allies. Hubert Humphrey recalled that the President prodded him to show that liberal "bomb throwers" could depart from their customary speech making long enough to produce tangible results.[28]

Passage of the 1964 act came at a crucial juncture in the administration's involvement with the civil rights movement. Preparing to campaign for the presidency, Johnson did not want chaotic scenes of black agitation to frighten white voters into the camp of Barry Goldwater, the conservative Republican candidate who had voted against the civil rights bill. After the ceremony signing the measure into law, the President spoke privately with a group of civil rights leaders and admonished "that there be an understanding of the fact that the rights Negroes possessed could now be secured by law, making demonstrations unnecessary and possibly even self-defeating."[29] Agreeing with the chief executive, each of his listeners except representatives from the Congress of Racial Equality (CORE) and the Student Nonviolent Coordinating Committee (SNCC), the most militant of the groups, urged blacks to suspend large-scale protests until after the November election. Although sporadic violence flared both in the South and the North, Johnson easily won the contest. However, brutal assaults on civil rights workers spending a summer in Mississippi and riots by blacks in urban ghettos of the North flashed ominous warnings that racial strife would bring new problems for the administration.[30]

Elected President in his own right, Johnson preferred to postpone further legislative action on civil rights, but the resumption of mass protests in Selma, Alabama, in 1965 forced him to change his mind. The struggle for passage of the 1965 Voting Rights Act has received the fullest treatment of any aspect of Johnson's civil rights policies. Using documents in the Johnson Library, David Garrow's *Protest at Selma* and Steven Lawson's *Black Ballots* conclude that before Martin Luther King launched his demonstrations in Alabama, Johnson had authorized the Justice Department to sketch possible legislation removing obstacles that impeded black voter registration in the South. Lawyers at the Justice Department were roughing out their drafts when state troopers viciously assaulted a parade of protesters attempting to walk from Selma to Montgomery on Sunday, March 7, 1965. Both authors conclude the bloody attack ensured that the eventual bill "would be enacted into law, and with only minimal delay and no weakening amendments."[31]

In a most interesting departure for others to follow, Garrow compares the unusually prompt passage of the Voting Rights Act with the prolonged deliberations that had preceded approval of the civil rights law a year earlier. He suggests that Congress reacted with greater speed to the Selma demonstrators than those in Birmingham because the former remained nonviolent and stuck to a single issue. This analysis emphasizes the impact of media coverage in shaping congressional responses to racial confrontations. Consideration should also be given to Johnson's augmented influence with the eighty-ninth Congress, which seated far more liberal members than those who had watched events unfold in Birmingham. Furthermore, a bill devoted to voting rights, long considered the foundation of representative government, had political advantages over a measure addressing the more controversial issues of education and employment. A comparison of mail received by the White House during the course of debates on the two civil rights bills might reveal the differences in public perception of the need for each piece of legislation. Nevertheless, in both instances, the violence inflicted upon peaceful civil rights activists in due course swung sentiment behind reform measures.

In contrast, the moral indignation that fostered enactment of these two powerful measures had subsided by the time a third proposal became law in 1968. The final legislative component in Johnson's civil rights trilogy, it combatted racial discrimination in housing and jury selection and punished those who interfered with civil rights workers encouraging the exercise of constitutionally guaranteed rights. Reflecting changing times, the act also included penalties for individuals who traveled across state lines to foment or participate in a riot. The consensus that sustained earlier legislative victories had fractured under the stress of the Vietnam War and ghetto riots, thus making passage of this omnibus bill a significant feat. A full investigation of the attempts to secure this controversial proposal from 1966 through 1968 can offer insight into Johnson's endurance in extending first-class citizenship to blacks, and it may also provide a glimpse of the President's attitudes toward the altered contours of the civil rights movement.

Unlike the situation in 1964 and 1965, no single crisis with the drama of Birmingham or Selma mobilized the administration into action. However, a series of well-publicized slayings of civil rights workers in the South and the subsequent acquittal of the accused murderers did prompt the Justice Department to search for ways of strengthening impartial jury selection. After Alabama prosecutors failed to obtain a conviction in the murder case of Viola Liuzzo, a pilgrim to Selma, Joseph Califano, who coordinated the president's domestic legislative programs, reported to his boss on October 25, 1965, that there was "an increasing likelihood . . . that we will have for consideration in the civil rights area next year proposals on jury selection systems."[32] Before the end of the year, Attorney General Nicholas Katzenbach had added to the legislative list items for ex panding "federal jurisdiction to investigate civil rights crimes and enhance personal security."[33] By the time President Johnson delivered his civil rights message to Congress on April 28, 1966, the administration had broadened its proposal to include provisions banning racial discrimination in housing, the most controversial features of the omnibus measure.

The protracted, uphill struggle to obtain passage of the bill has received the least detailed treatment of any of Johnson's civil rights laws.[34] Perhaps the shift in emphasis after 1965 from integration toward the development of a separate black consciousness has lessened interest in studying the persistence of traditional civil rights goals in the late 1960s. Nevertheless, James C. Harvey has outlined the basic chronology of events leading to enactment of the 1968 statute. Written before the Johnson Library officially opened its doors, the description in *Black Civil Rights during the Johnson Administration* relies on data from newspapers, periodicals, and government documents. Since then, the library's civil rights papers have become available; they await inspection by scholars attempting to explain how the measure passed with powerful odds against it. In doing so, researchers will evaluate Harvey's conclusion that while "the president did utilize a number of levers at his disposal, . . . [in] the case of the Civil Rights Act of 1968 . . . Clarence Mitchell [the NAACP's Washington lobbyist] deserves more credit for its passage than Johnson himself."[35]

A large collection of archival sources covers the 1968 Civil Rights Act, permitting an inquiry from several directions. The Justice Department, the White House Staff, officials of civil rights groups, congressional leaders, and the President assumed key roles in the battle. The Justice Department's *Administrative History* describes the successive stages in drafting the measure to satisfy civil rights organizations and to meet objections raised by Senator Dirksen, without whose support once again, Attorney General Ramsey Clark reported, "we are pessimistic about being able to vote cloture."[36]

During congressional deliberations on the bill in 1966, the House of Representatives added an antiriot amendment, thereby weakening the measure. Although the President opposed it, he still had to answer the clamor for tough action in the wake of summer uprisings in northern ghettos. His concern was reflected in late November and December as an intergovernmental task force on civil rights met to map out plans for the coming legislative session. Summoned by Joseph Califano, this group of representatives from the White House Staff and the Department of Justice advised the President that a civil rights bill "would probably not pass unless an 'anti-riot' proposal is included." In plotting strategy, the task-force members recommended that "it might be better to include an acceptably narrow 'anti-riot' provision in the proposal—over which we would have a degree of control—than to have a broader 'anti-riot' provision added by Congress."[37]

The housing sections posed another serious problem for the administration. The White House came under intense pressure to adopt even stronger civil rights provisions than it had originally introduced. The most forceful suggestions emerged from the White House Conference on Civil Rights held in early June 1966. The vast records of the conference, including working papers, transcripts of proceedings, and reports, reveal that recommendations adopted by the panelists exceeded in scope those authorized by the task force and accepted by the President.[38] At the same time, the real estate industry organized a potent lobby against the housing measures, and its efforts seemed to strike a responsive chord in public opinion. Some White House aides bluntly warned that the "housing proposal will be impossible to enact," but the President stood by his original proposal. He emphatically insisted that support must be built "for all of the package and not just for parts of it."[39]

Johnson maintained this stance for two years, and in March 1968, he watched his supporters choke off a filibuster after three unsuccessful cloture attempts. The bill was about to clear its final congressional hurdle in the House when large-scale rioting broke out following the assassination of Martin Luther King. The impact upon Congress of King's death and the disorders that it unleashed remains undetermined, but the judgment of Barefoot Sanders, the President's legislative liaison, is instructive. The murder of King did not have much effect, Sanders recalls, "because the yeas and nays cancelled each other out."[40] Much of the sympathy for the bill prompt-ed by the slaying gave way to anger as members of Congress on their way to the Capitol inhaled smoke from burning buildings torched by mobs rampaging through Washington, D.C. When the civil rights leader died in Memphis, the House was considering what route to take on the administration bill already approved by the Senate. The lower chamber could endorse the measure or call for a conference committee which would delay final acceptance and probably result in dilution of the bill. The lawmakers chose the first alternative. Ap-parently, the administration broke the legislative stalemate by hold-ing in line the votes secured before the tragic killings and the subse-quent turbulence.

The most important issues arising from a study of the Civil Rights Act of 1968 concern Lyndon Johnson's responses to the chang-ing configuration of the racial struggle. As the civil rights coalition diminished in size and white reactionary forces grew, Johnson re-fused to order a major retreat on the legislative front. However, in honoring his moral commitment to extend first-class citizenship, the President had to take into account the political considerations up-setting his legislative consensus. Critics have accused him of back-ing away from his firm support of civil rights after northern white voters exhibited their hostility not only to riots but to black mili-tancy in general. James Harvey speculates that Johnson did not push the civil rights bill in 1966 because "he was thinking about the growing white backlash."[41] However, such a conclusion, besides re-quiring verification, ignores the possibility that black agitation may have stiffened Johnson's resolve to persist in prying loose the civil rights bill from Congress.

The effects of rising black aggressiveness on White House pol-icy offer exciting avenues for research. As SNCC and CORE aban-doned white liberals and blacks in the ghettos spontaneously re-leased their rage against symbols of white authority, the Johnson administration rushed to reinforce advocates of peaceful change. The prospects of racial violence in the cities, beginning with the summer of 1964, prompted Johnson advisers to find ways, as Eric Goldman notes, "to help the established Negro leaders, who may well be losing control of the civil rights movement, to reestablish control and keep the movement going in its legitimate direction."[42] To accomplish this aim demanded sensitivity and finesse. Harry McPherson, who succeeded Lee White as Johnson's principal coun-selor on race, recalls the problem facing his boss: "Johnson . . . understood that while he needed [Whitney] Young and [Roy] Wilkins and [A. Philip] Randolph and [Bayard] Rustin, that his embrace of them would endanger them after a short time with the Negro community. And yet he needed them and did use them in urgent situations."[43] An exchange of memoranda in September 1966 between McPherson and Attorney General Katzenbach delineates this thorny dilemma. The White House aide pointed out that "our lines of communication to the movement run generally . . . to the older Negro establishment. We have very few contacts with younger Negro leaders. We *must* develop these contacts." Katzenbach responded on a note of pessimism, contending that the "younger leaders who now exist are precisely those who . . . have consistently chosen an 'outside course': that is, Stokely Carmichael." Nevertheless, he did recommend that the NAACP, the Urban League, and the Southern Christian Leadership Conference (SCLC) consider "establishing a militant but peaceful organization of young people who could successfully compete with SNCC."[44] Nothing specific came of the idea, but the administration's attempts to develop alternatives to black violence and to bolster the position of conventional civil rights leaders merit a full investigation.

The annual outbreak of summer riots made matters worse for the White House. In contrast to the brutality suffered by peaceful protesters, the violence perpetrated by black mobs preaching physical retaliation hurt the administration politically. Recognizing that "every night of rioting costs us the support of thousands," one Johnson lieutenant suggested that the chief executive "appeal to the good sense and conscience of the country both white and Negro. Denounce violence, but recognize frustration. Be firm in the insistence on obedience to law."[45] Plagued by urban upheavals that increased in intensity each year during his second term, Johnson adopted a moderate course of action. Aimed at extending victories won by his loyal civil rights allies, the President's program also acknowledged the fears for personal safety voiced by Americans, white and black. McPherson echoes the difficulty liberals experienced in striking a delicately balanced response: " 'By God, there's law and order here. You can't get away with this,' followed by 'Of course we understand why you rioted. We know you could hardly do anything else.' "[46] How to respond to social and economic maladies infecting the ghettos without "rewarding the rioters" continuously perplexed the President and his advisers.[47]

Disorders in Watts, Newark, and Detroit raise a number of questions. Did the White House learn from the initial explosions any lessons that it applied to later problems? Did partisan political considerations, such as the presence of a Democratic or Republican governor, affect Johnson's handling of particular riots? A comparison of the strife in Newark with that in Detroit offers a good case study of this point. In pacifying insurrections in the North, did the administration follow the same principles as it did in answering requests by civil rights workers in the South for federal protection from white racists? Besieged by demands to repair the breakdown of law and order that hampered the civil rights movement in Dixie, the Justice Department customarily refrained from intervening, contending that the federal system delegated law enforcement duties to local officials.[48]

In the past, Presidents had established commissions to study volatile civil rights problems and to recommend solutions. Following this tradition, Johnson created a group of inquiry headed by Otto Kerner to examine the urban disorders. However, when the panel suggested strong measures and condemned white racism, the White House ignored its proposals. Why did Johnson choose to scuttle the Kerner Commission's report? By doing so, he left the impression that he viewed it "as an attack on [his] administration calling for too much Federal spending while the Vietnam war is going on."[49]

The Vietnam War earned some dividends for civil rights advocates while it also unsettled their ranks and drained funds and attention from their struggle. The need to build and maintain a consensus in support of escalation in Southeast Asia may have influenced Johnson's support of additional civil rights measures after 1965. Although SNCC and CORE attacked the administration's Vietnam policy from the start, the NAACP, the Urban League, and the SCLC attempted to divorce foreign and domestic affairs. Whitney Young of the Urban League derided white liberals who ignored the President's "impressive record of accomplishing what they have been fighting for for years and work themselves into a lather over Vietnam." NAACP Executive Secretary Roy Wilkins spent "a considerable amount of his time . . . keeping the 'peace in Viet Nam movement' from becoming too big a factor in the civil rights movement."[50] In defending the war, the majority of black leaders sought to maintain Johnson's backing for their unfinished programs in housing, employment, and education. Vietnam and the riots isolated the President from black radicals, but drew him closer to such moderates as Wilkins and Young.

It remains for historians to estimate the impact of the Vietnam War on civil rights. The heavy combat load shouldered by blacks overseas gave civil rights leaders ammunition to use in fighting their battles on the home front. "For the first time," a black adviser to the President declared, "the U.S. has fielded a truly democratic team in Vietnam," a situation that provided the premise for arguments for extending racial equality.[51] The threat posed to this ideological weapon by antiwar groups urging withdrawal from Vietnam may help explain the vehemence with which black leaders loyal to the President attacked the dissenters. In selling the war to their constituents, Negro leaders cemented presidential support for their goals, but they paid a high price for their endorsement. Not only did the conflict splinter the civil rights forces, but the war also crowded vital domestic programs off the list of top priorities. By 1968, according to Ramsey Clark, Johnson had shifted "his concerns and time . . . so far toward Vietnam that his involvement [in civil rights] was very, very limited."[52]

One of the casualties lost in the war was the President's association with Martin Luther King. In winning some of his greatest victories from 1963 through 1965, King had come to depend on the power of the federal government. Although viewed as a militant, he was considered a responsible leader who usually listened to White House reason. King enjoyed administration cooperation as long as he kept private his reservations about the war. The breach that developed between Johnson and King after 1967 closed off to each side options for pursuing racial advancement.[53]

Public opposition to the Vietnam War soured King's relationship with Johnson. Soon after passage of the Voting Rights Act in August 1965, administration advisers began expressing concern over King's "trying to get into the Vietnam act."[54] Over the next two years, presidential aides tried to compute the most "difficult part of the equation: . . . what Martin Luther King will do next." During that time, King's name continued to appear on White House invitation lists, and he or one of his assistants attended high-level strategy sessions on civil rights. However, by April 1967 King had openly denounced Johnson's policy of escalation, and the White House and its black allies sought to discredit "the crown prince of the Vietniks."[56] Shortly before King's assassination, some of the President's people responded to King's plans for a poor people's march on Washington by angrily lumping together the winner of the Nobel Peace Prize with such purveyors of violence as Stokely Carmichael and Rap Brown.[57] An inquiry into the administration's response to the subsequent march may pinpoint some of the consequences resulting from the deterioration of the alliance between the chief executive and the black leader.

Johnson's disenchantment with segments of the civil rights movement can also be discerned by examining the events surrounding the White House Conference in 1966. A speech delivered by the President to the graduating class of Howard University on June 4, 1965 triggered plans for a conference to address the unfinished business remaining on the nation's civil rights agenda. Beginning a new phase in pursuit of racial emancipation, the address emphasized affirmative action to remove the remnants of past discrimination. The president declared, "We seek not just freedom but opportunity"—not just legal equality but human equity—not just equality as a right and a theory, but equality as a fact and a result."[58] In preparing to deliver these remarks, Johnson explained to his principal speech writer: "It was like you couldn't pick up the blanket off a Negro at one corner, you had to pick it all up."[59]

However, the bright expectations aroused by the President's stirring message soon dissolved into acrimony. Disputes erupted over whether to schedule workshops at the projected conference on the controversial Moynihan report, a treatise widely misinterpreted as attributing the plight of Afro-Americans to a degenerate family lifestyle. Although the conference planners finally scratched the topic from the scheduled discussions, other sources of discord persisted. The conference took place amidst undercurrents of tension between the administration and civil rights militants over Vietnam and black power. Over two thousand delegates attending the meeting ratified far-reaching proposals for massive governmental and private action, but in contrast to the year before, the President now showed little enthusiasm for jumping into "the next and most profound stage of the battle for civil rights."[60]

The standard account of the White House conference appeared a year after the event in Lee Rainwater and William L. Yancey's *The Moynihan Report and the Politics of Controversy.* The authors criticize Johnson for intentionally orchestrating the conference to persuade black Americans "that he was now in charge of the civil rights movement."[61] A valuable book based on conversations with key public officials and civil rights leaders, it can nevertheless be updated. Fresh answers are needed to explain why Johnson called the conference and what degree of control the White House exerted over the proceedings. Some have charged that Johnson intended the affair to drive a wedge in the civil rights movement, allowing him to lessen pressures "to produce such a major program at the time he was escalating the war in Vietnam and couldn't do both." Harry McPherson, who helped organize the gathering and wrote his own version of it, dismisses this charge. He insists that until the middle of 1967, the President thought he could wage wars simultaneously at home and abroad.[62] Still unaccounted for are Johnson's reasons for shelving the suggestions offered by the conferees.[63]

In siding with the moderates over the militants, Johnson tried to guide the course of the civil rights struggle. Sharing the sentiments of Rainwater and Yancey, Bruce Miroff suggests that the President sought to manipulate the sometimes unruly forces for racial advancement into acceptable avenues of progress. "Threatened by the independence, dynamism, and unpredictability of black political activity," Miroff asserts, "the White House attempted to find means of directing this activity into safer and more controlled channels."[64] Civil rights proponents believed that American government was crisis oriented, that it responded most rapidly to direct confrontation. Following outbursts of militancy, officials in Washington sought to accomplish reform in piecemeal fashion, only to have a new crisis precipitate calls for more immediate and sweeping action. Critics on the left, like Miroff, aimed their attacks more at the pluralist system than at the particular chief executive who presided over it. Condemning liberals for striving to reduce conflicts through rational negotiations between competing interest groups, they preferred instead a decision-making process which encouraged a heightening of tensions through mass political demonstrations.[65]

Although seeking to keep turbulent civil rights pressures from shattering its fragile reform consensus, the Johnson administration seriously doubted that it could harness black activism. According to Nicholas Katzenbach, the President was "the country's leader toward civil rights, but this is something different from being a civil rights leader." The attorney general warned that "one of the principal difficulties of established Negro leadership has been and will continue to be taking positions that are at the same time responsible and practical—and clearly independent of the Administration."[66] Nevertheless, the White House intended to exert a calming influence on civil rights protesters. Before a discussion with Martin Luther King in 1964, Lee White suggested that "some thought should be given to providing . . . constructive channels to energies for the summer," and he endorsed the holding of religious rallies, voter registration drives, and community job programs.[67]

The desire of presidents to ameliorate disruptive social conflicts is not surprising; more importantly, historians should analyze what policy choices are selected from the available options. Two separate questions must be raised: How skillfully and imaginatively did Johnson and his staff operate within the existing framework of political institutions? How effectively did the solutions devised by liberal reformers promote genuine equality of opportunity? These queries furnish different yardsticks for measuring the overall performance of the Johnson Administration in responding to black unrest.

Those judging the ability of Johnson to obtain remedies for curing racial ills must also consider how well he administered the prescribed treatments. An evaluation from this perspective turns the spotlight away from the White House and toward the departments in the executive branch. Gary Orfield has correctly pointed out that enactment of a law "means very little until the resources of the executive bureaucracies are committed to its implementation."[68] Thus, studies of the way federal agencies enforced congressional legislation are essential for reaching conclusions about the progress of civil rights during the Johnson years.

A full-scale analysis of these efforts can be undertaken with only partial assistance from the Johnson Library. Enforcement responsibilities centered primarily in the Justice Department; the Department of Health, Education, and Welfare; the Department of Housing and Urban Affairs; and the Equal Employment Opportunity Commission. Their records are destined for deposit in the National Archives. Without looking through these office files, it is impossible to document substantially how agencies promulgated their guidelines and carried out their rules and regulations. Nevertheless, the Johnson Library affords the researcher opportunities to gather additional data from administrative histories, the White House Central Files, and transcribed interviews with department chiefs.[69]

Investigations of federal enforcement efforts provide an added dimension to the examination of the Johnson administration's responses to convulsions within the civil rights movement. Implementation activities took place mainly during a period when black radicals directed their anger against white liberals, and the mood of whites across the nation swung from sympathy for civil rights activists to hostility against black militants. In this highly charged political atmosphere, Johnson had to calculate the risks not only to his legislative program but also to his enforcement plans.

Johnson has been sharply criticized for not paying closer attention to the vital details of bureaucratic operations. Allan Wolk contends that the President "used his legislative skills to get Congress to act, but then assumed somewhat of a laissez faire attitude in which he allowed enforcement to proceed without his help or hindrance."[70] James Harvey also chides the chief executive: "Without his pressure and support the bureaucracy was often unable or unwilling to cope with counter-pressures of strategically placed southern Congressmen and the recalcitrance of their white constituents in opposition to implementation of civil rights laws."[71] Gary Orfield agrees that federal agencies performed cautiously, but he argues that moderation was occasionally necessary to ensure lasting changes within a federal system which put a premium on cooperation between Washington and local governments.[72]

Some commentators have implied that the President deliberately thwarted strong enforcement endeavors. They bemoan a decision reached by Johnson in late 1965 assigning overall supervision of civil rights activities to the Justice Department. In doing so, the chief executive reversed a short-lived experiment designating Vice-President Humphrey as civil rights coordinator for the White House. Critics maintain that enforcement was handicapped by this transfer of duties away from Humphrey, known as an innovator in civil rights, to Attorney General Katzenbach, who was inclined to pursue a methodical, legalistic approach.[73] The reorganization decision came at a time when Johnson and the civil rights movement had reached a crossroads; thus, researchers might consider whether it was a signpost indicating new departures in administration policy.

Two excellent monographs have already discussed the swirling currents of change affecting the performance of the bureaucracy. Orfield's penetrating study of Title VI of the 1964 Civil Rights Act analyzes executive operations within a dynamic political context. The author demonstrates that to a large extent enforcement efforts depended on congressional approval. Agency officials either had "to come to terms with its existing constituency or to try to create a new constituency able to generate broadly based support in Congress."[74] After 1965, legislators were horrified by the ghetto riots sweeping the nation, and they took out their wrath by pinching needed funds from federal programs. James Button's *Black Violence* suggests that administration responses to black revolts varied according to the level and intensity of the disturbances, the attitude of public officials toward the groups participating in the disorders, the availability of government money to satisfy the protesters' demands, the clarity of the demonstrators' goals, and the concomitant deployment of nonviolent forms of dissent. Using these criteria, Button discerns a generally sympathetic reaction from Washington to urban unrest from 1963 to 1965 in contrast to a position of retrenchment in 1967 and 1968. These findings, along with those of

David Garrow's on Selma, indicate that the effects of violence on administration policy shifted with the political moods of Congress and the nation.[75]

Explorations of the Johnson years naturally focus on Washington as the seat of governmental power. However, scholars have studied official business transacted in the nation's capital without examining political life in the city itself. The District of Columbia offers a microcosmic view of Lyndon Johnson's pursuit of racial equality. Deprived of home rule, the district, when Johnson took office, was governed by three commissioners appointed by the President. However, Congress made crucial decisions affecting the city, including those involving finances. The House and the Senate each had a committee which closely monitored Washington affairs. The House Committee on the District of Columbia provided the chief stumbling block for home-rule advocates. Traditionally chaired by white Southerners, the House panel had resisted attempts over the years to extend self-government to a city whose black residents comprised a majority of the population.

Under these circumstances, Washington resembled a southern city depriving blacks of an effective voice in government. After 1965 Washington Negroes listened carefully to exhortations on black power by Stokely Carmichael, a graduate of the district's Howard University, and they increasingly sought to apply his lessons to their city. Although the absence of self-government also handicapped whites living in Washington, the home-rule issue revolved around race. The white chairman of the Board of Commissioners, an advocate of autonomy, declared that the "real reason for opposition to home rule is the fear that Washington might be run by its Negro citizens."[76] One northern member of Congress considered home rule as "a sort of 'civil rights' issue" and recommended that it "might do a little coat-tail riding in a successful civil rights fight in the House."[77]

As President, Johnson sponsored self-government measures in Congress, culminating in an intense legislative battle that narrowly failed in 1966. After the House declined to modify its own version of a bill to conform with one passed in the Senate, the chief executive took other steps toward home rule. In 1967, he won congressional approval for a reorganization plan dissolving the three-member governing board and replacing it with an appointed mayor and city council. Adoption of this halfway measure did not reflect a desire on Johnson's part to stop short of pursuing the goal of "full elective local government"; rather, the President insisted, "successful operation of the new government will strengthen our case before the Congress."[78]

Despite obvious implications for civil rights, historians have neglected the home-rule fight. One of the rare acknowledgements of its importance, Robert Sherrill's *The Accidental President*, portrays Johnson unfavorably. Sherrill argues that the President felt scant enthusiasm for home rule and gave little help to extend it to "the only major city in America where black power could become an immediate fact."[79]

A plentiful supply of documents exists in the Johnson Library for investigators wanting to test the validity of Sherrill's harsh judgment. Details of administration strategy in managing the issue can be located in the files of several White House aides, most notably in those of Charles Horsky, who advised the President on District of Columbia matters through most of the home-rule campaign. Additional information can be found in the White House Central Files as well as in the oral histories of Charles Diggs, a black member of the House district committee; Barefoot Sanders, the legislative liaison; and Joseph Rauh, a civil rights lawyer active in the Democratic party organization in the nation's capital. A perusal of these materials will add to an overall estimation of Johnson's role in advancing equal rights for Afro-Americans. Attention should be devoted to the impact of the black power persuasion on presidential thinking concerning home rule. Furthermore, scholars examining the riot in Washington following Martin Luther King's assassination and the subsequent assembly of poor people can determine how, after five years of siege, the administration regarded continuing racial unrest and civil rights protests.

The Johnson years were a watershed in the struggle for racial equality in the United States. More than any president before him, Lyndon Johnson helped blacks discard the legal barriers blocking the attainment of first-class citizenship. Most of the uncompleted civil rights items on the legislative agenda he had inherited upon taking office in 1963 were enacted by the time he retired to his Texas ranch in 1969. The kind of president capable of ordering the public execution of Jim Crow, Johnson was not Eric Goldman's "wrong man from the wrong place at the wrong time under the wrong circumstances."[80] Combining moral fervor and a finely honed sense of political timing, Johnson translated the ideals of civil rights protesters into practical statutory language.

However, as the goals of the racial struggle leaped beyond integration and strict equality under law, the President displayed the limitations of modern liberal reformers. By philosophy and style, he was suited for achieving legislative breakthroughs within the traditional boundaries of the constitutional system. But, when administration achievements boosted black expectations of immediate economic and political power, the conventional remedies of color-blind treatment decreed by law were inadequate. The Civil Rights Act of 1964 opened up public accommodations to black patrons, but it did not enable them to acquire the funds to afford admission. The 1965 Voting Rights Act removed discriminatory suffrage requirements in the South, but it stopped short of eliminating methods of diluting the franchise, and it did not supply the resources for mobilizing the potency of black ballots. The Civil Rights Act of 1968 outlawed racial bias in the sale of houses and the rental of apartments, but it did not address the problem of furnishing adequate incomes so that blacks could escape the slums. In this second Reconstruction as in the first, the unconquered frontier bordering full emancipation was economic.

The Johnson administration's approach to solving racial problems by a redistribution of economic and political power should be examined. In his Howard University address, the President passionately asserted the need to transcend ordinary solutions. He pointed the way toward affirmative action to compensate for past abuses, and investigators should search for documentary clues to measure how much success his regime had in reversing the effects of previous discrimination in education, politics, and employment. How did the chief executive view busing? What did he do to foster realignment of the Democratic party in fulfillment of its 1964 convention pledge to encourage increased representation by minorities?[81] How did the administration view quotas for hiring? These questions and others must be asked to determine how far Johnson was willing to move in challenging the vestiges of racial inequality.

By liberal standards, Lyndon Johnson was the foremost practitioner of civil rights ever to occupy the White House. His greatest successes, T. Harry Williams notes, emerged from "measured manipulated change within the system and a consensus built on compromise."[82] However, in staking out a middle ground of reform between white conservatives and black militants, he had trouble holding the center together. The challenge for future historians of the Johnson administration is to improve upon these extemporaneous comments of Harry McPherson:

Johnson and I and Bill Moyers and many of us around the White House were Southern liberals. We believe in integration, we believe in reason, we believe that things are going to be fine if men of good will get together and if we put down the racists. We thought that if we could be a sort of super YMCA saying "You can go to school with us, we'll educate you, train you, will get better housing" and all that sort of stuff. But we haven't really fixed it at the base which is money, security, families holding together, some power that is given to them by money.[83]

In utilizing the archives of the Johnson Library to reach an assessment of civil rights during the Johnson years, researchers should heed several warnings. Researching a history of the Johnson administration uncovers the thinking of the White House staff and agency officials more than it does the President's. The files contain volumes of evidence testifying to the opinions of presidential advisers who counseled their boss or wrote letters for his signature, but they usually lack statements penned in the chief executive's hand. The Johnson system of answering staff memoranda by checking off "yes," "no," or some other possible listing at the bottom of the page precluded an extensive written dialogue. Although one might safely assume that a presidentially scrawled check mark constituted Johnson's point of view on a particular issue, historians must allow the chief executive's actions to speak louder than his written words.

Aggravating the problem of deciphering Johnson's personal beliefs is the President's predilection for conducting important business over the telephone. Fortunately, Johnson's assistants maintained a detailed log of incoming and outgoing calls, including those at the Texas White House, and these records are deposited at the Johnson Library. In most instances, however, the subject of the conversation is not listed, though sometimes an aide jotted down on a sheet a brief description of the discussion. This practice occurred more frequently with respect to personal meetings involving the President. Notations outlining these sessions come closest to documenting the President's private thoughts. Although most conversations were unrecorded, the Diary Backup Files nevertheless help identify the individuals who advised the chief executive on routine matters and in times of racial crisis.[84]

Oral histories may also fill in some of the gaps in the written materials. More than forty transcribed interviews in the Johnson Library touch upon the subject of civil rights. The respondents include government officials and private citizens, and supporters and opponents of civil rights measures. However, these interviews suffer from some shortcomings. They vary in quality depending on the pertinence of the questions raised and on the candor and memory of the interviewees. Furthermore, the library needs to supplement its collection by arranging to add oral memoirs of a number of individuals presently absent from the project.[85]

Presidential libraries have inherent drawbacks. Like its counterparts, the Johnson Library presents a view of the past from the top, obviously reflecting in its records the presidential vantage point of social change. This tendency stems from the organization of manuscript collections around specific administrations, an arrangement that may misdirect the civil rights researcher by suggesting presidential omnipotence in shaping race relations. In choosing to focus on the Johnson administration, one orients a study toward Washington and away from the grass roots level from which the civil rights struggle derived most of its creative energies. In countering the presidential bias, investigators must carefully examine the interplay of forces, governmental and private, national and local.

To date, the initial judgment that Lyndon Johnson played a striking role in promoting racial equality remains intact. The 1972 symposium that unveiled the civil rights papers brought to the speaker's rostrum Julian Bond, a former SNCC member, a caustic critic of Johnson's Vietnam policy, and one of the first blacks elected to the Georgia legislature after the Voting Rights Act of 1965. Addressing an audience gathered at the Johnson Library, the young lawmaker remarked about the library's namesake that "when the forces demanded and the mood permitted, for once an activist, human-hearted man had his hands on the levers of power and a vision beyond the next election. He was there when we and the Nation needed him, and, oh my God, do I wish he was there now."[86] After inspecting the library's holdings it may be asked, are these words any less timely three presidential regimes later?

Notes

1. Bayard Rustin Oral History Interview, Lyndon B. Johnson Library, Austin, Texas.

2. Doris Kearns, *Lyndon Johnson and the American Dream* (New York: Harper and Row, 1976), p. 391.

3. George F. Will, "Fashions in Heroes," *Newsweek* 94 (August 6, 1979): 84.

4. Bruce Miroff, "Presidential Management of Black Politics: The Johnson White House," p. 17 (ms. in the author's possession).

5. Ronald Radosh, "From Protest to Black Power: The Failure of Coalition Politics," in *The Great Society Reader: The Failure of American Liberalism*, ed. Marvin Gettleman and David Mermelstein (New York: Random House, 1967), pp. 282, 292.

6. James C. Harvey, *Black Civil Rights during the Johnson Administration* (Jackson: University of Mississippi Press, 1973), p. 225. For similar criticisms, see Pat Watters and Reese Cleghorn, *Climbing Jacob's Ladder* (New York: Harcourt, Brace, and World, 1967).

7. John Herbers, *The Lost Priority: Whatever Happened to the Civil Rights Movement in America?* (New York: Funk and Wagnall, 1970), p. 176.

8. Clarence Mitchell Oral History Interview, Johnson Library.

9. See Anthony Lewis, "The Professionals Win Out over Civil Rights," *Reporter* 22 (May 26, 1960): 26–30.

10. Monroe Billington, "Lyndon B. Johnson and Blacks: The Early Years," *Journal of Negro History* 62 (January 1977): 42.

11. Steven F. Lawson and Mark I. Gelfand, "Consensus and Civil Rights: Lyndon B. Johnson and the Black Franchise," *Prologue* 8 (Summer 1976): 66–68.

12. Joe B. Frantz, "Opening a Curtain: the Metamorphosis of Lyndon B. Johnson," *Journal of Southern History* 45 (February 1979): 25.

13. T. Harry Williams, "Huey, Lyndon, and Southern Radicalism," *Journal of American History* 60 (September 1973): 284.

14. Leonard Baker, *The Johnson Eclipse: A President's Vice Presidency* (New York: Macmillan, 1966), ch. 4; Carl Brauer, *John F. Kennedy and the Second Reconstruction* (New York: Columbia University Press, 1977), pp. 245–46.

15. Telephone conversation of Johnson with Theodore Sorenson, June 3, 1963, transcript, pp. 12, 14, Johnson Library.

16. Ibid., pp. 4–5.

17. Additional papers of Hobart Taylor can be found at the University of Michigan. Liberals faulted Vice-President Johnson, who as president of the Senate refused to give a parliamentary ruling that would have aided cloture reform. Was he acting under Kennedy's orders?

18. "Notes on Senator Johnson's remarks to Clarence Mitchell and other delegates to January 13–14, 1960, Legislative Conference on Civil Rights," box 13, Johnson Senatorial Papers, Johnson Library.

19. Tom Wicker, *JFK and LBJ: The Influence of Personality upon Politics* (Baltimore: Penguin Books, 1969), p. 176.

20. Williams, "Huey, Lyndon, and Southern Radicalism," p. 287.

21. Kearns, *Lyndon Johnson*, p. 191.

22. Daniel Berman, *A Bill Becomes a Law* (London: Macmillan, 1966). Clifford M. Lytle, "The History of the Civil Rights Bill of 1964," *Journal of Negro History* 51 (October 1966): 275–296, is a superficial account by a for-

mer official of the Community Relations Service, an agency created by the act. Perhaps the best analysis of the passage of the measure appears in James Sundquist, *Politics and Policy: The Eisenhower, Kennedy, and Johnson Years* (Washington, D.C.: Brookings Institution, 1968).

23. Brauer, *John F. Kennedy*, p. 310. This view has been endorsed in Arthur M. Schlesinger, Jr., *Robert F. Kennedy and His Times* (Boston: Houghton Mifflin, 1978), pp. 644–45. In contrast, Rowland Evans and Robert Novak believe that Johnson guaranteed a stronger bill than one his predecessor might have produced. "Now fully emancipated from his Southern base, there was no need to trim his civil rights position to please Dixie. On this issue, Johnson's political imperatives as a *Southern* President foreclosed compromise, whereas Kennedy's would not have," the reporters assert in *Lyndon B. Johnson: The Exercise of Power* (New York: New American Library, 1966), p. 379.

24. Lyndon B. Johnson, *The Vantage Point* (New York: Holt, Rinehart, and Winston, 1971), pp. 58–59.

25. Eric Goldman, *The Tragedy of Lyndon Johnson* (New York: Dell, 1969), pp. 80–84. On Senator Dirksen, see Neil MacNeil, *Dirksen: Portrait of a Public Man* (New York: World Publishing, 1970). Dirksen's papers are deposited in the senator's library and congressional center in Pekin, Illinois.

26. Department of Justice, *Administrative History*, 7:53, Johnson Library.

27. Lee White to the President, April 15, 1964, Hu 2, box 2, Executive File, White House Central Files, Johnson Library. See also Stewart Udall to the President, May 7, 1964, Hu 2, box 65, Ibid., and Mike Manatos to Lawrence O'Brien, May 11, 1964, Hu 2, box 2, Ibid.

28. Hubert Humphrey Oral History Interview, Johnson Library.

29. Lee White memorandum to the files, July 6, 1964, Le Hu 2, box 2, Executive File, White House Central Files, Johnson Library.

30. On the deteriorating relations between Johnson and the black radicals after the 1964 freedom summer, see James Forman, *The Making of Black Revolutionaries* (New York: Macmillan, 1972); Hanes Walton, *Black Political Parties* (New York: Free Press, 1972); Waters and Cleghorn, *Climbing Jacob's Ladder*; and Anne Cooke Romaine, "The Mississippi Freedom Democratic Party through August 1964" (master's thesis, University of Virginia, 1969).

31. David J. Garrow, *Protest at Selma: Martin Luther King, Jr., and the Voting Rights Act of 1965* (New Haven: Yale University Press, 1978), p. 134; Steven F. Lawson, *Black Ballots: Voting Rights in the South, 1944–1969* (New York: Columbia University Press, 1976), ch. 10. For the role of the Community Relations Service in mediating the Selma dispute, see Thomas R. Wagy, "Governor LeRoy Collins of Florida and the Selma Crisis of 1965," *Florida Historical Quarterly* 57 (April 1979): 403–420. The day-to-day events in the Alabama battleground are best described in Charles E. Fager, *Selma, 1965* (New York: Charles Scribner's Sons, 1974).

32. Joseph Califano to the President, October 25, 1965, Hu 2, Confidential File, White House Central Files, Johnson Library.
33. Nicholas Katzenbach to Joseph Califano, December 12, 1965, Le Hu 2, box 65, Johnson Library.
34. For a detailed examination of one section of the proposed bill, see Thomas J. Seess, "Federal Power to Combat Private Racial Violence in the Aftermath of *Price, Guest*, and the Civil Rights Act of 1968," (Ph.D. diss., Georgetown University, 1972). The Johnson Library has conveniently placed on its shelves a large number of theses covering the Johnson era.
35. James C. Harvey, *Black Civil Rights*, p. 224.
36. U.S., Department of Justice, *Administrative History*, Reports on Legislation, September 2, 1966, box 26, Johnson Library.
37. Ramsey Clark, "Report of the Civil Rights Task Force," Joseph Califano Files, Johnson Library. See also the 1966 Civil Rights Task Force, "Summary Notebook," box 12, Task Force Files, Johnson Library.
38. See the records of the White House Conference on Civil Rights and Hu 2/Mc, White House Central Files, Johnson Library for pertinent material.
39. Henry Wilson to the President, March 11, 1966, box 11, Henry Wilson Files, Johnson Library; April 28, 1966, Le Hu 2, box 65, Appointment File, Diary Backup, Johnson Library.
40. Barefoot Sanders Oral History Interview, Johnson Library.
41. Harvey, *Black Civil Rights*, p. 40. Nicholas Katzenbach disagrees with this view. He remembers "that open housing was not an important issue in the 1966 election, although everybody predicted it would be. So I think the fact that we pushed it in 1966 helped, because [members of Congress] tested it out with the public and it was really surprising." Katzenbach Oral History Interview, Johnson Library.
42. Eric Goldman to the President, May 4, 1964, Le Hu 2, box 65, Executive File, White House Central Files, Johnson Library.
43. Harry McPherson Oral History Interview, tape 7, Johnson Library.
44. Harry McPherson to the President, September 12, 1966, box 21 (2), Harry McPherson Files, Johnson Library; Nicholas Katzenbach to McPherson, September 17, 1966, Ibid.; McPherson to Katzenbach, September 20, 1966, Ibid. See also Harry McPherson to George Christian, August 1, 1967, Hu 2, box 6, Executive File, White House Central Files, Johnson Library.
45. Jack Valenti (?) to the President, July 27, 1964, Hu 2, box 3, Ibid.
46. Harry McPherson, Oral History Interview, tape 6, Johnson Library.
47. Harry McPherson to George Christian, August 1, 1967, Hu 2, box 6, Executive File, White House Central Files, Johnson Library. With respect to traditional racial objectives, the administration pushed the omnibus civil rights measure, accepting with it an antiriot rider. Nevertheless, the White House was not enthusiastic about the provision. Joseph Califano reported that Deputy Attorney General Warren Christopher declared, "Enactment of a Federal Act runs the risk of appearing to do more than we can really ac-

complish—it won't prevent riots and will lead to pressures upon the Justice Department to prosecute in dubious situations, but it could be used as leverage to enact other points of your program which may be in trouble." Joseph Califano to the President, January 29, 1968, Le/J1, box 79, Executive File, White House Central Files, Johnson Library.

48. For discussions of the Kennedy and Johnson administrations' view of the federal system and civil rights, see Burke Marshall, *Federalism and Civil Rights* (New York: Columbia University Press, 1964); Brauer, *John F. Kennedy*, ch. 4; Howard Zinn, *SNCC* (Boston: Beacon Press, 1964); Victor Navasky, *Kennedy Justice* (New York: Atheneum, 1971); and Lawson, *Black Ballots*. Students of the riots will find in the Johnson Library the records of the National Commission on Civil Disorders and the oral histories of Ramsey Clark, John McCone, Edmund Brown, and Richard Hughes. There is no oral history with George Romney, the governor of Michigan, but his papers are at the University of Michigan. Ramsey Clark recalls in his oral history that the Justice Department emphasized that in dealing with riots "local authority must act first or we're going to have garrison cities and federal police."

49. Harry McPherson to the President, March 18, 1968, box 53, Harry McPherson Files, Johnson Library.

50. Young's statement appears in his newspaper column, May 10, 1966, Hu 2, box 4, Executive File, White House Central Files, Johnson Library; Wilkins's activities are noted in Bill Moyers to the President, August 30, 1965, Hu 2, box 3, Ibid. See also Roy Wilkins's column, January 15–16, 1966, attached to a memorandum from Jack Valenti to Frank A. Clark, January 21, 1966, Hu 2, box 4, Ibid.; and David Halberstam, "The Second Coming of Martin Luther King," *Harper's* 235 (August 1967): 40.

51. Louis Martin to Marvin Watson, August 16, 1965, NC 19/CO 312, Johnson Library. Charles Evers and Aaron Henry telegraphed the President from Mississippi: "Inasmuch as you have seen fit to send observers to Vietnam to see that 'free and democratic' elections are held, . . . it would mean much more to America and particularly 22 million Negroes if you would use your influence and call for new elections in many sections of Mississippi and send representatives to make certain Negroes and Negro candidates are assured justice and fair play in all elections" (August 30, 1967, Pl/St 24, box 53, General File, White House Central Files, Johnson Library). Harry McPherson remarked on the connection between Vietnam and the domestic war against racism: "The war in Vietnam threatened to estrange the Democratic party from the President. If he was to retain the support of the national Democrats, . . . he would have to remain liberal at home, talking less of stopping crime than of its causes" (*A Political Education* [Boston: Little, Brown, and Co., 1972], pp. 382–83).

52. Ramsey Clark Oral History Interview, Johnson Library.

53. The administration's dealings with King from Selma to Memphis are noted in the neatly indexed White House Daily Diary and Backup Files,

Johnson Library. On King's role in the civil rights movement, see David Lewis, *King*, 2nd ed. (Urbana: University of Illinois Press, 1978); August Meier, "On the Role of Martin Luther King," *New Politics* 4 (Winter 1965): 52–59; Garrow, *Protest at Selma*.

54. Louis Martin to Marvin Watson, August 16, 1965, ND 19/CO 312, Johnson Library; Clifford Alexander to the President, January 7, 1966, Hu 2, box 3, Executive File, White House Central Files, Johnson Library.

55. Harry McPherson to the President, April 4, 1967, box 14, Harry McPherson Files, Johnson Library; George Christian to the President, April 8, 1967, Hu 2, box 4, Executive File, White House Central Files, Johnson Library.

56. Harry McPherson Oral History Interview, tape 7, Johnson Library.

57. Larry Temple to the President, February 14, 1968, Hu 2, box 7, Executive File, White House Central Files, Johnson Library; Ben Wattenberg to the President, February 29, 1968, filed Douglass Cater, FG 11-8-1, Confidential File, White House Central Files, Johnson Library.

58. *Public Papers of the Presidents, Lyndon B. Johnson* (Washington, D.C.: Government Printing Office, 1965), 2: 636.

59. Harry McPherson Oral History Interview, Johnson Library. Richard Goodwin drafted the speech, and his files are in the library.

60. *Public Papers*, p. 636. Daniel Patrick Moynihan was assistant secretary of labor when he wrote the report. The document was originally intended for internal use. See John W. Leslie to Frank Erwin, July 30, 1965, Hu 2, box 3, Executive File, White House Central Files, Johnson Library; Lee White to the President, August 10, 1965, Hu 2, box 3, Ibid.; Lee White to Bill Moyers, August 12, 1965, box 6, Lee White Files, Johnson Library.

61. Lee Rainwater and William L. Yancey, *The Moynihan Report and the Politics of Controversy* (Cambridge, Massachusetts: M.I.T. Press, 1967), p. 16.

62. Harry McPherson Oral History Interview, tape 6, Johnson Library. See also McPherson, *A Political Education*, ch. 10. On this issue the Johnson Library contains the voluminous files of the White House Conference on Civil Rights, which can be supplemented with material from the White House Central Files and the presidential aide files of Harry McPherson and Lee White. Also available are the oral histories of several conference planners and participants. In particular see the memoir of Ben Heineman, the chairman of the conference.

63. For McPherson's depiction of subsequent events, see *A Political Education*, pp. 350–52.

64. Bruce Miroff, "Presidential Management of Black Politics," p. 1.

65. Ibid., p. 17; Francis Fox Piven and Richard A. Cloward, *Poor People's Movements: Why They Succeed, How They Fail* (New York: Pantheon Books, 1977).

66. Nicholas Katzenbach to Harry McPherson, September 17, 1966, box 21, Harry McPherson Files, Johnson Library.

67. Lee White to the President, March 11, 1964, Hu 2, box 2, Executive File, White House Central Files, Johnson Library. See also Richard Goodwin to the President, May 4, 1964, Hu 2, box 2, Ibid. Goodwin explained: "A lot of this is essentially uncontrollable. It will happen no matter what the federal government does. A wave of violence, federal intervention etc. might have serious political repercussions, North and South. But we should plan for the worst, hope for the best."

68. Gary Orfield, *The Reconstruction of Southern Education: The Schools and the 1964 Civil Rights Act* (New York: John Wiley and Sons, 1969), p. 307.

69. Federal agencies processing civil rights complaints, particularly the Departments of Justice and Health, Education and Welfare, have some material in the White House Central Files, federal government (FG) groupings. Other pertinent records can be found in the human rights (Hu) category divided into specific subjects, e.g., employment (Hu 2-1), education (Hu 2-5).

70. Allan Wolk, *The Presidency and Black Civil Rights: Eisenhower to Nixon* (Rutherford, New Jersey: Fairleigh Dickenson University Press, 1971), p. 247.

71. Harvey, *Black Civil Rights*, p. 224. See also Herbers, *Lost Priority*, p. 176; Harrell R. Rodgers, Jr. and Charles S. Bullock, III, *Law and Social Change: Civil Rights Laws and Their Consequences* (New York: McGraw-Hill, 1972).

72. Orfield, *Reconstruction of Southern Education*, p. viii.

73. Wolk, in *The Presidency and Black Civil Rights*, charged that the "Justice Department was a useful front, perhaps appearing to liberals as an affirmative control unit of coordination. But more often than not it assumed a restraining role in its interdepartmental relations" (p. 189). This view was shared by Samuel F. Yette, a former special assistant on civil rights in the Office of Economic Opportunity. See *The Choice: the Issue of Black Extermination in America* (New York: Berkley Medallion Books, 1975), pp. 61ff. For appraisals of the Justice Department's enforcement of the Voting Rights Act, see Lawson, *Black Ballots*, pp. 329–39; Garrow, *Protest at Selma*, pp. 179–93; U.S. Commission on Civil Rights, *Political Participation* (Washington, D.C.: Government Printing Office, 1968); and L. Thorne McCarty and Russell B. Stevenson, "The Voting Rights Act of 1965: An Evaluation," *Harvard Civil Rights-Civil Liberties Review* 3 (Spring 1968): 357–411.

74. Orfield, *Reconstruction of Southern Education*, p. 307. The author also covered the politics of northern-style de facto school desegregation, concentrating on Chicago. The task of comparing enforcement of racial policies in the North and South should be undertaken. On the subject of educational desegregation, two oral histories in the Johnson Library are particularly useful: those of former Commissioners of Education Francis Keppel and Harold Howe, II.

75. James Button, *Black Violence* (Princeton: Princeton University Press, 1978), pp. 174–76. On the implications of the Button and Garrow

studies, see August Meier's and Elliot Rudwick's review in the *Journal of American History* 66 (September 1979): 466.

76. This statement by Walter Tobriner was quoted in a WTOP (Washington, D.C.) radio editorial, March 10 and 11, 1965, 1117, Charles Horsky Files, Johnson Library. For a concise background of the issue see Martin F. Nolan, "The Negro Stake in Washington House Rule," *The Reporter* 35 (August 11, 1966): 18–21.

77. Charles Horsky to Larry O'Brien, October 25, 1963, 1125, Charles Horsky Files, Johnson Library. For background on this issue, see Constance McLaughlin Green, *The Secret City: A History of Race Relations in the Nation's Capitol* (Princeton: Princeton University Press, 1967).

78. Lyndon Johnson to David Carliner, November 15, 1967, FG 216, box 267, Executive File, White House Central Files, Johnson Library.

79. Robert Sherrill, *The Accidental President* (New York: Grossman Publishers, 1967), p. 196.

80. Eric Goldman, *The Tragedy of Lyndon Johnson*, p. 628.

81. The records of the Democratic National Committee during the Johnson years chart the changing fortunes of Afro-Americans and the party of the President. Comprised mainly of newspaper clippings and pamphlets, these files in the Johnson Library contain important material documenting the work of the Special Equal Rights Committee, which sought to expand black participation in Democratic affairs.

82. Williams, "Huey, Lyndon, and Southern Radicalism," p. 292.

83. Harry McPherson Oral History Interview, tape 6, Johnson Library.

84. The Appointment File, Diary Backup contains briefing papers preparing the president for scheduled meetings.

85. Some possibilities are Justice Department lawyers John Doar and Stephen Pollak; White House counselor Clifford Alexander; Deputy Chairman of the Democratic National Committee Louis Martin; Berl Bernhard, a staff director of the U.S. Civil Rights Commission and planner of the White House Conference on Civil Rights; Roger Wilkins, director of the Community Relations Service; Carl Rowan, a journalist and chief of the United States Information Agency; Dorothy Height, head of the National Council of Negro Women; and Charles Horsky, the District of Columbia specialist.

86. Robert C. Rooney, ed., *Equal Opportunity in the United States: A Symposium on Civil Rights* (Austin: University of Texas, 1973), p. 128.

4 | The War on Poverty
by Mark I. Gelfand

"A DECENT PROVISION FOR THE POOR," declared the English man of letters Samuel Johnson, "is the true test of civilization." For Lyndon Johnson, an American politician extraordinaire, the War on Poverty represented his first initiative as President and the supreme test of his struggle to create a Great Society. Just as the Vietnam War dominated Johnson's foreign policy, the War on Poverty overshadowed his other domestic programs. To study the War on Poverty is also to explore the climax of more than a half century of liberal reform.

The story of the War on Poverty is marked by superlatives. "Nothing about the War on Poverty is commonplace," wrote a former government official turned analyst in 1969. "In the zeal of its administration, in the freshness of their ideas, in the innovations of organization and policy approach, it stands alone." But most remarkable of all was the war's objective: "to do what no people had ever done—to eliminate poverty from the land."[1] In 1928, presidential nominee Herbert Hoover promised the Republican party that "we shall soon, with the help of God, be in sight of the day when poverty will be banished in the nation." After a decade of depression and nearly two decades of unparalleled prosperity, Lyndon Johnson had no intention of waiting on the good works of the Almighty. "Having the power," he exhorted the nation, "we have the duty."

Although the 1960s and 1970s witnessed sharp debates about the definition and extent of poverty, there has surely been no poverty of literature about the war against want.[2] Because of the uniqueness of the venture and the character of the people who directed the fighting, the Great Society's "unconditional war on poverty" has spawned an abundance of critiques and reminiscences. Sociologists and economists, along with a sprinkling of political scientists, have been prolific and swift in publishing. But historians, who, unlike their social science colleagues, were not participant-observers, must rely upon the documentary record, and thus have scarcely entered the field.[3]

As they do begin to investigate, historians will find the resources of the Lyndon B. Johnson Library of limited assistance. Despite the President's close association with the War on Poverty in the public mind, researchers will uncover surprisingly little material linking the chief executive or even the White House staff to the major engagements of the conflict. Aside from a few key legislative and political battles, the War on Poverty was fought in the bureaucratic trenches and in hundreds of communities across the nation. Unlike the civil rights struggle, which presented the President with basic moral and political choices he could not and would not ignore, the War on Poverty quickly fell into the hands of his generals and their field commanders. And unlike the war in Southeast Asia, which required almost daily decisions at the very top of government, the War on Poverty was essentially an administrative operation needing and receiving scant consideration in the Oval Office. Indeed, as the racial issue became complicated by ghetto rioting and the Vietnam policy of escalation met rising protests at home from liberals, the poverty program lost its once-favored status at the White House.[4]

Origins

Although opinions differ about the underlying motivation for the declaration of war on poverty, it is widely accepted that President Johnson seized the issue as a means to put his personal stamp on the office he had inherited so suddenly and tragically. For although John Kennedy had left his successor a long list of stalled legislative proposals, including federal aid to education, Medicare, tax cuts, and an omnibus civil rights bill, poverty had not been a focal point of liberal interest and had not yet entered the public consciousness. The irony is that while Johnson may have been the first political leader to make poverty a national concern, Kennedy had bequeathed that subject to him too.

Records in the Johnson Library leave no doubt about this Kennedy legacy. Administrative histories prepared by the Council of Economic Advisers (CEA) and the Office of Economic Opportunity and documents collected in the file, "Legislative Background of the Economic Opportunity Act of 1964," reveal how a "Kennedy offensive against poverty" was taking shape during the summer and fall of 1963. In charge of this effort was the chairman of the CEA, Walter W. Heller. "We did not formulate a program until after the assassination," Heller reminded Johnson in the fall of 1964. "It was in process at that time, and I discussed it with President Kennedy on November 19, 1963. As I had told you on November 23, Kennedy had said to go ahead with our work on a program, but gave us no guidance as to the specific contents. That was to come later."[5] On November 23, at the end of Johnson's first full day as President, the chief executive gave Heller his enthusiastic authorization to "move full-speed ahead" with the "attack on Poverty. . . . That's my kind of program. It will help people."[6]

What prompted Kennedy to scout and Johnson to implement an antipoverty program has puzzled observers. Since at least the New Deal, strong pressure groups had set the country's political agenda; the federal government had been a reactive agent rather than an independent force. As there was no organized movement of poor people in 1963–1964, why did the two Presidents prove so adventurous? Intimates and outsiders have typically explained Kennedy's behavior as the product of his intellect, great capacity for growth, and political instincts. His reading of John Kenneth Galbraith, Michael Harrington, and Leon Keyserling, which alerted him to the problems of "the other America"; his campaigning in West Virginia, which exposed him to a world very different from the sheltered one he had grown up in; and his need to make the New Frontier appear truly innovative lay behind his instructions to Heller to look into the matter.[7] In Johnson's case, political advantage is commonly offered as both necessary and sufficient cause for his support. Even those who are willing to admit that Johnson's own less-than-privileged youth might have inspired his reflexive response to Heller's description of the CEA's activities think it more likely that he acted from a need to establish his own leadership and liberal credentials before the presidential contest in 1964.[8]

A few commentators have attempted to place the War on Poverty in a wider context. Economist Lester C. Thurow, who served as a CEA consultant during the 1960s, suggests that the antipoverty program be viewed as part of the Cold War. In order to prevent the Soviet Union from overtaking the United States economically, the nation's productivity rate had to be raised. This goal required that the poor as well as the rich and middle class be put to work. According to Thurow, the obsession with increasing productivity explains not only the source of the antipoverty program but also that program's stress on manpower-training endeavors to the exclusion of income-maintenance strategies.[9] The elimination of poverty would occur merely as the byproduct of a much more pressing national concern: keeping the United States first among the world's economic systems.[10]

Political scientist Frances Fox Piven and sociologist Richard A.

Cloward, whose earlier writings contributed to the development of the poverty program and the response to it, take a different view.[11] From Piven and Cloward's perspective, the antipoverty campaign arose out of the recognition of national Democratic politicians that local Democratic leaders were alienating urban blacks by denying them patronage and adequate municipal services, thus seriously threatening Democratic control of the White House. If the critical black vote was to be kept loyal, national assistance would have to be sent directly to the ghetto. "The managerial powers of the presidency," Piven and Cloward contend, "were used to forge programs to deal with the political problems of the presidency, and the publicity-making powers of the presidency were used to stir up the issues to justify the programs." Impressed by "the scale of federal action and its distinctive administrative features," Piven and Cloward conclude that the Great Society "could best be understood as a [coherent political] response to a major political disturbance in the United States."[12]

If Piven and Cloward are correct, then Johnson succeeded only to fail. His antipoverty program kept the blacks in the Democratic fold but drove millions of middle class whites into the GOP.[13] It was a risk the President was aware of, but whether he saw his options in precisely the terms Piven and Cloward describe remains unclear.[14] For, as British journalist Godfrey Hodgson has noted, the War on Poverty was "the archetypal liberal program . . . inspired by a characteristic blend of benevolence, optimism, innocence and chauvinism."[15] In the intoxicating days of 1963–1964, Johnson could believe that he might have it all ways: the country would meet its commitment to the less fortunate; the affluent would feel uplifted by their good deeds; there would be a full-employment economy of abundance; and the Democrats would build a broad national consensus. Why it did not work out that way is the question underlying the discussion that follows.

Strategy I

(*The events described in this section have been related in several published accounts with slightly different information in each version, some based on first-hand recollections, others on interviews and partial access to documents. None of the accounts adequately identifies its sources.*)[16]

In the two months following Johnson's go-ahead signal to Heller, the administration struggled to reach its own consensus on what

form the War on Poverty should take. The President made two critical decisions as discussions began: the antipoverty program would
receive special attention in the state-of-the-union message, and it
would be allotted $500 million in the new budget. Johnson's critics
have repeatedly bemoaned the disparity between the huge publicity
lavished on the antipoverty war and the small sums appropriated for
it, but in December 1963 and January 1964 the White House was not
only seeking consciously to dramatize the program's originality but
also searching desperately for ways to spend the money. During this
period the various possible components of the antipoverty effort
emerged. Because of the failure to resolve the many ambiguities that
swirled around these approaches and around the very nature of the
poverty problem itself, the program got off to a shaky start from
which it never truly recovered.

As the War on Poverty moved from a gleam in Kennedy's eye to
the focus of Johnson's domestic policy, responsibility for its design
shifted from the Council of Economic Advisers to the Bureau of the
Budget (BOB). Significantly, while the bureau's critical role can be
traced in documents of the Johnson Library file, "Legislative Background to the Economic Opportunity Act of 1964," the Budget Bureau's internally prepared *Administrative History* makes no reference to these events. This omission undoubtedly reflects the
bureau's sense of defeat and embarrassment. Besides losing its position of leadership, the bureau also saw the administrative device it
had championed distorted beyond recognition.[17]

For anyone familiar with only the subsequent history of the
community action program, the bureau's advocacy of community
action agencies as the centerpiece of the War on Poverty must surely
come as a surprise. How could this bastion of sound management
techniques have supported a mechanism that would so disturb the
peace? How could this apostle of frugality have given such aid and
comfort to profligate spenders? The answer is obvious—the bureau
meant to do nothing of the kind. It envisioned the community
action agency as a coordinating body for an economical yet comprehensive attack on poverty. Careful planning and evaluation in
a few localities would precede any additional federal commitment
of funds. The whole objective was to prevent haste, waste, and
disruption.[18]

The Budget Bureau's prescription for a well-ordered, measured
War on Poverty appeared headed for ready acceptance when it ran
into two roadblocks, the Labor Department and the President.
Whereas the other old-line departments and agencies were content

to leave design of the antipoverty drive to the White House, the leaders at the Labor Department were not. They had their own idea about how to help the poor: a large-scale employment program encompassing both job training and job creation. That this approach was expensive and controversial meant less to the Labor Department than that it would add directly to the income of the poor people. Not only would the BOB plan fail to accomplish this objective, but it would also take so long for the community action program to have substantive impact that Congress and the nation would quickly lose interest in the project.[19]

The latter part of the Labor Department's demurrer was not lost on the President. Though Johnson could dismiss the department's jobs proposal as simply an effort to expand its own programs, he could not ignore the fickle nature of public opinion. The people and their elected representatives would want concrete results right away; by the Budget Bureau's own admission, its organizational emphasis would be heavy on experimenting with means and light on delivering ends. Not happy with this arrangement, Johnson decided to call in someone fresh to whip his pet program into shape. On February 1, 1964, he announced the appointment of R. Sargent Shriver as director of the Office of Economic Opportunity.

Momentous consequences would flow from Shriver's selection. Although the ideas for the various facets of the War on Poverty came from others, it was Shriver who developed the strategy of drafting the legislation presented to Congress in mid-March as an omnibus package. Inclusion, not exclusion, became the hallmark of Shriver's tenure as "poverty czar." Job training, work relief, remedial and adult education, rural assistance, small loans, and a domestic Peace Corps joined the community action concept in the administration's bill. The measure now carried a price tag of $962.5 million, but only $500 million of this was new money; the remainder came from agency requests already in the budget. Finding in Shriver the same passion for getting things done that consumed him, Johnson gave his whole-hearted blessing to what Shriver had wrought. Together they offered promises that would haunt liberals for years to come.

Unfortunately, the records at the Johnson Library do not convey a good picture of this decision-making process. The depth of the President's involvement is unclear. Journalists Rowland Evans and Robert Novak have suggested that Johnson was not deeply interested in the bureaucratic wrangling that accompanied the birth of the War on Poverty; he saw his function as primarily evangelical, converting the public to his mission of eradicating poverty.[20] But even if he did not concern himself with the fine details, certain key decisions could only be made by the President, and these are not documented at the library. Historians will want to examine the Budget Bureau's loss of favor and Johnson's response to the Labor Department's persistent efforts to shape the antipoverty war to its own blueprints. A large gap in primary sources exists in relation to Shriver's role. Beyond the obvious question of how and why Johnson chose the Peace Corps director to head his White House Task Force on the War on Poverty, there is also the issue of how this group functioned. Several participants have provided accounts which give a glimpse of what went on, but these only heighten the confusion about what the task force intended.[21] The only task force document presently available is the bill sent to Capitol Hill, a measure notable for its broad sense of purpose, broad grants of authority, and ambiguous language.

On the Hill

A little more than five months elapsed between transmittal of the President's proposed Economic Opportunity Act to Congress and the elaborate bill-signing ceremony opening the War on Poverty. From March until August 1964, the Congress worked at breakneck speed to give Johnson this innovative plank in his election-year platform. The contrast with the long-delayed Medicare and federal-aid-to-education bills could not have been starker; their time would come, but not until another Congress had been seated. Instead of encountering an obstacle course on Capitol Hill, the antipoverty program found a smooth and quick route through the legislative morass, something no domestic reform proposal had seen since the glory days of the New Deal.

By all accounts Lyndon Johnson is credited with this success.[22] Having served his political apprenticeship under Franklin Roosevelt and having built up an inventory of information and contacts during his more than twenty years in Congress, Johnson pulled out all the stops for his antipoverty bill. It was a textbook example of the President as chief legislator. The tactic, for example, of persuading Representative Phil Landrum (D-Ga) to serve as the measure's floor manager in the House was a stroke of political genius. By going with the Georgian instead of Adam Clayton Powell (D-NY), who as chairman of the Education and Labor Committee would normally have been asked to act as the bill's sponsor, the administration not only sidetracked some potentially nasty racial issues but also gained a superb parliamentarian with solid ties to conservative southern Democrats whose votes were indispensable for the bill's passage. The White House combined intensive lobbying with a willingness to accept amendments that attracted doubtful supporters but did not alter the basic structure of the program.

One aspect of the "Johnson treatment" remains controversial—the Adam Yarmolinsky Affair. Yarmolinsky, on leave from the Defense Department, was Shriver's number two man on the White House task force, and it was widely assumed that a top-level job awaited him once the War on Poverty got underway. But many southerners associated Yarmolinsky with the Defense Department's hardening line on integration, and a group of congressional members warned the White House that unless Yarmolinsky was blackballed from the new antipoverty agency, they would vote against the bill. The President gave them the pledge demanded. When news of the deal broke in the press, Johnson denied that he had ever intended to appoint Yarmolinsky, but the question of Yarmolinsky's martyrdom persists. Johnson did not mention the episode in his memoir, and Shriver's public comments left the issue clouded and have not subsequently been amplified.[23]

The swift legislative triumph was sweet, but political analysts have expressed reservations about its long-term costs. By identifying the War on Poverty so completely with himself in the year he was running for the presidency, did Johnson burden the program with the stigma of partisanship? Republicans were placed in an uncomfortable position by Johnson's strategy. To be doubtful about the War on Poverty, one GOP congressman lamented, is to put one "under the suspicion of being in favor of poverty." The Republicans never ceased trying to dismantle the apparatus Johnson had created.[24] Furthermore, by preparing the program with no congressional input and then by pushing the bill through the legislature almost without debate, the President left the War on Poverty dependent almost entirely on his own prestige. The antipoverty program would be denied "the base of reliable and continuing congressional and public support accorded those measures that were the product of the legislative branch's own initiative and tedious processes of refinement."[25] Was the President's victory on Capitol Hill in 1964, therefore, a Pyrrhic one? Had he deluded himself into believing that a valid consensus existed? Was the nation really committed to an all-out war against poverty? Only one point is certain: Johnson had driven the poverty issue indelibly into the national consciousness. The country might not eliminate the problem, but it could not forget one was there.[26]

Strategy II

The President had declared war on poverty and the Congress had sanctioned that war, but neither had a clear idea how the war was to be fought—or what constituted victory. The summer of 1964 witnessed the passage of two significant pieces of legislation, the Gulf of Tonkin Resolution and the Economic Opportunity Act. Both set the nation on activist courses, but neither had specificity or policy. Each was capable of being all things to all people. Over the next four years the Tonkin Resolution became a primary instrument of White House policymaking; during the same period the Economic Opportunity Act became increasingly a presidential orphan. The fate of the latter was closely tied to the use of the former, but the war in Vietnam was not the only cause for the War on Poverty's distress.

In early 1969 there appeared one of those books whose publication marks a political fault line. Just as John Kenneth Galbraith's *The Affluent Society* (1958) had provided Kennedy-era liberals an intellectual base, so Daniel Patrick Moynihan's *Maximum Feasible Misunderstanding* supplied the incipient neoconservative movement with a basic text. The author's own career was instructive. A former Labor Department official in the Kennedy and Johnson administrations, Moynihan was the freshly appointed urban affairs adviser to the new President, Richard Nixon. Through his political shift and his book, Moynihan highlighted the ideological confusion engendered by the events of the late 1960s.

The thrust of *Maximum Feasible Misunderstanding* is that social scientists with idealistic notions about the organization of society but little common sense about human behavior persuaded national officials to turn the War on Poverty into a war on the political establishment. In the same fashion that the Manhattan Project had realized physical science abstractions, the Community Action Program (CAP) was a vehicle to realize social science abstractions; CAP was intended to put into practice social theories about alienation and participatory democracy. According to Moynihan, CAP was actually little more than occupational therapy for members of the white middle class who were alienated from their own community background.

Moynihan was not the first to identify the central role of social theorists. Sociologists Peter Marris and Martin Rein in their book *Dilemmas of Social Reform* (1967), had traced the design of the War on Poverty to efforts of social scientists, foundation executives, and federal officials to shake up old-line local bureaucracies. But whereas Marris and Rein took the sympathetic view that these were attempts to make the government more responsive to the poor, Moynihan denounced the whole approach as ill conceived and ultimately harmful to the poor. With his scathing criticism of misguided academics and their poorly advised political friends, Moynihan supplied political opponents of the War on Poverty with prestigious scholarly ammunition. The book also raised anew a question that had long fascinated observers of the antipoverty war: how did community action take on its adversary form?

The roots of community action are well known; less clear is whether its early proponents understood and then tried to hide its disruptive potential. Experimental projects in mobilizing the poor were started at the close of the 1950s under the auspices of the "gray areas" program of the Ford Foundation. After its creation in 1961, the President's Committee on Juvenile Delinquency sponsored similar endeavors. Neither the Ford Foundation nor the President's committee had fully evaluated these projects by the late fall of 1963 when the Bureau of the Budget came around looking for new ideas on which to base the War on Poverty; nonetheless, the President's committee recommended the community action approach as a coordinating device in a limited number of neighborhood experiments. Committee information on the troubled history of the existing community action agencies and the conflicting interpretations being drawn from them was apparently not transmitted to the Budget Bureau.[27]

Nor did the Shriver task force fully explore community action. Put forth as an organizational and planning mechanism, the community action concept held little attraction for the performance-oriented Shriver. Only personal intervention by Attorney General Robert Kennedy, chairman of the President's Committee on Juvenile Delinquency, prevented Shriver from jettisoning CAP.[28] The insertion of language requiring the "maximum feasible participation" of the poor was preceded by almost no discussion, although subsequent accounts of the Shriver task force's deliberations have revealed great differences of opinion about what people thought it meant. In the hurried congressional consideration of the administration bill, the community action title was left untouched and the "maximum feasible participation" mandate escaped floor scrutiny altogether.[29]

Over the next four years, however, Shriver's Office of Economic Opportunity (OEO) became virtually synonymous with the Community Action Program. Other OEO undertakings such as Head Start, VISTA, Job Corps, and Upward Bound attracted attention, but none came near the headline-making capacity of CAP. And whereas the other programs were appraised within the bounds of traditional reformer-conservative debates of equal opportunity vs. individualism and a helping hand vs. boondoggle, CAP created a whole new set of concerns. Was OEO fomenting revolution against the very governmental and political systems of which it was a part? Could American democracy function with the active participation of the poor? Because of CAP, the economic goals of OEO were lost in intense political controversy that blurred the old liberal-conservative divisions.

The process by which OEO and CAP emerged as a threat to local politics as usual has yet to be thoroughly researched, although many hypotheses have been made. Moynihan blames social scientists for leading astray agency heads who should have known better. Piven and Cloward credit astute national politicians with recognizing the need for change. Paul Peterson and J. David Greenstone, two political scientists, attribute CAP's militancy to OEO's instincts for self-preservation: community action presented OEO with the opportunity to create a constituency of its own, thereby reducing its dependence on the President.[30] Marris and Rein suggest that OEO had no choice but to take the "maximum feasible participation" route. Ghetto militancy was already too high, they argue, for conventional programs administered by noncommunity agencies to have been welcomed. If the War on Poverty was to be waged at all, the poor would have to be actively involved.

Whatever the sources of OEO's conduct, it surely did not meet with favor in the Oval Office. Less than a year after OEO was established, James Rowe, a former Roosevelt aide and Johnson friend, was warning the President that the local community action agency was staging protests against Democratic leaders in the District of Columbia. Johnson's response was emphatic; in a handwritten note to Bill Moyers he demanded, "For God's sake get on top of this and put a stop to it at once."[31] After mayoral complaints about CAP had intensified during the summer of 1965, Budget Director Charles Schultze told the President in September that the "maximum feasible participation" requirement was receiving the wrong kind of emphasis. Instead of giving the poor jobs, getting them to volunteer, and keeping them informed about the progress of programs, CAP was focusing on putting the poor onto local poverty boards, holding elections, and organizing the poor. The chief executive approved Schultze's suggestion that OEO be instructed to get CAP out of the business of setting up "competing political groups."[32]

But the White House differences with OEO over community action would not go away easily. When newspaper articles in November 1965 broke the story of the BOB order to OEO, Shriver lashed out in public against the Budget Bureau and sent a strongly worded message of protest to the President. Claiming that the revelations had severely damaged the poverty agency's standing with the poor, Shriver charged the White House staff and BOB with leaking the information. The OEO director contended that the "maximum feasible participation" issue had been all but settled ("90 percent over the hump") before the articles appeared; however, "now it is becoming a storm."[33] This particular dispute soon blew over, but the clouds of controversy hanging over CAP never dissipated. Johnson had his 1967 poverty message rewritten to include the admonition that CAP be kept out of politics, and the congressional antipoverty legislation that year limited the poor to one-third of the seats on local antipoverty councils.[34]

Evaluations of CAP have been as ambiguous as the community action concept itself. While Moynihan argues that it was politically and socially destructive, Peterson and Greenstone praise it for opening the political system to groups previously denied access. Although sharing the latter appraisal, Piven and Cloward do not view it in a favorable light. In their view, the War on Poverty succeeded in "absorbing and directing many of the agitational elements in the black population," thereby defusing a potentially revolutionary situation and preserving the Democratic party.[35] Instead of real change, the poor got more welfare. It was an outcome Lyndon Johnson could not have been happy with, either.

The Poverty Warriors

The War on Poverty may have been fought in the field by several federal departments, but the headquarters were indisputably in the Office of Economic Opportunity. The decision to establish this presidential agency resulted from two considerations: the desire to dramatize Johnson's commitment to the struggle and the need to coordinate the antipoverty war's far-flung operations. The latter objective worked out better on paper than in practice, but OEO more than lived up to expectations as an attention getter. In a positive way with such in-house originated programs as Head Start and Upward Bound, and in a more negative fashion with CAP and Job Corps, OEO became the nerve center and lightning rod for the War on Poverty.

Just as Robert McNamara dominated the nation's other war-making department during the 1960s, so Sargent Shriver's presence gave OEO its distinctive features. Director of OEO for its first four years, Shriver generated such enthusiasm both within and outside the agency for what OEO was doing that even an unsympathetic Richard Nixon had to move cautiously to eliminate the agency. It is fair to say that if someone besides Shriver had run OEO during those years, the War on Poverty would have been conducted differently; therefore, the absence of a Shriver oral history leaves a gaping hole in the Johnson Library's coverage of the topic.[36]

Perhaps the most intriguing question concerning Shriver was his relationship with the President. In addition to Shriver's boundless energy, the other attribute which may have originally attracted Johnson to him was his connection to the Kennedy family. As the brother-in-law of the late President, Shriver could lend legitimacy to the antipoverty war and the entire Johnson regime, a serious concern to LBJ in 1964. But as the years passed, Johnson was undoubtedly troubled by Shriver's ties to Robert Kennedy. Further adding to the potential for misunderstanding was Shriver's penchant for staffing his agency with bold, sometimes unconventional aides who either refused or did not know how to play the political game to which Washington was accustomed. Shriver and OEO were so indistinguishable that Johnson's feelings about one were sure to affect his attitude toward the other.

Materials at the Johnson Library offer glimpses of this tangled web. Wilbur Cohen, Johnson's last secretary of health, education, and welfare, recalls in his oral history that every time a matter concerning OEO came up during his conversations with the President, Johnson would complain that "the OEO people were always trying to undermine him." When Cohen sought to appoint some OEO personnel to jobs in his department, the President's initial response was negative because he believed everybody in OEO was "disloyal to him"; Johnson, however, eventually acceded to Cohen's request.[37] According to the oral history of Herbert Kramer, OEO's director of public affairs, the President had no basis to question Shriver's allegiance: "He was at all times a loyal subject" of Johnson.[38] When

Shriver attempted to resign in December 1966, Bill Moyers made a point of telling the President that Shriver wanted his departure "handled in a way that does not give the appearance of bad blood between him and the White House."[39] Johnson's response was to invite Shriver and his wife to spend Christmas at the LBJ ranch, where Johnson apparently talked him out of resigning. When Shriver did leave OEO in early 1968, it was to take up the ambassadorial post in France.

There is little in the Johnson Library's documentary holdings illuminating either the long-range strategy or the operating style of OEO.[40] Most of the correspondence between White House staff and Shriver's agency deals with specific details of particular projects. Neither Bill Moyers nor subsequently James Gaither, the White House liaison, seemed to have developed any firm ideas about the antipoverty war beyond their belief that it was a necessary effort.[41] The President's counsel, Harry McPherson, was more thoughtful. "There is no real agreement," he wrote Johnson at the end of 1966,

> on how to go about improving the job situation, or education, or family income in the slums.
>
> I think we have about all the social programs we need—already authorized. We may have too many. There are too many mouths to feed—too many social program constituencies trying to get our attention and support.
>
> It will take more than political judgment on whether this or that program can pass, or whether they will be funded, or whether they will cause trouble with the mayors.
>
> You need to ask: what is this program trying to accomplish? How well has it done? What *should* we be trying to accomplish in this area?[42]

No such review appears to have been attempted.

Far more than most agencies, OEO performed in the glare of publicity. A good deal of this exposure was OEO's own doing; its press relations staff, at Shriver's direction, actively sought coverage as a means of building popular backing.[43] But in the news-conscious 1960s, the media were not content to report solely what the OEO provided. OEO was taking controversial actions with its money. Just as the evening news on television portrayed the Vietnam War in the form of daily battles that did not give viewers an appreciation of the subtleties of the conflict, so too the antipoverty war was presented in terms of episodic engagements. The substantive programmatic issues were lost in the midst of charges, countercharges, and demonstrations.[44] This constant uproar had an effect on OEO's operating style. "At the end of the day," wrote one OEO official, "I have reacted to a dozen crises and leave my desk with a feeling that I have advanced not a foot. The whole system is like a giant pinball machine. Problems, like steel balls, are periodically shot out—one by one all the desks light up—the ball bounces from station to station, and finally at the end of the day, drops out of sight. Whatever happens to yesterday's crisis?"[45] As they sort their way through OEO press clippings, historians will face the difficult challenge of separating the ephemeral from the consequential.

OEO remained concerned with its image to the very end. Its *Administrative History* runs to more than seven hundred pages and is based on internal documents, interviews, and published accounts. It is indispensable but, like all such products, it must be used carefully.

Hunger and the Poor People's Campaign

In the spring of 1968, Joseph Califano, Johnson's chief assistant for domestic affairs, wrote a memorandum to the lame-duck President. "You have clearly made your mark," Califano declared, "in the fields of education, health, jobs and poverty and housing. The one area remaining is food."[46] Califano's observation was offered after a year of steadily increasing public awareness of hunger among the poor. Appreciation of this particular problem owed much to Lyndon Johnson's earlier and forthright depiction of poor people's plight, but the President's handling of the food issue in the latter part of his administration cast a long shadow over his entire antipoverty record.

Hunger suddenly became news in the spring of 1967 with the trip by a bipartisan group of senators to rural Mississippi. Sickened by their discovery of malnutrition and even starvation among the black children they visited, all nine members of the Senate poverty subcommittee signed a letter to the President demanding prompt federal action. They sought a much larger food stamp program that would reach more people and supply them with adequate diets. Because the need was so basic and the pictorial testimony so vivid, the hunger problem aroused concern in a nation otherwise tired of crusades.

For the last eighteen months of the Johnson administration, the public was treated to the spectacle of an executive branch at war with itself over what to do about food for the poor. The White House alternated between denying that any problem existed, leaking various agency schemes for bolder and more expensive programs, and arguing that a tight federal budget would not permit significantly greater spending. Even when his subordinates agreed unanimously on the details of a generous food package, the President shot it down. Not until his farewell budget message to Congress in January 1969 did Johnson endorse a larger appropriation for food stamps, but by this time his power to achieve it was completely gone.

Journalist Nick Kotz, who has described this phase of the antipoverty war in his book, *Let Them Eat Promises: The Politics of Hunger in America*, suggests several explanations for the President's dismal performance.[47] As always, Robert Kennedy influenced Johnson's position. Since Kennedy had been among the first to highlight the problem and continued to draw attention to it, Johnson undoubtedly believed the matter to be more of political than of humanitarian concern. The President also had reservations about food stamps. "I just don't know about these programs," he told his secretary of agriculture. "Food comes and food goes. You don't get anything for it. Education and job training get more for the money."[48] Dividends aside, finances certainly entered into the President's calculations. In order to get his tax surcharge through Congress, Johnson had promised fiscal conservatives that the spending side of the federal ledger would be held in check; to go full-speed ahead on a food stamp program was simply not possible within this pledge.

Nor did Johnson appreciate the behavior of those needing help. The long, hot summers of urban disorders had been tragic and counterproductive in the President's view, but there was some solace in the fact that they had been the spontaneous outbursts of unorganized individuals living at the fringes of society.[49] Not so with the Poor People's Campaign and Resurrection City in 1968. Leaders who should have known better were attempting to apply pressure on legislators, bureaucrats, and a chief executive who would not take kindly to this sort of public tactic. Johnson would not be pushed around; he would not see Reverend Abernathy or Mrs. King, and he would not lobby for their program in Congress. He thought he could accomplish more if they would go home and stay there.

Yet the White House could not totally ignore a group that wanted what the administration wished it had the means to provide. Looking to the past for guidance, staff aides found a message in the writings of Arthur M. Schlesinger, Jr., otherwise not among the favored authors at 1600 Pennsylvania Avenue. Urging that his boss study Schlesinger's account of the Bonus March, an assistant to Califano noted, "The historians have judged Hoover and the Congress harshly, and we can learn from their mistake. I believe we can deal with the Poor People's Campaign in a more civilized manner."[50] Another Califano assistant sent the same piece to Harry McPherson, together with the recommendation that the President meet with the campaign's leaders: "It will be important in the long run for the Government to have appeared concerned, compassionate and sympathetic to the objectives of the Campaign."[51] In a memorandum of his own to Johnson, Califano stressed that no program would be expanded or added in response to the campaign's demands, although there would be some administrative changes "to give Abernathy something to report back to his people." But, Califano hastened to append, "no changes are being made merely because Abernathy requested them."[52] It was a strange and sad denouncement of the War on Poverty: the liberators of the poor were besieged by those they were seeking to free, and neither camp was able to communicate with the other.

The Road Not Taken

When the Johnson administration embarked upon the antipoverty crusade in 1964, there were three broad alternatives open to its planners. First they might seek to change the basic socioeconomic framework of the country so as to distribute its rewards more evenly. But this option was never seriously considered because no one in high government circles believed the existing system was fundamentally wrong. Indeed, the fact that poverty was confined to a minority of the population was strong testimony to the system's essential soundness. Furthermore, as the subsequent experience of CAP demonstrated, any effort to upset prevailing power relationships would generate tremendous political shockwaves, the very antithesis of the consensus Johnson desired. If society was not to be transformed, then the poor would have to be.

The second alternative assumed that people were poor because they lacked the incentives or skills necessary to get decent paying jobs, hence the emphasis on education, training, and the notion of equal opportunity. The poor would be offered the chance to fulfill the American dream, and the War on Poverty could easily be defended as the natural extension of liberal reform.[53]

The third approach, income transfer, lacked this badge of legitimacy. While not as revolutionary on the surface as the first alternative, it was nonetheless perceived to be just as subversive of American ideals. The 1964 annual report of the Council of Economic

Advisers noted both the attraction of income transfer and its unacceptability: "Conquest of poverty is well within our power. The majority of the nation could simply tax themselves enough to provide the necessary income supplements to their less fortunate citizens. . . . But this 'solution' would leave untouched most of the roots of poverty. Americans want to *earn* the American standard by their own efforts and contributions." The War on Poverty rejected an income transfer strategy in favor of a service strategy that stressed investment in human capital. There would be no raid on the pocketbooks of middle class Americans; the aid extended would be a "hand up," not a "hand-out."[54]

The rejection of income transfer invites additional study for at least two reasons. First, this very approach dominated public discussion of poverty issues in the 1970s.[55] Why were the two decades so different? And second, despite the President's strong opposition to the idea, income transfer came up time and time again in the internal deliberations of the Johnson administration. In its very first National Anti-Poverty Plan, prepared in the fall of 1965, the OEO's Office of Research, Plans, Progress and Evaluation recommended a negative income tax as a way out of the "welfare mess." Over the next few years, OEO received support for the negative income tax and its variations from staff members of the Council of Economic Advisers and from the annual interagency task forces on income maintenance.[56] In early 1968 after considerable delay, Johnson established the President's Commission on Income Maintenance Programs. Its report, released after Johnson left office, would lend encouragement to President Nixon's Family Assistance Plan.[57] This line of continuity needs to be traced.

That Other War

Writing to Joseph Califano in the summer of 1966 about a recent meeting in New York between the presidential aide and a group of liberal academics, William Leuchtenburg observed, "Like Banquo's ghost, Vietnam was the unwelcome guest at the feast." The historian's literary allusion neatly summarizes the problem faced by the antipoverty warriors: they were not waging the country's only fight. Indeed, as the conflict in Southeast Asia continued to escalate, the poverty war could count on less and less public support, either moral or financial. "So long as the President persists in these [Vietnam] policies," Leuchtenburg warned, "there is no hope at all for expanding the Great Society."[58]

That the Vietnam War crippled, if it did not destroy, the War on Poverty is nearly universally accepted, but we need to define more precisely this impact.[59] To what extent did the foreign war set domestic budgetary restraints upon the President? In what ways did the foreign war unleash forces at home harmful to the poor? Did the rise of liberal opposition to Vietnam make the President less sympathetic to domestic reform? Was Harry McPherson being anything other than a good defense lawyer preparing a case for his client when he wrote Johnson in the spring of 1967: "It is a lot easier to make Vietnam the villain than to face (1) the problem of managing the new programs, (2) the apparent failure of Negroes and other minorities to make substantial gains, or (3) the reluctance of Congress and the voting public to support new programs, or adequate funds for existing programs."[60] Has the Vietnam War been unfairly blamed for a failure that was inevitable?

Evaluating the War on Poverty

Was the War on Poverty indeed a failure? No other question is more likely to be asked and less likely to be answered satisfactorily. Can we distinguish between the impact of the War on Poverty programs and influences exerted by other policies and programs? Is it reasonable, putting aside the admittedly overblown rhetoric of the mid-1960s, to set any time limit for the successful completion of the struggle to eliminate poverty? By what standards is the war to be judged?[61]

How, for example, does one treat a 1979 study on hunger released by the Field Foundation? In 1967 the foundation sponsored medical teams that helped uncover the prevalence of inadequate diets in the rural South; a decade later the foundation underwrote a follow-up survey on the federal response. The report's major conclusion: "There is nowhere the same evidence of gross malnutrition" witnessed earlier. Infant mortality had declined by about 33 percent; there had been a 50 percent drop in malnutrition-related deaths. Impressive statistics, but the good news they tell is diminished by another, less positive figure: "The current food aid programs have never reached more than 60 percent of the people who need them."[62]

This refrain of "better but" is to be encountered in nearly every appraisal of the antipoverty program.[63] The conclusions drawn are most likely to be a function of the evaluator's philosophical inclinations. Conservatives are prone to stress the shortcomings, label the

whole effort a failure, and demand a rollback of federal intervention.[64] Radicals are likely to employ similar characterizations but
call for greater federal control of the economy (or, alternatively,
more community autonomy) in the pursuit of real equality.[65] Liberals tend to concede the limits of the gains, place the blame on inadequate resources, and urge more social welfare programs and more
money.[66] When they join the social scientists in the debate, historians will probably divide along the ideological camps already
established.

If that is all historians do, they will be gravely misallocating
their energy. Larger questions are presented by the War on Poverty
than simply its hits and misses—issues regarding the relationship of
the government to its citizens and the structure and strategy of politics, matters of great interest to Lyndon Johnson.

The War on Poverty produced a classic instance of the American habit of substituting good intentions for cold, hard cash. In declaring the nation's commitment to the war, Johnson requested a little less than $1 billion to start the battle. Always the supreme
legislative tactician, Johnson held first-year program costs low in
order not to frighten a frugal Congress. Appropriations did rise in
subsequent years, but never to the scale implied in the original message, because newer programs kept coming along, and siphoning off
funds. This gap between promise and delivery, repeated time and
again, led to "frustration and loss of credibility,"[67] as one memorandum by the budget director conceded. To what extent was the government responsible for the heightened expectations and deeper dis-
appointments of the poor in the 1960s? Were the ghetto riots the
Great Society's fault?[68]

The President's—and therefore the government's—credibility
was further eroded by unwillingness to admit that programs might
not be working. Just as the Vietnam War body counts diverted attention from the real but intangible losses piled up by administration
policy, the antipoverty war's incessantly upbeat publicity campaign
sought to obscure that program's problems. Johnson had his reasons;
as he explained to Doris Kearns,

> I wish it had been different. I wish the public had seen the task
> of ending poverty the same way as they saw the task of getting
> to the moon, where they accepted mistakes as a part of the sci-
> entific process. I wish they had let us experiment with different
> programs, admitting that some were working better than oth-
> ers. It would have made everything easier. But I knew that the

moment we said out loud that this or that program was a failure, then the wolves who never wanted us to be successful in the first place would be down upon us at once, tearing away at every joint, killing our effort before we even had a chance.[69]

Must a representative government be less than candid with its people? Can the modern welfare state ever reach the politically inarticulate and economically downtrodden? Will, indeed, the poor always be with us?

Notes

1. James L. Sundquist, "Introduction," in *On Fighting Poverty*, ed. James L. Sundquist (New York: Basic Books, 1969), p. 3.

2. The early writings are listed in Dorothy Campbell Tompkins, comp., *Poverty in the United States during the Sixties—A Bibliography* (Berkeley: University of California, Institute of Governmental Studies, 1970).

3. Before poverty became a public issue in the mid-1960s, American historians had almost totally ignored the subject. Robert Bremner's *From the Depths: The Discovery of Poverty in the United States* (New York: New York University Press, 1956) was itself a discovery for historians, but not one quickly followed up. With the appearance of Roy Lubove's *The Progressives and the Slums* (Pittsburgh: University of Pittsburgh Press, 1962) and Stephan Thernstrom's *Poverty and Progress: Social Mobility in a Nineteenth Century City* (Cambridge: Harvard University Press, 1964), the two main avenues of historical inquiry were laid out: the study of social reformers and the quantitative examination of poor people's climb up the economic ladder. The rising interest in social history since 1964 has led to a flood of books on the many facets of poverty. A recent overview is James T. Patterson, "Poverty and Welfare in America, 1930–1975" (paper delivered at the Annual Meeting of the American Historical Association, 1979). Patterson is engaged in a full-scale investigation of this subject.

4. For the purposes of this paper the War on Poverty has been defined rather narrowly: the activities of the Office of Economic Opportunity. With only scattered exceptions, all the major domestic programs of the Johnson administration can be considered as having been directed toward the elimination of poverty; these would include macroeconomic policies as well as the civil rights effort, Medicare, aid to education, and the Model Cities Program. But as their primary objective was not to uplift the economic underclass, they have not been dealt with here. Nor is there discussion of the non-Office of Economic Opportunity poverty programs administered by the Departments of Labor; Agriculture; and Health, Education, and Welfare; and by other agencies. They were peripheral to the War on Poverty and attracted far less attention.

5. Walter W. Heller to Lyndon Johnson, November 16, 1964, Council of Economic Advisers, *Administrative History*, Vol. 2, Documentary Supplement, Part 4, Lyndon B. Johnson Library, Austin, Texas.

6. Heller, speech, March 25, 1965, Indiana State College, Indiana, Pennsylvania. Johnson's account of his choice of words differs from Heller's: "I'm interested. I'm sympathetic. Go ahead. Give it the highest priority. Push ahead full tilt" (*The Vantage Point* [New York: Holt, Rinehart and Winston, 1971], p. 71). In his notes on the meeting, dictated immediately after returning to his office, Heller provided this version: "The new President expressed his interest in it, his sympathy for it, and in answer to a point-blank question, said we should push full-tilt on this project" ("Notes on Meeting with President Johnson, November 23, 1963," box 7, Walter W. Heller Papers, John F. Kennedy Library, Boston). The Heller collection at the Kennedy Library has good material on the War on Poverty's beginnings.

7. Arthur M. Schlesinger, Jr., *A Thousand Days: John F. Kennedy in the White House* (Boston: Houghton Mifflin, 1965), pp. 1005–1012; James L. Sundquist, *Politics and Policy: The Eisenhower, Kennedy and Johnson Years* (Washington: Brookings Institution, 1968), pp. 112–114.

8. See, for example, David Burner, Robert D. Marcus, and Thomas R. West, *A Giant's Strength: America in the 1960s* (New York: Holt, Rinehart and Winston, 1971), pp. 95–96.

9. Robert H. Haveman, ed., *A Decade of Federal Antipoverty Programs* (New York: Academic Press, 1977), pp. 26–28.

10. Ibid., pp. 118–119.

11. Richard Cloward and Lloyd Ohlin, *Delinquency and Opportunity: A Theory of Delinquent Groups* (Glencoe, Ill.: Free Press, 1960), provided the sociological concepts for the experiments in organizing the poor that evolved into the Community Action Program. See also Richard A. Cloward and Frances Fox Piven, "A Strategy to End Poverty," *Nation* 202 (May 2, 1966): 14–17. Cloward and Piven are usually credited with sparking the welfare rights movement and the resulting interest in some form of guaranteed income (Ibid., pp. 510–517).

12. Frances Fox Piven and Richard A. Cloward, *Regulating the Poor: The Functions of Public Welfare* (New York: Pantheon, 1971), pp. 250–263; Cloward and Piven, *The Politics of Turmoil* (New York: Pantheon, 1974), pp. 268, 273. Although the way the programs operated would tend to support this view, Piven and Cloward do not provide evidence that either Kennedy or Johnson or their advisers ever actually articulated such a strategy.

13. In addition to the question whether politicians saw the War on Poverty in racial terms is the issue of how the general public perceived it. To what extent was the decline of popular support attributable to the shift in the antipoverty campaign's focus from helping white Appalachia to serving the inner-city ghettos?

14. Johnson cited just such a warning by his aide, Horace Busby, in *Vantage Point*, p. 71. Kennedy, too, had been alerted to the possible dangers of a

close identification with poverty issues (Theodore C. Sorensen, *Kennedy* [New York: Harper and Row, 1965], p. 104).

15. Godfrey Hodgson, *America in Our Time* (Garden City, N.Y.: Doubleday, 1976), p. 270. One example of this innocence was the inability to define who were the poor. It is by no means clear that the White House had a definite idea whom it was trying to assist.

16. See John C. Donovan, *The Politics of Poverty* (New York: Pegasus, 1967); John Bibby and Roger Davidson, *On Capitol Hill: Studies in the Legislative Process* (New York: Holt, Rinehart, and Winston, 1967); Sundquist, *Politics and Policy*; Daniel Patrick Moynihan, *Maximum Feasible Misunderstanding* (New York: Free Press, 1969); Sar A. Levitan, *The Great Society's Poor Law* (Baltimore: Johns Hopkins Press, 1969). Also see the proceedings of the Conference on Poverty and Urban Policy, sponsored by the John F. Kennedy Library and the Florence Heller Graduate School of Social Work, Brandeis University, 1973 (a copy is available at the Johnson Library). Arthur M. Schlesinger cited an unpublished manuscript by William Cannon, "The Dangerous Abuse of the Lower Class," in his *Robert F. Kennedy and His Times* (Boston: Houghton Mifflin, 1978), p. 991, n. 84. A rich source is Richard Blumenthal, "Community Action: The Origins of a Government Program" (honors thesis, Harvard College, 1967). A recent study based on archival materials is Carl M. Brauer, "Origins of the War on Poverty" (paper delivered at the Annual Meeting of the American Historical Association, 1979).

17. Bureau of the Budget, *Administrative History*, Johnson Library. Budget Bureau records, which are not yet opened, may shed additional light on this matter. The papers of Kermit Gordon, the Budget Bureau director during this period, are on deposit at the Kennedy Library.

18. The Budget Bureau materials contained in the file, Legislative Background of the Economic Opportunity Act of 1964, Johnson Library, confirm in the view of this writer the argument that the bureau did not envision an advocacy role for community action agencies.

19. W. Williard Wirtz to Theodore C. Sorensen, January 23, 1964, box 37, Sorensen Papers, Kennedy Library.

20. Rowland Evans and Robert Novak, *Lyndon B. Johnson: The Exercise of Power* (New York: New American Library, 1966), p. 430.

21. See, for example, Adam Yarmolinsky, "The Beginnings of OEO," in *On Fighting Poverty*, ed. Sundquist, pp. 34–51; Moynihan, *Maximum Feasible Misunderstanding*; Sundquist, *Politics and Policy*; and Conference on Poverty and Urban Policy. The Johnson Library's oral history holdings on this subject include interviews with David Hackett, Frank Mankiewicz, Stephen Pollak, James Sundquist, Erich Tolmach, and Adam Yarmolinsky. Examination of the Hackett, Pollak, and Yarmolinsky materials requires the permission of the interviewees.

22. See particularly Bibby and Davidson, *On Capitol Hill*; Sundquist, *Politics and Policy*; and Jack Bell, *The Johnson Treatment* (New York:

Harper and Row, 1965), pp. 95–100. See also the Adam Yarmolinsky Oral History Interview at the Johnson Library.

23. Bell, *Johnson Treatment*, pp. 98–99. Yarmolinsky's papers, on deposit at the Kennedy Library, may shed light on both this incident and the operations of the task force.

24. William C. Selover, "The View from Capitol Hill: Harassment and Survival," in *On Fighting Poverty*, ed. Sundquist, pp. 160–166.

25. Sundquist, *Politics and Policy*, p. 494.

26. Because of Johnson's active support, Doris Kearns writes, "What had been largely the concern of a small number of liberal intellectuals and government bureaucrats became within six months the national disgrace that shattered the complacency of a people who always considered their country a land of equal opportunity" (*Lyndon Johnson and the American Dream* [New York: Harper and Row, 1976], p. 188).

27. In addition to Moynihan's harsh appraisal of the Mobilization for Youth project in *Maximum Feasible Misunderstanding*, there is the judicious treatment of the community action concept in Peter Marris and Martin Rein, *Dilemmas of Social Reform*, 2nd ed. (Chicago: Aldine, 1973), and the decidedly partisan account of the President's Committee on Juvenile Delinquency by two sociologists, Daniel Knapp and Kenneth Polk (*Scouting the War on Poverty: Social Reform Politics in the Kennedy Administration* [Lexington, Mass.: Heath Lexington Books, 1971]). Until 1992, the records of the President's committee are available at the National Archives, Washington, D.C. only with the permission of the Department of Justice.

28. Schlesinger, *Robert F. Kennedy*, pp. 638–639. In a memorandum to Johnson before Shriver's appointment to head the task force, Kennedy had argued that the antipoverty program "must involve the poor and must seek to make them self-sufficient." He also urged that the antipoverty war be directed by a cabinet-level committee with actual operations lodged in the existing departments (Kennedy to Johnson, January 16, 1964, box 39, Bill Moyers Files, Johnson Library).

29. Lillian B. Rubin, "Maximum Feasible Participation: The Origin, Implication and Present Status," *Annals* 385 (September 1969): 14–29.

30. Paul E. Peterson and J. David Greenstone, "Radical Change and Citizen Participation: The Mobilization of Low-Income Communities through Community Action," in *Decade of Federal Antipoverty Programs*, ed. Haveman, pp. 247–249, 253–256.

31. James Rowe to Johnson, with Johnson's handwritten note to Bill Moyers, June 29, 1965, box 56, Bill Moyers Files, Johnson Library; Bill Moyers to Sargent Shriver, July 1, 1965, Ibid.

32. Charles L. Schultze to Johnson, September 18, 1965, Ibid.

33. Sargent Shriver to Johnson, November 6, 1965, box 26, WE 9, Executive File, White House Central Files, Johnson Library; Charles Schultze to Johnson, November 6, 1965, Ibid.

34. Joseph Califano to Johnson, March 10, 1967, box 112, SP 2-3/1967/

WE 9, Poverty, White House Central Files; see also Harry McPherson to Johnson, August 10, 1967, box 30, WE 9, Executive File, White House Central Files, Johnson Library. The Johnson Library has an oral history interview with Theodore M. Berry, CAP's first director; the interviewee's permission is required in order to examine the transcript. Among the many studies of CAP are Kenneth B. Clark and Jeanette Hopkins, *A Relevant War against Poverty: A Study of Community Action Programs and Observable Social Change* (New York: Harper and Row, 1969); Stephen M. Rose, *The Betrayal of the Poor: The Transformation of Community Action* (Cambridge, Mass.: Schenkman, 1972); and J. David Greenstone and Paul E. Peterson, *Race and Authority in Urban Politics* (New York: Russell Sage Foundation, 1973). For local studies, see Stephan Thernstrom, *Poverty, Planning and Politics in the New Boston: The Origins of ABCD* (New York: Basic Books, 1969); Dale Rogers Marshall, *The Politics of Participation and Poverty: A Case Study of the Board of the Economic and Youth Opportunities Agency of Greater Los Angeles* (Berkeley: University of California Press, 1971); and John Hall Fish, *Black Power/White Control: The Struggle of the Woodlawn Organization in Chicago* (Princeton: Princeton University Press, 1973).

35. Piven and Cloward, *Regulating the Poor*, pp. 275–276. See also Nick Kotz and Mary Lynn Kotz, *A Passion for Equality: George A. Wiley and the Movement* (New York: Norton, 1977), p. 151.

36. Nor does Shriver have an oral history at the Kennedy Library. His papers are still in his personal possession. The Lyndon B. Johnson School of Public Affairs did conduct interviews with Shriver and other key OEO officials regarding the appointment process; transcripts of these interviews have been made available to the Johnson Library.

37. Wilbur J. Cohen Oral History Interview, tape 3, pp. 10–11; tape 4, pp. 5, 6, 9, Johnson Library.

38. Herbert J. Kramer Oral History Interview, p. 12, Johnson Library.

39. Bill Moyers to Johnson, with handwritten copy of Sargent Shriver to Johnson, December 19, 1966, box 125, FG 11-15, Executive File, White House Central Files, Johnson Library.

40. Office of Economic Opportunity materials at the Johnson Library consist of thirty-six rolls of microfilm and twenty-nine boxes. Except for rolls 4 and 5, which contain the chronological file of Shriver's office from April to December 1964, the first seventeen rolls cover the records of the Office of Research, Plans, Programs, and Evaluation. Rolls 18 to 36 are made up largely of press releases and information regarding grant applications. Of the boxes, nine contain press clippings, while the remainder hold printed and other materials from OEO's Washington and regional offices. OEO records at the National Archives, Washington, D.C. do not appear to be much more promising. Most of the 366 linear feet covering the years 1964 to 1972 contain raw data about the condition of the poor; there is also some material on the Job Corps, CAP, civil rights policies, and public affairs (U.S., National Archives and Records Service, *Preliminary Inventory of the Records*

of the Office of Economic Opportunity, RG 381). The Johnson Library has oral histories of Public Affairs Director Herbert Kramer; Bertrand Harding, OEO's deputy director (1966–1968) and director (1968–1969); Robert A. Levine, assistant director of the Office of Research, Plans, Programs, and Evaluation; Jule M. Sugarman, administrator of Head Start; and Otis Singletary, the first director of Job Corps. Other useful oral history interviews are with Donald Baker, William Crook, William P. Kelly, Robert Perrin, and William G. Phillips. The library also has Bertrand Harding's personal papers.

41. James Gaither's oral history provides little insight into the poverty program. In addition to isolated folders in the files of many presidential aides, the bulk of materials in the Johnson Library's White House Central Files relating to the War on Poverty is to be found in WE 9.

42. Harry McPherson to Johnson, December 19, 1966, box 21, Harry McPherson Files, Johnson Library.

43. Erwin Knoll and Jules Witcover, "Maximum Feasible Publicity," *Columbia Journalism Review* 5 (Fall 1966): 33–40.

44. See Herbert J. Kramer Oral History Interview, Johnson Library.

45. Bill Crook to Hayes Redmon, September 1, 1965, box 56, Bill Moyers Files, Johnson Library.

46. Joseph Califano to Johnson, June 25, 1968, box 7, Devier Pierson Files, Johnson Library.

47. Nick Kotz, *Let Them Eat Promises: The Politics of Hunger in America* (Englewood Cliffs, N.J.: Prentice-Hall, 1969). Kotz interviewed most of the key people involved and gained access to many documents circulated through the executive branch. Nothing in the Johnson Library directly contradicts or significantly adds to his account. There are records to be found in box 7, Devier Pierson Files; box 31, James Gaither Files, box 29, WE 9, Executive File, White House Central Files; box 35, BE 5-5/AG 7; box 30 LE/BE 5-5/AG 7; and the materials for June 28, 1968 in the Appointment File, Diary Backup. For a history of the food stamp program, see Gilbert Y. Steiner, *The State of Welfare* (Washington: Brookings Institution, 1971), pp. 191–236.

48. Kotz, *Let Them Eat Promises*, p. 188. The Johnson Library's oral history of Secretary of Agriculture Orville Freeman contains no references to the hunger issue.

49. The relationship between the War on Poverty and the series of ghetto riots that started in 1965 is complex. The poverty program's critics blamed OEO in general and CAP in particular for creating the climate for violence, if not actually instigating it; the program's defenders argued that War on Poverty agencies helped dampen the fires of unrest. On balance, the disorders probably hurt the antipoverty campaign. How the Johnson administration responded to the riots will undoubtedly be the subject of many books; see James W. Button, *Black Violence: Political Impact of the 1960s Riots* (Princeton: Princeton University Press, 1978). Determining the ad-

ministration's attitude will require examination of many different collections. Since the riots were seen in racial rather than class terms, there are many more materials in the civil rights than the poverty files.

50. Matt Nimitz to Joseph Califano, May 16, 1968, box 1, Legislative Background of Poor People's Campaign, Johnson Library.

51. James Gaither to Harry McPherson, June 21, 1968, Ibid. McPherson urged Johnson to see the two leaders (McPherson Oral History Interview, tape 8, pp. 2–4, Johnson Library).

52. Joseph Califano to Johnson, May 21, 1968, box 36, Gaither Files, Johnson Library.

53. Henry J. Aaron, *Politics and the Professors: The Great Society in Perspective* (Washington: Brookings Institution, 1978), pp. 27–28. George Wiley, the leader of the National Welfare Rights Organization, put the choice this way: "Whites might support a program which sought to correct defects in black people and poor people, but would oppose a program which said the defects were in white institutions which left millions unemployed and underemployed, in slum housing, and without adequate medical care." (Kotz and Kotz, *Passion for Equality*, p. 164).

54. Lawrence E. Lynn, Jr., "A Decade of Policy Developments in the Income-Maintenance System," in *Decade of Federal Antipoverty Programs*, ed. Haveman, pp. 64–66. James Tobin, a former member of the CEA, later wrote, "In eschewing this [income guarantee] approach . . . the administration carried to extreme its reluctance to face squarely the issue of income redistribution." ("The Political Economy of the 1960s," in *Toward New Human Rights: The Social Policies of the Kennedy and Johnson Administrations*, ed. David C. Warner [Austin: Lyndon B. Johnson School of Public Affairs, 1977], p. 46).

55. See Daniel Patrick Moynihan, *The Politics of a Guaranteed Income* (New York: Random House, 1973); and Vincent J. Burke and Vee Burke, *Nixon's Good Deed* (New York: Columbia University Press, 1974). In the Burkes's account, Wilbur Cohen is portrayed as the main opponent of the income transfer strategy in the Johnson administration, but his oral history does not touch on the issue.

56. For the 1965 OEO plan, see Sargent Shriver to Johnson, October 20, 1965, box 26, WE 9, Executive File, White House Central Files, Johnson Library. In his reminiscences of the War on Poverty, Robert A. Levine, the assistant director of the Office of Research, Plans, Programs, and Evaluation argued that the opportunity approach taken during the 1960s was misguided and that the income transfer approach should have been taken (*The Poor Ye Need Not Have with You* [Cambridge, Mass.: M.I.T. Press, 1970]). For CEA's role, see the agency's *Administrative History* and its "Draft History of the War on Poverty," in box 1, Legislative Background of the Equal Opportunity Act of 1964, Johnson Library. In addition to the reports of the various interagency task forces, there are also some items in box 232, James Gaither Files; box 15, WE 6, Executive File, White House Central Files, Johnson Li-

brary; and box 164, LE/WE 6, White House Central Files, Johnson Library.

57. President's Commission on Income Maintenance Programs, *Poverty amid Plenty: The American Paradox* (Washington: Government Printing Office, 1969). The records of the commission are in the National Archives, Washington, D.C. The oral history of Ben Heineman, the commission chairman, fails to mention this aspect of Heineman's public service.

58. William Leuchtenburg to Joseph Califano, July 6, 1966, box 27, WE 9, Executive File, White House Central Files, Johnson Library.

59. See, for example, the comments of James Tobin: "The political economy of the 1960s did not expect citizens to be altruistic. But it did assume a widespread popular faith that government and the economy would give all individuals and groups a fair deal, and a fair share of the fruits of a growing economy. The willingness of the taxpaying majority to help less fortunate citizens depended on such attitudes. . . . [But] the war [and its economic consequences] tragically rent the fabric of American society, the bonds of trust and compassion among citizens and between citizens and governments" ("Political Economy of the 1960s," p. 50).

60. Harry McPherson to Johnson, April 4, 1967, box 14, Harry McPherson Files, Johnson Library. See also Kearns, *Johnson and the American Dream*, p. 299.

61. Aaron, *Politics and Professors*, pp. 30–34; Robert S. Weiss and Martin Rein, "The Evaluation of Broad-Aim Programs: A Cautionary Case and Moral," *Annals* 385 (September 1969): 133–42; Louis A. Ferman, "Some Perspectives on Evaluating Social Welfare Programs," Ibid., pp. 143–56.

62. *New York Times*, May 1, 1979, p. B9.

63. See, for example, Robert A. Levine, "An Overview of the Policies and Programs to Guarantee a Decent Standard of Living," in *Toward New Human Rights*, ed. Warner, pp. 55–73; Robert J. Lampman, "Changing Patterns of Income, 1960–1974," in Ibid., pp. 109–126; Karen Davis and Cathy Schoen, *Health and the War on Poverty: A Ten Year Appraisal* (Washington: Brookings Institution, 1978); Robert D. Plotnick and Felicity Skidmore, *Progress against Poverty: A Review of the 1964–1974 Decade* (New York: Academic Press, 1975).

64. Michael Harrington, "The Welfare State and Its Neoconservative Critics," in *The New Conservatism: A Critique from the Left*, ed. Lewis A. Coser and Irving Howe (New York: Quadrangle, 1974), pp. 29–63.

65. Richard H. deLone, *Small Futures: Children, Inequality and the Limits of Liberal Reform* (New York: Harcourt Brace Jovanovich, 1979).

66. Sar A. Levitan and Robert Taggart, *The Promise of Greatness* (Cambridge, Mass.: Harvard University Press, 1976).

67. Charles L. Schultze to Johnson, November 11, 1966, box 28, WE 9, Executive File, White House Central Files, Johnson Library.

68. Rejecting the notion that the poor would have been silent if their political leaders had not stirred them up, Arthur Schlesinger observes: "I

would guess that television had far more than Lyndon Johnson to do with raising people's expectations in the 1960s" ("The Evolution of the National Government as an Instrument for Attaining Social Rights," in *Toward New Human Rights*, ed. Warner, p. 28).

69. Kearns, *Johnson and the American Dream*, p. 291.

5 | The Transformation of Federal Education Policy

by Hugh Davis Graham

WHEN PRESIDENT LYNDON JOHNSON signed the path-breaking Elementary and Secondary Education Act (ESEA) of 1965 into law, he dramatically flew to the one-room schoolhouse near Stonewall, Texas, where he had begun his own schooling. With his first teacher, Mrs. Kathryn Deadrich Loney—"Miss Kate"—at his side, he recalled once again the depressed circumstances of his youth and his early school-teaching career. He observed that "a pattern had come full circle in the course of fifty years" and had "brought me back to fulfill a dream."[1] Like Huey Long, Johnson was given to exaggerating the poverty of his youth, but his constantly reiterated faith in the almost panacean powers of education is universally conceded as genuine. The sixty education laws to his credit have attracted the attention of a substantial body of scholars—although in a rather lopsided way considering the sources available. This essay will briefly survey the historical background of federal aid to education and then assess the scholarly literature, especially the largely untapped archival evidence, as it bears on the process of policy formulation, legislation, and implementation in the radically transformed world of the federal educational structure.

Federal Aid to Education: Historical Background

In his memoir, *The Vantage Point*, Johnson claimed that "other Presidents and advocates had been trying to provide federal aid to the schools since the days of Andrew Jackson. None had succeeded."[2] This claim is not true as stated. On the contrary, federal aid to education predated the Constitution and the presidency; it was explicitly encouraged by the Congress of the Confederation in the Survey Ordinance of 1785 and the Northwest Ordinance of 1787. The continuity of this policy extended for a century and a half, through the statehood acts for Hawaii and Alaska. Land being the chief historic form of federal wealth, the federal government granted a total of 98.5 million acres to the states for supporting public schools.[3] This policy was extended to higher education by the Morrill Act of 1862 and was further reinforced in 1890 (Second Morrill Act), 1914

(Smith-Lever Act), and 1917 (Smith-Hughes Act). These acts funded the new land grant colleges for the expansion of agricultural extension and provided for mechanical-vocational training and home economics programs in high schools. World War II brought the "impacted" aid of the Lanham Act in 1940 for school districts overburdened by nontaxed military installations and the GI Bill in 1944. Finally, the Cold War brought the National Science Foundation Act of 1950 and—in response to Sputnik—the National Defense Education Act (NDEA) of 1958 to stimulate education in science, engineering, foreign languages, and mathematics.[4] The federal government was clearly willing to provide categorical aid, especially in times of national crisis. However, attempts to pass a general aid bill had foundered on constitutional objections, the church-state issue, fear of loss of local control, and the school desegregation controversy.[5]

Enter President John F. Kennedy in 1961 with a general federal-aid-to-education bill and a high commitment to its passage. According to Theodore Sorensen, "the one domestic subject that mattered most to John Kennedy [was] education. Throughout his campaign and throughout his Presidency, he devoted more time and talks to this single topic than to any other domestic issue."[6] The debate over federal aid had been accelerated by the discovery during the two world wars of widespread illiteracy among conscripts, by the postwar baby boom coming of age in the 1960s, and by the increasing inability of local tax sources to meet these challenges. Francis Keppel, who left Harvard to become Kennedy's commissioner of education in 1962, identified the demographic pressures: U.S. high school attendance had grown eighteenfold since 1900 (or six times the rate of population increase). New elementary and secondary school pupils would require 400,000 new classrooms in the late 1960s. College attendance had increased eightyfold since 1900 and by 1970 would increase by another 50 percent.[7]

Kennedy's 1961 general aid-to-education bill passed the Senate in the spring but was beaten in the House by a coalition of Republicans who opposed general aid, Catholics who resented fellow-Catholic Kennedy's exclusion of aid to parochial schools, and southerners who feared the civil rights wedge of federal school funds. In 1962 Kennedy's higher education bill foundered in conference committee. In 1963 after first adopting and then abandoning an omnibus general-aid bill, he settled for a makeshift package of separate, more traditional categorical measures that extended the popular impact laws and the NDEA and provided additional federal aid for vocational education, manpower training, the physically and mentally handicapped, and such specific educational facilities as libraries and medical schools. Despite this accomplishment, Sorensen's attempt to salvage Kennedy's reputation in education is less convincing than Arthur Schlesinger's admission (with rather unconvincing apologies) that Kennedy lacked the political will to risk frontal combat for civil rights, education, and Medicare.[8]

In *Decade of Disillusionment*, Jim Heath sees Kennedy's domestic record on education as a failure brought about partly by lack of nerve, partly by higher priorities in foreign affairs, and partly by weak leadership and thin Democratic margins in Congress.[9] General aid to education continued to be victimized also by seemingly intractable arguments over religion, states' rights, civil rights, academic freedom, balanced budgets, and financial equalization. A major and sympathetic study of the general aid question in the early 1960s was deeply pessimistic.[10] Yet in 1965 Congress passed massive aid to elementary and secondary education with a whoop; the circumstances of this remarkable turnaround following Kennedy's assassination reveal much about the political and policy process under the driving hand of Lyndon Johnson.[11] Subsequent scholarship has clustered in three areas: (1) the process of policy formulation that distinguished the Johnson administration, especially in relation to the secret task forces, particularly John Gardner's 1964 task force on education; (2) the changed circumstances surrounding the enactment of the ESEA of 1965 and related educational developments; and (3) the evaluation of legislative implementation, especially in light of subsequent debate over program failure. In addition to reviewing that literature, this essay will also propose an area of scholarship that has been largely neglected: a systematic reconstruction and analysis of the evolution of public policy in education based on archival sources.

The Johnson Task Force: Policy

In the spring of 1966 William Leuchtenburg published a tantalizing article in *The Reporter* entitled "The Genesis of the Great Society."[12] The article describes how in the spring of 1964 President Johnson, anticipating both a landslide victory over Goldwater and overwhelming Democratic dominance in the Eighty-ninth Congress a year later, planned a reform program of his own that would produce legislative proposals for presentation to the new Congress in January. In his "Great Society" speech at the University of Michigan commencement on May 22, Johnson said: "We are going to assemble the best thought and the broadest knowledge from all over the world. . . . I intend to establish working groups to prepare a series of White House conferences and meetings—on the cities, on natural beauty, on the quality of education, and on other emerging challenges. And from these meetings and from these studies, we will begin to set our course toward the Great Society."[13]

From this commitment sprang the Johnson task forces—ultimately 135 of them by present count.[14] Students of public administration have been fascinated by the President's use of task forces as an attempted short-circuit of the normal central-clearance process of legislative agenda formulation, whereby agencies routinely generated a program of bills and the executive packaged them for Congress.[15] As Phillip S. Hughes of the Bureau of the Budget candidly observed:

> The task force was the basic tool which made much of the success of the Eighty-ninth Congress. The routine way to develop a legislative program has been to ask the Departments to generate proposals. Each agency sends its ideas through channels, which means that the ideas are limited by the imagination of the old-line agencies. They tend to be repetitive—the same proposals year after year. When the ideas of the different agencies reach the departmental level, all kinds of objections are raised, especially objections that new notions may somehow infringe on the rights of some other agency in the department. By the time a legislative proposal from a department reaches the President, it's a pretty well-compromised product.[16]

Thus the task force device was designed to interrupt the normal bureaucratic flow, provide for innovation, combat the inherent inertia and boundary maintenance of the agencies, and maximize the leverage of the presidential battalion of a thousand short-term political appointees over the entrenched subgovernment army of 2.5 million civil servants and their constituency and congressional subcommittee allies.[17]

The Johnson task forces as described by Leuchtenburg were coordinated by Bill Moyers and after mid-1965 by Joseph Califano. These men along with Richard Goodwin, Walter Heller, and Kermit Gordon represented continuity with the Kennedy task forces.[18] Unlike the latter, however, which had leaked information and gotten Kennedy into political trouble, the Johnson task forces were to be secret. They would also be small and modestly staffed, would focus on policy rather than politics, and would link the administration to the university and practitioner world through an executive secretary from the government (mainly from the Bureau of the Budget) and a liaison person from the White House staff.[19] By early June 1964, Moyers and Goodwin were recruiting on the prestige campuses. By July 2, when Johnson first briefed his Cabinet on the task force plan, fifteen task forces were already at work, all but one of them on domestic matters (whereas fifteen of the twenty-nine Kennedy task forces had been concerned with national security and foreign affairs). While Johnson and the Cabinet worked on such immediate legacies from the Kennedy regime as the tax cut, the poverty program, and the civil rights bill, the fifteen initial task forces were to work toward a November 15 reporting date, after which their proposals would be filtered and refined toward the January 1965 legislative docket.

Since the publication of Leuchtenburg's bellwether article, much has been learned about the task force operation and its role in legislative policy formulation—although the rich lode of sources in the Johnson Library has scarcely been mined. Most of the literature has been generated by social scientists who typically employed systems analysis and model building based on case studies and who interviewed often anonymous participants rather than to wait, as historians must (or should), for the archives to open.[20] Nothing has attracted so much attention as John Gardner's 1964 task force on education, primarily because, as Leuchtenburg observed, "The history of the elementary-education bill is probably the best example of the success of the task force technique."[21]

The 1964 Gardner Task Force on Education: A Case Study in Policy Formulation

Because the Gardner task force was the prelude to the stunning ESEA victory of 1965, scholars have extensively studied the relationship between the two. As early as 1967 three book-length studies of this phenomenon appeared. The historian of public policy is struck by the degree to which the early studies suffer by comparison with the subsequent decade of literature. The reason is not that research builds on preceding scholarship or even that the passage of time enhances perspective. Rather, it is that crucial documentary evidence, especially in presidential libraries, was not available to the earlier researchers, who relied on public documents and interviews. Consider the case of the Gardner task force of 1964 and the ESEA of 1965.

In 1967 Philip Meranto published *The Politics of Federal Aid to Education in 1965*, which focused ably but almost exclusively on such accessible external factors as lobbies, interest groups, and their congressional interplay. The book was oblivious to the task force role.[22] Yet that same year Philip Kearney's dissertation compared the task force recommendations on elementary and secondary education to the five enacted ESEA titles, based on textual analysis of available evidence that apparently included a copy of the confidential task force report.[23] According to Kearney, the task force made essentially no contribution to Title II (instructional materials for public and nonpublic school students), was not "significant or essential" in developing Title I (the crucial, billion-dollar formulaic aid for poverty students) or Title V (aid to state departments of education), and "may have influenced" Titles III (supplemental educational service centers) and IV (educational research laboratories). Kearney concluded that the task force's contribution was minimal. It served most significantly as "a legitimating agent for ideas already in existence," and its relationship with the other, more important groups—i.e., the various congressional actors, administrators of the Department of Health, Education, and Welfare, and educational lobbyists—was at best indirect.

The third major study completed in 1967 was Edith Kern Mosher's dissertation, which relied on Kearney for evaluation of the task force role and concentrated on testing Eastonian systems analysis against external evidence drawn primarily from Government Printing Office documents generated by Congress and the relevant executive agencies.[24] The following year she joined Stephen K. Bailey in publishing *ESEA: The Office of Education Administers a Law*, which combined her competent external research with forty-eight interviews.[25] Her use of the classic Bailey case-study technique contains all the strengths of his pioneering, but the anonymity of the interviewees is irritating. Then in 1969 appeared *An Act of Congress*, by Eugene Eidenberg and Roy Morey,[26] which paralleled Bailey and Mosher in description and interpretation, although the Eidenberg-Morey experience and evidence skewed their focus heavily toward Congress, much as the Bailey-Mosher purpose and evidence skewed theirs toward the executive branch and the educational clientele groups.

These two useful books dominate the literature. Still unpublished, however, is a 1977 doctoral dissertation by political scientist Robert Hawkinson that is considerably more comprehensive.[27] Hawkinson grounded his research on the archival documents of the

Johnson Library and hence, unlike the early researchers, could follow the complex process of policy formulation and adoption from the nerve center of the administration. Hawkinson's analysis concentrates on the unusual telescoping of the development of the ESEA: many of the same actors simultaneously worked (1) on externally "selling" interest groups, primarily on the political compromises necessary to resolve the church-state impasse, and (2) on the internal process of specifying in detail the contents of the bill.[28] Hawkinson largely confirms the external descriptions of Eidenberg and Morey and to a lesser extent those of Bailey and Mosher. But the richness of his research lies in his unique documentary analysis of the internal process.

Although Hawkinson does not set out to magnify the importance of the task force in the achievement of the ESEA, his study does, on balance, challenge Kearney's external slot-machine comparison. While recognizing the considerable hand of the task force in four of the five ESEA titles, he agrees with Kearney that Congressman Hugh Carey (D-NY) was the prime mover behind Title II's $300 million program of instructional and library grants to nonpublic as well as public school children (Keppel's negotiated "sweetener" for the Catholics). Unlike Kearney, he gives the task force primary credit for the ESEA's final three titles, although their initially authorized budgets were relatively modest: $75 million for Title III's supplementary education centers, $70 million for Title IV's educational research laboratories, and $17 million for Title V's aid to strengthen state departments of education.[29] As for the crucial $1 billion Title I, it was "only generally anticipated in the task force's proposal for general aid and a suggestion that the aid-to-impacted areas mechanism be examined."[30] Here Hawkinson assigns less credit to the task force than to Commissioner Keppel, to the President and his staff, and to such key congressional entrepreneurs as Senator Wayne Morse (D-Ore) and Congressman Carl Perkins (D-Ky) and their committee staffs.[31] The central question is not how much credit the Gardner task force should receive but how it functioned in a broad network of communications and pressures and how it contributed to the complicated process of policy formulation that led to the ESEA of 1965.[32]

The ESEA of 1965: A Case Study in Policy Adoption

The disagreement over the role of Gardner's 1964 task force is in striking contrast for the broad agreement over the dramatically changed political circumstances of 1964–1965 and the Johnson strategy for the streamlined enactment of the ESEA. President Kennedy's assassination in November 1963 had generated a wave of grief and sympathy that sped the enactment of his originally proposed tax cut, civil rights law, and antipoverty program in the following year. Furthermore, Kennedy's death replaced a Catholic President with a Protestant, and the Civil Rights Act of 1964 submerged longstanding southern objections that the federal aid carrot would bring the civil rights stick—since the stick, in the form of Title VI's ban on racial segregation in federally aided programs, was now in federal hands anyway.[33] Then Goldwater's disastrous campaign and Johnson's powerful coattail effect brought 69 new Democrats into the House, wiping out more than 400 years of Republican seniority in the House and giving the Democrats a margin of 295 to 140 in the House and 68 to 32 in the Senate. The new congressional majority of urban liberals from the North and West greatly strengthened Johnson's leverage in the committees, especially the House Rules Committee, where Kennedy's previous general aid-to-education bill had died in 1961.[34]

Meanwhile Gardner submitted his task force report to the White House in mid-November. The rapid process of transforming its broad recommendations into legislative programs was begun by Francis Keppel and his staff; continued in early December by Douglass Cater and Bill Moyers within the higher echelons of the executive; and finished over Christmas by Johnson, senior aides, and Cabinet officers at the LBJ Ranch. On January 12 Johnson sent the bill and his educational message to Congress, where it was simultaneously introduced by Wayne Morse in the Senate (S. 370) and Carl Perkins in the House (H.R. 2362). On March 26 it passed the House by a roll-call vote of 263 to 153, and on April 9 the Senate approved the House bill by a huge 73 to 18 majority. Two days later the President signed the ESEA (P.L. 89-10) into law in Stonewall, Texas.

In 1976 Douglass Cater told a symposium at the LBJ School of Public Affairs that three great political accommodations cleared the way for the ESEA.[36] The first occurred in 1964, when the civil rights law at least temporarily disarmed the school segregation issue. The second accommodation disarmed the church-state controversy by employing the "child-benefit" theory approved in 1947 by the U.S. Supreme Court in *Everson* v. *Ewing Township* (310 U.S. 1). The Court upheld state expenditures to bus New Jersey parochial school students as a benefit to the individual children, not the schools. This potentially open-ended interpretation displeased Protestant lobbies like the National Council of Churches, however, as much as it pleased the United States Catholic Conference. So a third accommodation was reached: the child-benefit theory would be used to justify only indirect aid to parochial schools to assist in nonreligious instruction. The primary purpose of federal funds was to lift the educational level of poor children, whether in public or private schools.[36]

The Johnson administration linked the ESEA to the politically popular notions of the War on Poverty, impacted-areas aid, and specific categorical programs during a period of economic prosperity. The administration was enjoying a political honeymoon with the whopping liberal Democratic majorities in Congress. And the administration had laid a careful groundwork for the ESEA. These conditions produced a congressional debate that focused not on the hoary three R's of Race, Religion, and Reds, but on the formula for distributing Title I's proposed billion-dollar aid. The resulting political compromise favored urban slum and impoverished rural districts, but by targeting some funds to 90 percent of the nation's school districts and 95 percent of its counties, Title I's distribution formula offered something to virtually everybody.[37] In an astonishing piece of political artistry, observes Eric Goldman, "the Congress had passed a billion-dollar law, deeply affecting a fundamental institution of the nation, in a breath-taking eighty-seven days. The House had approved it with no amendment that mattered; the Senate had voted it through literally without a comma changed."[38] And every penny of it was categorical, not general aid. This represented a fundamental shift in federal education policy—"the abandonment of attempts to pass legislation authorizing general federal aid to elementary and secondary education and the adoption of an approach utilizing a broad range of categorical assistance programs designed to attack specific problems such as the education of economically disadvantaged children."[39]

Task Force Evolution: Outside and Interagency Groups

The extensive case studies of the 1964 Gardner task force and the ESEA of 1965 are instructive, but their narrow concentration has partially obscured the broader question of how federal educational policy was shaped through a series of educational task forces into the program initiatives that are our present legacy.[40] Of the 135 task forces established during the Johnson administration between 1964 and 1969, 17 appear to have figured importantly in federal educational developments. Before turning to them, it is necessary to sketch briefly the essential patterns and life cycle of the task forces, beginning with the 15 set up by Johnson in 1964 under the overall direction of Bill Moyers. Johnson emphasized confidentiality when he explained his task force operation to the cabinet on July 2, 1964: "They will operate without publicity. It is very important that this not become a public operation. The purpose of these task forces is to come up with ideas, not to sell those ideas to the public."[41] Johnson's hostility to the kind of leaking that had plagued the Kennedy task forces was legendary.[42] His insistence was reinforced by leaks to the *New York Times* from economist Joseph Pechman's 1964 Task Force on Inter-Governmental Fiscal Cooperation.[43]

The forty-three initial Johnson task forces were predominantly "outside" groups; i.e., most members worked outside the government. First Moyers and the inherited Kennedy aides and then Califano and his staff aides Fred Bohen, James Gaither, Larry Levinson, and Matthew Nimetz barnstormed university campuses in a series of "academic dinners" designed to identify both promising new ideas and potential task force members. From these visits and from agency submissions as well, Califano and his staff, together with Charles Schultze, Gardner Ackley, Harry McPherson, and Phillip Hughes would review one-page descriptions of the accumulated ideas and compile the most promising into an "idea book." President Johnson would then select those ideas substantive enough to merit outside task force investigation. Task force membership can be illustrated by Gardner's celebrated 1964 task force on education, which consisted of sixteen men (no women), including three university presidents, three professors, two state education officials, two business executives, one foundation president (Carnegie's John Gardner), one mayor, and one magazine editor, plus U.S. Office of Education Commissioner Francis Keppel, William B. Cannon representing the Bureau of the Budget, and Richard Goodwin acting as White House liaison.[44]

Outside task force membership was often even more heavily academic. For instance, the 1966 Task Force on Child Development, which generated unusual excitement and enthusiasm over its extremely optimistic assessment of early-childhood learning potential, was chaired by psychologist Joseph McV. Hunt of the University of Illinois and counted eight academics among its fourteen members. Generally, the blue-ribbon outside task forces were provided with staff and expenses (and glamorous White House entrée), were charged with broad brainstorming responsibilities without regard to political impediments or cost constraints, and were given a full year to report.

When Califano replaced Moyers in July 1965, he began developing the "inside" or interagency form of task force. These working groups tended to be smaller than the outside task forces, with membership consisting entirely of representatives from the government. For instance, the 1965 Task Force on Education was chaired by Commissioner Keppel and consisted only of Keppel, a deputy assistant secretary of the Department of Health, Education, and Welfare, an assistant secretary of the Treasury, William Cannon of the Bureau of the Budget, and White House liaison Douglass Cater. The charges of interagency task forces tended to be much narrower and more specific: to respond to outside task force proposals, to coordinate agency approaches, and to attempt to resolve interagency disputes. They were usually given only three or four months to report and were required to cost out their recommendations through detailed pricing estimates. Both types of task force were customarily formed at the beginning of the fiscal year in July. The outside groups had a year's headstart, allowing the interagency groups to begin reviewing the outside recommendations during the summer and to submit their own recommendations in mid-autumn for review by Califano and his staff, together with representatives from the Bureau of the Budget, the Council of Economic Advisers, and appropriate agency heads. By December President Johnson would select proposals he wished to incorporate into his legislative program, and he would either highlight these in his January state-of-the-union message or subsequently send special messages to the Congress.

Task Force Reports: Education and Government Reorganization

Of the seventeen task forces dealing most directly with major educational developments, nine were outside and eight were interagency. Five dealt with such special educational areas as early childhood, gifted students and international education.[45] Although they bear less centrally on my primary concerns than do the remaining dozen, they remain prime candidates for the kind of intensive case-study analysis that links policy origin with program adoption, implementation, and evaluation—an especially promising example being the relationship between the 1966 Joseph Hunt and William Gorham task forces on early childhood, and the evolution of such preschool projects as Head Start.

Of the other twelve task forces, seven were involved with educational policies and programs in general, and five dealt with broad questions of government organization and reorganization. The most celebrated example of the former group is the Gardner task force. This emphasis is understandable but in one sense unfortunate, for it reflects a dual imbalance in attention and scholarship. Even the extensive research on the Gardner task force has not produced a published study analyzing the internal archival evidence. Worse, the subsequent task forces, which were crucial to the developmental sequence, have been largely ignored. In 1965 Francis Keppel chaired an interagency task force that concentrated on translating the new policy proposals into program implementation; John Gardner himself chaired another in 1966. Also in 1966, the president of the University of North Carolina, William Friday, chaired a high-powered outside task force (including Sidney Marland, John Fischer, Fred Harrington, Edward Levi, Thomas Pettigrew, and William Cannon) that produced an ambitiously comprehensive, 150-page report calling for a "moon shot" for the poor that would double educational appropriations.

Lest interagency task forces be regarded as less important or less interesting than outside task forces or as mere follow-through procedures concerned with implementing strategies rather than substantive policies, consider the 1967 report of the Gardner interagency task force on education. The prologue to this fascinating document constitutes a political analysis of revealing candor and acuity. It pictures a profusion of fragmented federal categorical-aid programs, scattered in an uncoordinated fashion throughout fifteen federal departments and agencies, with the U.S. Office of Education alone operating more than one hundred programs authorized under more than seventy legislative titles. All were chronically underfunded, the report complains, with an excessive proportion of the scarce resources going to support state and local administrative superstructures rather than field operations to maximize classroom impact. While appropriations for ESEA Title I had increased annually, federal funding nevertheless began to fall behind the growth of student populations, providing less aid per child. Contradicting the William Friday task force report of the previous year, the Gardner study recommended more general aid rather than categorical aid.

By 1967, growing frustration over program underfunding reflected the administration's intensifying and inflationary struggle with the competing demands of the Great Society's domestic commitments and the deepening involvement in the Vietnam War. But there were older sources of frustration as well, stemming from the unwieldy structures of the federal government. Over the years a series of big and little Hoover commissions and special task forces had tried to improve government efficiency by reorganizing a bureaucratic structure that had allegedly grown into a labyrinth of rigid and jealously competing departments and agencies preoccupied with boundary maintenance, turf protection, and empire building. Even the more sympathetic post-Weberian students of public administration deplored the historic intractability of such constituency-bound departments as Agriculture, Commerce, Labor, and the Interior.[46]

But the Office of Education, since its birth as an anemic bureau in 1867, had scarcely evolved into such a monster.[47] The Johnson White House, many in the Congress, and Commissioner Keppel saw a different problem: how, in view of the massive new commitments embodied in the ESEA of 1965 and its companion, the Higher Education Act (HEA) of 1965, to transform this statistics-gathering and report-writing staff agency into an efficient, program-operating line organization.[48] To work on the problem, Keppel appointed Henry Loomis of the Voice of America as his deputy, and Johnson appointed an interagency task force on education headed by Dwight Ink, then assistant general manager of the Atomic Agency Commission. In mid-June after only two months of study, the Ink task force recommended a thorough reorganization of the Office of Education by target educational level rather than by function. The subsequent reorganizational blitzkrieg under the iron hand of Loomis was traumatic in the extreme. Bailey and Mosher's study contains a sprightly chapter on the resultant turmoil and anguish in the Office of Education, observing that "the ensuing, if temporary, administrative chaos was shattering."[49]

Interestingly, Bailey himself had served on the 1964 Task Force on Government Reorganization chaired by Donald K. Price, a dean of the Harvard Graduate School of Public Administration who had been counselor to President Kennedy since 1961. This task force had called for a radical restructuring of the executive branch's domestic departments. The Price report had boldly proposed the creation of five new cabinet-level departments: Education, Transportation, Housing and Community Development, Economic Development, and Natural Resources. This plan would have detached the Office of Education from the Department of Health, Education, and Welfare and would have cannibalized much of Commerce, Labor, and the Interior. In 1966 Johnson appointed yet another task force on government organization, this one headed by Ben Heineman, chairman of the Chicago and Northwest Railway and of the President's Council on Civil Rights. The Heineman report stoutly resisted the creation of new clientele-based departments such as Education and Health and called instead for the appointment just below the President of a domestic czar to oversee the cabinet agencies. Through ten consolidated federal regions, the czar would coordinate the Great Society functions currently being performed through the fragmented efforts of the Departments of Health, Education, and Welfare, Labor, and Housing and Urban Development, and the Office of Economic Opportunity. In this grand design, the conglomerate HEW was seen as a model to be built upon, not one to be broken up. *"In many ways HEW is the department of the Great Society,"* the Heineman report concluded. "It administers the majority of Federal social legislation— *old and new. It has the potential to become a superdepartment."*[50]

At this point two caveats are in order. First, this line of inquiry leads intriguingly toward the contemporary departmentalization of Education. Care must be taken, however, not to cheat and look ahead but rather to retain the focus on policy and program development in the political context of the 1960s. The Heineman task force made its controversial recommendations in June 1967, just five months before Gardner issued his pessimistic political analysis from an interagency perspective. The following spring Johnson announced that he would not run for reelection, and that fall Wilbur Cohen's apparently unenthusiastic interagency Task Force on Education was reduced to recommending little more than administrative tinkering and enhanced state roles. That same anticlimactic autumn the interagency Task Force on Higher Education cochaired by Ivan Bennett and Alice Rivlin foreshadowed the battles over higher education and educational research of the early Nixon administration.

Although the formidable innovative programs of the Great Society bear impressive witness to the efficient rhythm of the Johnson administration's policy planning process, it clearly didn't always work that way. Indeed, the evidence suggests a kind of pathological cycle that parallels the flow and ebb of presidential power generally; the glow of early success generates expectations that performance cannot match and enthusiasm cannot sustain. As Johnson's honeymoon eroded under the pressures of domestic violence, the Vietnam War, and inflation, the early euphoria of the Great Society faded, congressional resistance stiffened, and Johnson's popularity plummeted. Innovative outside task forces increasingly gave way to inter-agency groups in which agency resentments festered and competition for scarce resources increased. Seasoned Cabinet officers resented the directives of Califano and his young staff. The evidence implies that HEW Secretaries Gardner and Cohen virtually ignored Califano's later appointments to task force chairmanships and instead chose men like Office of Education Commissioner Harold Howe II as acting chairmen. Wilbur Cohen chaired a 1968 Task Force on Older Americans; according to Harry Cain's dissertation, which analyzed it as a case study under those conditions and at that late date, it not surprisingly fell into the vacuum and was ignored.[51] By 1968 the extraordinary Johnson task forces, like the beleaguered Johnson administration, had pretty well run their course.

Archival Evidence for the 1960s

The second caveat is that although the documents of the seventeen task forces—the reports, idea books, and education subject files—are rich and largely untapped resources, they do not interpret themselves and often raise more questions than they answer. They must be interpreted within the context of the presidential-aide files and associated White House Central Files (WHCF), administrative histories, and oral histories in the Johnson Library. Particularly with presidential-aide files, manuscript and archival research becomes more art than science, with a liberal admixture of good and bad luck. Despite the labors of well-trained archivists to organize the files, documents can surface in the most wondrous and puzzling locations—or not at all. Compared to the Johnson Library, the Kennedy Library holdings on education are modest and the Nixon archives remain closed.[52] Fortunately, in the Johnson Library most internal memoranda and correspondence pertaining to the task force operations are centered in the rather massive files of presidential staff assistant James C. Gaither (138 linear feet). Even more fortunately, the Johnson Library has assembled from the Gaither and other files a general reference task force file. The WHCF files of the senior Johnson aides are similarly substantial: Bill Moyers (91 LF), Lawrence O'Brien (35 LF), Joseph Califano (77 LF), and Douglass Cater (37 LF). The next echelon of aides includes Harry McPherson (26 LF), Fred Bohen (5 LF), Matthew Nimetz (5 LF), and Lee White (2 LF).[53] Many of the Johnson WHCF Confidential Files have been opened for educational research, and the personnel files of John

Macy, chairman of the Civil Service Commission, contain 300 LF on persons considered for appointment between 1961 and 1969, although their classification status varies.

During his tenure as President, Lyndon Johnson directed federal departments and agencies to prepare narrative histories with supporting documents for inclusion in the presidential archives. These sixty-four administrative histories vary widely in volume and quality, ranging from the eighteen volumes and twelve archive boxes on the Department of Health, Education, and Welfare, to a slim report on the Committee on Purchases of Blind-Made Products. Fortunately, the thousand-page history of the U.S. Office of Education is one of the most objective and richest in detail.

Finally, the oral history collections continue to grow. Holdings in the Kennedy Library appear to be modest concerning education and consist mainly of interviews with Wilbur Cohen, Francis Keppel, and Theodore Sorensen. The Johnson Library holdings, however, are quite extensive.[54] Most promising for educational research are interviews with the following: Francis Bator, Ivan Bennett, Joseph Califano, Douglass Cater, Anthony Celebrezze, James Coleman, James Gaither, John Gardner, Samuel Halperin, Ben Heineman, Donald Hornig, Harold Howe, Dwight Ink, Francis Keppel, Harry McPherson, John Macy, Sidney Marland, Matthew Nimetz, David Seeley, and Lee White.[55] Until these archival riches are more seriously researched, we shall have to make do with the external secondary literature. This literature falls roughly into four categories; thus far I have dealt only with the first two, which essentially involve getting the laws on the books.

The Implementation and Evaluation of Education Programs

I earlier surveyed the literature that analyzes (1) educational policy formulation, with emphasis on the task force role and the work of inventors and innovators, and (2) policy adoption, focusing on the passage of the ESEA and the work of brokers and entrepreneurs. Not surprisingly, this literature tends to be highly Washington-centered, and researchers in presidential archives are well advised to caution themselves against the inherent danger of White House myopia. On the other hand, research on (3) program implementation emphasizes the work of public administrators in the agency and in the field; it is implicitly concerned with (4) the evaluation of policy outcomes—with what works or doesn't, in this case ultimately in the classroom. Such assessments are inherently con-

troversial, and because the ESEA contained unprecedented requirements for systematic evaluation, the effectiveness of the Great Society's transformation in federal education policy was early brought
under intense public scrutiny.[56]

Controversy over the evaluation of ESEA-type social programs
that were designed to intervene in the poverty cycle began even before the ESEA was passed. In response to Title IV of the Civil Rights
Act of 1964, which had mandated a report within two years on the
availability of equal educational opportunity, the Office of Education appointed James Coleman of Johns Hopkins University to lead a
mammoth nationwide survey. The resulting "Coleman Report" created a storm of controversy when it was released in the summer of
1966, primarily because Coleman's regression analysis suggested
that, in comparison with family background and socioeconomic factors, "school factors" accounted for only a small fraction of the depressed achievement of minority students.[57] Also in 1965, Commissioner Keppel encouraged Carnegie and Ford Foundation funding for
Ralph W. Tyler's Exploratory Committee on Assessing the Progress
of Education. When the White House Conference on Education was
held in July 1965 under the chairmanship of Carnegie Foundation
President John Gardner, the Tyler committee's national assessment
attracted heated debate among the delegates, with opponents stressing the dangers of monolithic federal control of curriculum.[58] It was
in this volatile climate that Senator Robert Kennedy, who feared
that school administrators would ignore the wishes and interests of
the poor in spending Title I funds, demanded and got inclusion in
the ESEA of a unique provision for systematic evaluation of the program's effectiveness in meeting the "special educational needs of
disadvantaged children."[59]

Senator Kennedy's suspicions were well founded. As early as
1968, Bailey and Mosher concluded that while evaluations of the
impact of the ESEA to date were "largely impressionistic and self-
serving," the "limited, hard evidence that does exist on attempts to
improve the educational performance of low status children by
providing additional money and services is devastatingly pessimistic."[60] In 1972 Joel Berke and Michael Kirst published the report of
the major 1968–1969 Gardner study, funded by the National Urban
Coalition (and hence heavily by the Ford Foundation) and sponsored
by the Maxwell Graduate School of Citizenship and Public Affairs at
Syracuse.[61] This evaluation was based on data from 575 school districts during the ESEA's initial implementation period, 1965–1969,
and the results were depressing in the extreme to the champions of

equity through federal aid. The new infusion of federal aid, Berke and Kirst concluded, was too small in relation to total educational expenditures to have any significant redistributionist impact; school district wealth, not need, continued to determine per-pupil expenditures.[62] The affluent continued to benefit most from the overall school expenditures, and the "religion of localism" still governed. Worse, the urban redistributionist effect of ESEA Title I was countered by the effects of ESEA Titles II (textbooks and libraries) and III (teacher service centers), by NDEA Title III (instructional equipment), and by vocational aid, all of which tended to flow disproportionately toward suburb and countryside. In brief, concludes the report, "the story in general is grossly disappointing."[63]

In 1975 Milbrey Wallin McLaughlin published the Rand Educational Policy Study of the ESEA Title I evaluations from 1965 through 1972.[64] She was testing the hopes of reformers like Robert Kennedy, who viewed mandated evaluation as a means of achieving *political* accountability, and of those like HEW's William Gorham, who sought *management* accountability by applying cost-benefit principles of the Planning-Programming-Budgeting System, a Washington fad associated most notably with Robert McNamara's "whiz kids" in the Pentagon. McLaughlin's major conclusion is that seven years and $52 million worth of evaluation efforts produced dismal failure, an "empty ritual" that "may have done more harm than good." She finds the roots of failure in (1) the multiple and diverse goals of broad-aim social action programs, which are difficult to transform into measurable objectives, and (2) the federal system itself, in that the Office of Education did not really "run" Title I. Rather, 30,000 Local Educational Agencies (LEAs) ran it according to the preferences of entrenched local interests. Their resistance to federal data-collection efforts functioned "to undermine [the educational system] and to demoralize education personnel at all levels."

Norman C. Thomas reaches a similar gloomy conclusion in *Education in National Politics*. A political scientist, Thomas agrees that policy implementation was less exciting than formulation and adoption, but he insists that it was equally important, if not more so:

> Organized interests, especially education clientele groups and the bureaucrats, recognized this as did some members of Congress, most notably Edith Green, and the careerists in the Bureau of the Budget. But the failure of Congress to exercise more careful and exacting oversight, and the inability of the Presi-

dency to mount effective monitoring of the bureaucracy, resulted in a considerable amount of slippage in the achievement of policy objectives once programs had been authorized and funded. Much of this slippage occurred because of the symbiotic relationship that existed within the policy triangles between the agencies, Congressional subcommittees, and clientele groups which [Theodore] Lowi has characterized as "interest group liberalism."[65]

The politics of pluralism was "highly elitist in composition and provided an inhospitable environment for substantial policy changes." It favored defenders of the status quo or at best the cautious custodians of incremental change. The required sequential approvals provided a multiplicity of access points for organized interests to thwart initiatives and frustrate action.

Finally, the emerging scholarly suspicion that after a decade of operation, the ESEA and its associated educational programs had basically failed—as had the bulk of the Great Society's social programs—was reinforced in 1978 by the publication of Julie Roy Jeffrey's *Education for the Children of the Poor.*[66] Jeffrey's ambitious book began as a historical dissertation on the origins and implementation of the ESEA but emerged as a broad-ranging and damaging assessment of the antipoverty war in general and particularly of education as an instrument of social reform and upward mobility—as, in Lyndon Johnson's words, "the only valid passport from poverty." Her bibliographical grasp is extensive, although it does not basically extend beyond 1972. Because her survey is both descriptive and critical, it relieves this essay of the burden of tracing such important storms of controversy in the running educational debate as those that centered on the arguments of James Coleman, Charles Silberman, Arthur Jensen, Christopher Jencks, the Rand report on school effectiveness, and the like.[67] Jeffrey shares with policy analysts McLaughlin and Thomas an indictment of the American polity's systematic resistance to substantive change, and she is highly skeptical of education's—or at least schooling's—leverage on social mobility. As a historian she is keenly attuned to the impact of specific historical events that uniquely characterize the decade during which the Great Society's liberal consensus "disappeared under the strains of the country's frustrating Vietnam involvement, deep divisions within the black community, race riots, and violence."

Summary

Social scientists have dominated research in the important educational developments of the Johnson years to such an extent that historians have been virtually invisible. For such recent history, this is neither surprising nor altogether undesirable. Considering the literature's dominant example of the Gardner task force of 1964 and the passage of the ESEA in 1965, within three years we received five major studies of essentially the same broad series of events, yet redundancies were surprisingly minimal. Kearney compared Gardner's task force report to the ESEA titles, while Meranto looked primarily at the behavior of Congress, constituent groups, and lobbies. Mosher used Bailey's classic case-study technique in her competent dissertation to link policy formulation to agency implementation. Congressional Fellows Eidenberg and Morey concentrated on Capitol Hill.

In addition to being both prompt and prolific, this social scientific research was theoretically informed by the interdisciplinary thrust of the policy sciences—especially, in the late 1960s, in the form of systems analysis. This invites some criticism of intellectual fadism and input-output jargon, but overall the quest for theoretical vigor forced conceptualization beyond mere taxonomy and toward an awareness of continuous, interrelated processes. As for the evidence with which to test the theoretical models, the general openness of the legislative process was reinforced by prompt GPO publication of committee hearings and reports, and the more closed sanctuaries of the executive agencies were probed by mostly anonymous interviews. We quickly learned a great deal from these studies, while the few historians who dared to deal with contemporary events and the fewer still who cared to work in educational affairs were waiting at least a decade for the archives to open.

But what price was paid for the advantages of these early studies? The competitive advantage of speed carries obvious costs, especially in light of the historian's hindsight. For example, Meranto seemed to know next to nothing about the Gardner task force of 1964. Kearney did investigate, but he could barely penetrate the almost paranoid veil of Johnsonian secrecy with his nine elite interviews (his honesty about this is rare and becoming), so he repaired to a rather mechanistic comparison of task force recommendations and ESEA titles in an exercise whose usefulness is greatly dimmed by subsequent research. Bailey and Mosher boldly attempted to assess the administration of a law scarcely two years old, whose titles had only recently been funded and whose implementing agency had been newly and radically reorganized. They thoughtfully listed their forty-eight major interview informants in an appendix but never revealed them in the text, and Eidenberg and Morey's forty interviewees remain altogether anonymous. Clearly, candor in contemporary interviews customarily demands such confidentiality, but historians' training and instincts are otherwise; when they belatedly pursue research and writing, they reveal names responsibly.

Perhaps what I call disadvantages in this type of social science research simply represent historians' preferences. Be that as it may, I submit that what historians lose in lapsed time, they gain in access to internal as well as external evidence, in emphasis on perspective rather than immediacy and book sales, in the use of a holistic approach as opposed to episodic writing and case studies, in construction of a critical narrative rather than a categorical analysis. Still, contemporary history benefits from the power of social scientific analysis, just as social science needs the corrective of historical perspective. Happily, in the past dozen years the ahistorical (indeed at times antihistorical) behaviorism of the 1950s and 1960s has begun to yield to a renewed historical awareness that has deepened social analysis. With regard to education research, this has been most notable in the felicitous reunion of political science and education. Interdisciplinary students of the politics of education perceive that education has historically been political and that the professional legacy of America's Progressive reformers is not immutable.[68] Also, "post-Weberian" students of organizational theory and the politics of bureaucracy can sharply contrast the American democratic experience with Weber's cynical insistence upon the European technocratic tyranny of the bureaucratic careerist. Students of public administration in general and of the politics of education in particular seem increasingly aware that a historical understanding of the uniqueness of the American educational experience is crucial to contemporary policy planning.

Nevertheless, what is needed now that the Johnson presidential archives are open through 1969 is a history well grounded in the increasingly rare and always lonely and expensive enterprise of documentary research. The Johnson Library contains a cornucopia of riches that extend far beyond the standard lures of the Gardner task force of 1964 and the ESEA of 1965. Despite widespread fascination with the secret Johnson task forces among students of the presidency, the 135 task force files and the 64 administrative histories remain virtually untapped. Beyond information on the task forces, the

ESEA, and the reorganization of the Office of Education and the Department of Health, Education, and Welfare, there are data on a swarm of related federal programs that have taken a back seat to the ESEA, including the Higher Education Act of 1965, Educational Professional Development Assistance (EPDA), the two National Endowments, and myriad supportive programs to aid the disadvantaged in education. Of course, much of this has been externally described. But such external-document and internal-interview studies of Congress and agency, law and program, need to be supplemented by the largely missing and explicitly documented perspective of the presidential archives. Only when we have constructed such soundly based history can we enjoy the full luxury of historiographical debate.

Notes

1. Lyndon Baines Johnson, *The Vantage Point: Perspectives of the Presidency 1963–1969* (New York: Holt, Rinehart and Winston, 1971), p. 212. For a typical description of Johnson's reverence for education, see Theodore H. White, *The Making of the President, 1964* (New York: Atheneum, 1964), pp. 418–421.

2. Johnson, *Vantage Point*, p. 206.

3. A useful survey is Sidney W. Tiedt, *The Role of the Federal Government in Education* (New York: Oxford, 1966). Influential in the Kennedy and Johnson administrations was the Brookings Institution analysis of Alice M. Rivlin, *The Role of the Federal Government in Financing Higher Education* (Washington, D.C.: Brookings Institution, 1961). See also Homer D. Babidge, Jr. and Robert M. Rosenweig, *The Federal Interest in Higher Education* (New York: McGraw-Hill, 1962); and Donald R. Warren, *To Enforce Education* (Detroit: Wayne State University Press, 1974).

4. An excellent analytical summary of the evolution of federal aid from the Lanham Act through the Elementary and Secondary Education Act (ESEA) of 1965 is Norman C. Thomas, *Education in National Politics* (New York: McKay, 1975), ch. 2. The Lanham formula for impacted aid in lieu of taxes, which in 1950 was extended through P.L. 81-815 for school construction and through P.L. 81-874 for operating expenses, became highly popular with Congress and public school beneficiaries because it imposed virtually no federal controls, it was easy and inexpensive to administer, and its aid was widely distributed.

5. Historic resistance to general federal aid is reflected in the defeat of the Hoar, Perce, and Burnside bills of the 1870s, the Blair bills of the 1880s, and the Smith-Towner bill of 1919. See Gordon C. Lee, *The Struggle for Federal Aid* (New York: Teachers College, Columbia University Bureau of Publications, 1949); and Anne Gibson Buis, "An Historical Study of the Federal

Government in the Financial Support of Education" (Ph.D. diss., Ohio State University, 1953). An excellent survey of the postwar federal-aid struggle is James L. Sundquist, *Politics and Policy: The Eisenhower, Kennedy, and Johnson Years* (Washington, D.C.: Brookings Institution, 1968), pp. 155–220. On Kennedy's role in education from 1947 to 1963 see William T. O'Hara, ed., *John F. Kennedy on Education* (New York: Teacher's College Press, 1966).

6. Theodore C. Sorensen, *Kennedy* (New York: Harper and Row, 1965), p. 358.

7. See Francis Keppel's valedictory, *The Necessary Revolution in American Education* (New York: Harper and Row, 1966); and U.S., Congress, House, *The Federal Government and Education*, 88th Cong., 1st sess., 1963, no. 159.

8. Arthur M. Schlesinger, Jr., *A Thousand Days: John F. Kennedy in the White House* (Boston: Houghton-Mifflin, 1965), p. 724. For a carefully researched defense of Kennedy's record in civil rights, see Carl M. Brauer, *John F. Kennedy and the Second Reconstruction* (New York: Columbia University Press, 1977).

9. Jim F. Heath, *Decade of Disillusionment: The Kennedy-Johnson Years* (Bloomington: Indiana University Press, 1975), pp. 143–147.

10. Frank J. Munger and Richard F. Fenno, *National Politics and Federal Aid to Education* (Syracuse: Syracuse University Press, 1962). Kennedy's Catholicism heightened his administration's vulnerability to the whiplash legislative veto of the three R's—race, religion and reds (meaning federal control).

11. An essential secondary resource for analysis of political issues and federal government performance during the postwar era is *Congress and the Nation 1945–1964* (Washington, D.C.: Congressional Quarterly, 1965), especially pp. 1195–1224 on education; and *Congress and the Nation 1965–1968* (Washington, D.C.: Congressional Quarterly, 1969), especially pp. 709–733 on education.

12. William E. Leuchtenburg, "The Genesis of the Great Society," *The Reporter* (April 21, 1966), pp. 36–39. See also Adam Yarmolinsky, "Ideas into Programs," *The Public Interest* (Winter 1966), pp. 70–79. Patrick Anderson, *The President's Men* (Garden City, N.Y.: Doubleday, 1968), pp. 334–334, credits Richard Goodwin for pressing the task force ideas on Johnson, and Bill Moyers for organizational brilliance in launching them.

13. *Public Papers of the President of the United States: Lyndon Johnson 1963–64* (Washington: U.S. Government Printing Office, 1965), 1:705. For Johnson's retrospective assessment of the task forces, see *Vantage Point*, pp. 326–28.

14. An invaluable aid to research on the task forces is "Presidential Task Force Operation during the Johnson Administration," an eighteen-page mimeographed guide prepared by Johnson Library archivist Nancy Kegan Smith in June 1978 (Lyndon B. Johnson Library, Austin, Texas). This guide lists the 43 outside and 92 interagency task forces by box numbers, year,

title, chairperson, and reporting date—e.g., box No. 1, 1964 Task Force on Education, chairman John Gardner, reporting date 11/15/64. The Johnson Library lacks reports of backup papers for 3 of the 135 task forces—Sargent Shriver's outside Task Force on the War Against Poverty, 1964; Leonard Mark's interagency Task Force on Educational Television, 1966; and Donald Hornig's interagency Task Force on Networks for Knowledge, 1968.

15. The leading student of the function of task forces in policy formulation is Norman C. Thomas. See Norman C. Thomas and Harold Wolman, "Policy Formulation in the Institutionalized Presidency: The Johnson Task Forces," in *The Presidential Advisory System*, ed. Thomas E. Cronin and Sanford D. Greenberg (New York: Harper and Row, 1969); Norman C. Thomas and Harold Wolman, "The Presidency and Policy Formulation: The Task Force Device," *Public Administration Review* 29 (September/October, 1969): 459–70; Norman C. Thomas, "Presidential Advice and Information: Policy and Program Formulation," *Law and Contemporary Problems* 35 (Summer 1970): 540–72; Thomas E. Cronin and Norman C. Thomas, "Educational Policy Advisors and the Great Society," *Public Policy* (Fall 1970), pp. 659–86; and Norman C. Thomas, "Policy Formulation for Education: The Johnson Administration," *Educational Researcher* 2 (May 1973): 4–8, 17–18. See also Nathan Glazer, "On Task Forcing," *The Public Interest* (Spring 1969): 40–45.

16. Leuchtenburg, "Genesis of the Great Society," p. 38.

17. Two veterans of the Bureau of the Budget have expressed sympathy for the President's bureaucratic problem, but are critical of the task forces: William D. Carey, "Presidential Staffing in the Sixties and Seventies," *Public Administration Review* 29 (September/October 1969): 450–58; and Harold Seidman, *Politics, Position, and Power: the Dynamics of Federal Organization* (New York: Oxford, 1970).

18. Additionally, Wilbur Cohen worked extensively with Theodore Sorensen on the Kennedy education proposals. Texts of the Kennedy task force reports were promptly published in *New Frontiers of the Kennedy Administration* (Washington, D.C.: Public Affairs Press, 1961). Also working with Bill Moyers on the initial Johnson task force operation were presidential aides Myer Feldman, Lee White, Douglass Cater (who joined the staff in May from *The Reporter*), Donald Hornig (from the Office of Science and Technology), and Francis Bator (of the Council of Economic Advisers). Especially revealing on tensions between aides and cabinet and on the task force device as a source of leverage are "The White House Staff vs. the Cabinet: Hugh Sidey Interviews Bill Moyers," *Washington Monthly* (February 1969), pp. 2–9, 78–80; and the Joseph Califano Oral History Interview with Robert Hawkinson, Lyndon B. Johnson Library, Austin, Texas.

19. Harry P. Cain, "Confidential Task Forces: A Case Study in National Policy-Making" (Ph.D. diss., Brandeis University, 1974) is an able analysis of task force operations, although its case study concerns Wilbur Cohen's largely ineffective 1968 Task Force on Older Americans.

20. Two notable exceptions in recent educational research are Richard A. Dershimer's *The Federal Government and Education R & D* (Lexington, Mass.: Heath, 1976), which makes good use of the Johnson papers; and Robert E. Hawkinson's "Presidential Program Formulation in Education: Lyndon Johnson and the 89th Congress" (Ph.D. diss., University of Chicago, 1977). Hawkinson concentrates on the ESEA case study of 1965 and 1966 and is mainly concerned with constructing and testing models of "presidential legislative agenda formulation." His superior work clearly merits publication.

21. Leuchtenburg, "Genesis of the Great Society," p. 38. When the education papers were opened in the Johnson Library in 1972, Wilbur J. Cohen delivered a refreshingly substantive address placing the Gardner task force in context. See Cohen, "Education Legislation, 1963–68, from Various Vantage Points," in *Educating a Nation: The Changing American Commitment*, ed. Kenneth W. Tolo (University of Texas at Austin: Lyndon B. Johnson School of Public Affairs, 1973), pp. 24–39.

22. Philip Meranto, *The Politics of Federal Aid to Education* (Syracuse: Syracuse University Press, 1967).

23. Philip Kearney, "The 1964 Presidential Task Force on Education and the ESEA of 1965" (Ph.D. diss., University of Chicago, 1967), pp. 277–283.

24. Edith Kern Mosher, "The Origins, Enactment, and Implementation of the Elementary and Secondary Education Act of 1965: A Study of Emergent National Policy" (Ph.D. diss., University of California at Berkeley, 1967). The Kearney and Mosher dissertations were for educational doctorates and are generally of high quality. The ESEA was a popular topic among education graduate students in the late 1960s, but none of the dozen other theses and dissertations I have read merit mention here.

25. Stephen K. Bailey and Edith Kern Mosher, *ESEA: The Office of Education Administers a Law* (Syracuse: Syracuse University Press, 1968). While the Bailey-Mosher interviewees are not identified in the footnotes "to protect the confidentiality of sources," they are listed alphabetically in Appendix E.

26. Eugene Eidenberg and Roy Morey, *An Act of Congress* (New York: W. W. Norton, 1969). Eidenberg and Morey were participant-observers as congressional fellows of the American Political Science Association during the passage of the ESEA. Their book contains reference footnotes and a 1½ page note on sources but no general bibliography, and their forty interviewees remain unnamed.

27. Hawkinson, "Presidential Program Formulation in Education."

28. Crucial in this effort were Francis Keppel, Wilbur Cohen, Douglass Cater, and the lesser known William Cannon, who as executive secretary of the task force and as chief of the Education, Manpower, and Science Division of the Bureau of the Budget supervised the evaluation and costing out of the proposals. See Hawkinson, "Presidential Program Formulation in Ed-

ucation," pp. 95–119. The task force itself, according to Hawkinson, tended to be dominated by Gardner, Keppel, and Cannon.

29. Title V was proposed by task force member James Allen, Commissioner of Education for New York, but was most powerfully pushed by Keppel both as a task force member and as a spokesman for Office of Education interests who wanted strengthened state help in administering the program. Keppel was also the key to negotiating Title II, which the task force report ignored. His dual roles underline the conscious overlapping of Johnson's task force representation.

30. Hawkinson, "Presidential Program Formulation in Education," p. 103.

31. Wilbur Cohen claims primary credit for the antipoverty pupil aid formula that eventually resolved the church-state controversy. See the transcripts of the Wilbur J. Cohen Oral History Interview, tape 4, pp. 13–17, Johnson Library.

32. The intriguing Johnsonian secrecy with its implicit flattery and self-attention may tempt academics to inflate the importance of the task forces, much as it clearly prompted irritated officials in the line agencies to downgrade task force efforts. For a somewhat cynical inside view of the academic role in the task forces, see Harry McPherson, A Political Education (Boston: Little, Brown, 1972), pp. 292–296. More generous is Joseph A. Califano, Jr., A Presidential Nation (New York: Norton, 1975), p. 239; and the Califano Oral History Interview with Robert Hawkinson, Johnson Library. For keen academic receptivity to the task forces, see Bertram M. Gross, ed., A Great Society! (New York: Basic Books, 1968).

33. See Gary Orfield, The Reconstruction of Southern Education: The Schools and the 1964 Civil Rights Act (New York: Wiley-Interscience, 1969). Even so, in the final House vote on the ESEA, fifty-four of the fifty-seven Democrats voting against the bill were Southerners, as were fifteen of the seventeen Republicans, and the only opposing Democratic votes in the Senate were from the South. In 1966, after a bitter battle, Congress approved antibusing language that attempted to prohibit the assignment or transportation of students or teachers to overcome racial balance. The Department of Health, Education, and Welfare's subsequent use of federal school aid to achieve desegregation is well known.

34. Eidenberg and Morey, Act of Congress, ch. 3.

35. Douglass Cater, "The Political Struggle for Equality of Educational Opportunity," in Toward New Human Rights: The Social Policies of the Kennedy and Johnson Administrations, ed. David C. Warner (Austin, Texas: Lyndon B. Johnson School of Public Affairs, 1977), pp. 325–340.

36. Dean N. Kelley and George R. LaNoue, "The Church-State Settlement in The Federal Aid to Education Act," Religion and the Public Order, 1965 (Chicago: University of Chicago Press, 1966), pp. 110–160. The Eighty-ninth Congress contained the first Roman Catholic plurality in the House—107 Catholics compared to 88 Methodists (the largest Protestant bloc).

37. Thomas, Education, pp. 29–30; Eidenberg and Morey, Act of Con-

gress, pp. 96–168; Bailey and Mosher, *ESEA*, pp. 37–71; Cater, "Political Struggle," p. 333.

38. Eric F. Goldman, *The Tragedy of Lyndon Johnson* (New York: Knopf, 1969), p. 307. Johnson had been solicitous of Wilbur Mills and flexible toward House bargaining on the medicare bill, but he was determined to ram the ESEA through Congress without delay, and Morse was determined to avoid a conference committee by deflecting all Senate attempts to amend the House bill.

39. Thomas, *Education*, p. 28. Thomas gives substantial credit for this shift, and especially for the innovative programs in the ESEA, to the 1964 Gardner task force.

40. A superior model of the illumination that historical analysis can cast on federal policy planning, although it is not based primarily on archival research, is Otis L. Graham, Jr., *Toward a Planned Society: From Franklin D. Roosevelt to Richard Nixon* (New York: Oxford, 1975). See especially ch. 4, "The Democrats, 1961–1969," pp. 126–187.

41. Cabinet remarks of President Johnson, July 2, 1964, p. 3, Legislative Background—Four Year Farm Program, Foundation for Action folder, box 1, Johnson Library.

42. James Gaither, "Policy Formulation," p. 5, box 300, Johnson Library.

43. Joseph A. Pechman Oral History Interview, pp. 14–15, Johnson Library.

44. Johnson repeatedly admonished his aides not to overrely on the Ivy League and the Berkeley-Stanford-UCLA axis. See the Joseph Califano Oral History Interview, Johnson Library; McPherson, *A Political Education*, pp. 292–296.

45. These were Dean Rusk's Task Force on International Education (1965), Joseph Hunt's Task Force on Early Childhood Development (1966), Champion Ward's Task Force on Gifted Persons (1966), Paul Miller's Task Force on Urban Educational Opportunities (1966)—all outside task forces, and William Gorham's interagency Task Force on Child Development (1967).

46. A balanced analysis is Francis E. Rourke, *Bureaucracy, Politics, and Public Policy* (Boston: Little, Brown, 1969).

47. For a sympathetic but critical study, see Warren, *To Enforce Education*.

48. For the critical literature on the historic inadequacies of the U.S. Office of Education, see Bailey and Mosher, *ESEA*, p. 19, footnote 28; Warren, *To Enforce Education*, ch. 7; and the refreshingly candid self-assessment contained in the introduction to the Department of Health, Education, and Welfare, *Administrative History*, vol. 1, Part 4, pp. iii–ix, Johnson Library.

49. Bailey and Mosher, *ESEA*, ch. 3, pp. 72–97.

50. President's Task Force on Government Organization, *Final Report*, 17, box 4, Johnson Library. In addition to Heineman, this weighty group in-

cluded McGeorge Bundy, William Capron, Hale Champion, Kermit Gordon, Herbert Kaufman, Richard Lee, Bayless Manning, Robert McNamara, Harry Ransom, and Charles Schultze.

51. Cain, "Confidential Task Forces." Although the Johnson Library was opened in 1972, Cain based his social work dissertation primarily on published reports, the secondary literature, and twenty-nine interviews. Cain's analysis of a failed task force is especially provocative in its speculation about the causes for the erosion of momentum and effectiveness toward the end of the Johnson administration. It is instructive to note that of the 135 Johnson task forces, only 2 have received serious case-study analysis.

52. The subject file on education of the John F. Kennedy Library in Boston contains only 2 linear feet. Compared to the Johnson Library aide files, a distressing proportion of the Kennedy White House Staff Files (WHSF) and the collections of personal papers remain either "closed" or "closed pending review," and their linear footage appears quite small. Most promising are Myer Feldman (14 LF), Lawrence O'Brien (13 LF), and Lee White (10 LF) in the WHSF; and Theodore Sorensen (45 LF) in the collection of personal papers. The 1978 catalog of historical materials in the Kennedy Library lists the papers of both Richard Goodwin and Francis Keppel as closed. The papers of the Nixon administration remain closed in the National Archives in Washington, D.C. until protracted litigation clarifies their status. Furthermore, the Presidential Recordings and Materials Preservation Act of 1974 requires that the Office of Presidential Libraries reverse precedent by opening the controversial papers first, such as those of H. Robert Haldeman and John D. Erlichman. A generous estimate, then, is that the Nixon education papers—wherever they may be—will not be opened sooner than 1986. A superior insider's view of the important educational developments during the Nixon administration is Chester E. Finn, Jr., *Education and the Presidency* (Lexington, Mass.: Heath, 1977). See also Lawrence E. Gladieux and Thomas R. Wolanin, *Congress and the Colleges* (Lexington, Mass.: Heath, 1976), for an analysis of the politics of higher education during the Nixon years.

53. A curiosity of the Johnson Library's presidential aide files is the disparity between Johnson's pervasive presence as the central point of reference and the infrequency with which he speaks directly through the documents, either through his own directives or through notations on the memoranda and queries of his aides. This lacuna partially reflects the general trend toward oral and electronic communications that hampers the work of contemporary historians and makes oral history increasingly important. But it also reflects an idiosyncrasy of Johnson's decision-making process—which Wilbur Cohen referred to as a "triangular" mode. Johnson would rarely respond directly to an aide's memorandum of policy recommendation by checking either "I agree" or "I disagree." Rather, he would seek out a third opinion and respond to the aide later, or sometimes not at all. This practice of delay and indirection in making strategic decisions, which was

often so frustrating to Johnson's aides, contrasted sharply with his equally characteristic tendency to make tactical and personnel decisions with rapid-fire finality.

54. The Johnson Library listed 947 transcribed oral history interviews as of January 1980. For a personal interpretation by a historian centrally involved in directing the Johnson interviews, see Joe B. Frantz, "Opening a Curtain: The Metamorphosis of Lyndon B. Johnson," *Journal of Southern History* 45 (February 1979): 3–26.

55. The Joseph Califano Oral History Interview with Robert Hawkinson in the Johnson Library is excellent on the task forces, but Califano has not submitted to an interview on anything else nor has Bill Moyers or Richard Goodwin. Presidential libraries hold oral histories in varying degrees of restriction. Most, however, are open and available on interlibrary loan. The libraries provide names and addresses of interviewees from whom written permission is required.

56. In addition to the ESEA, the Great Society included such major educational innovations as the Higher Education Act (HEA) of 1965, which authorized federal scholarships and loans for undergraduate students for the first time and established the National Teacher Corps. HEA also transferred the antipoverty war's work-study and Upward Bound programs to the Office of Education and aided teacher training, cooperative education, and "developing institutions." By 1969 the Johnson legacy in education also included programs for the physically and mentally handicapped, bilingual education, school dropout prevention, Head Start, Follow Through, adult education, an expanded National Science Foundation, and National Endowments for the Arts and the Humanities. But none of these important developments was as dramatic as the ESEA and, not surprisingly, none has attracted as much scholarly analysis.

57. James S. Coleman et al., *Equality of Educational Opportunity* (Washington, D.C.: U.S. Government Printing Office, 1966). A reanalysis of the Coleman data conducted at Harvard corrected many alleged errors but generally sustained Coleman's main conclusion. See Frederick Mosteller and Daniel P. Moynihan, eds., *On Equality of Educational Opportunity: Papers Deriving from the Harvard Faculty Seminar on the Coleman Report* (New York: Random House, 1972); and Gerald Grant's review of the Harvard restudy in *Harvard Educational Review* 42 (February 1972): 109–125.

58. Martin T. Katyman and Roland S. Rosen, "The Science and Politics of the National Assessment," *The Record* 71 (1971): 571–586.

59. Samuel Halperin, "ESEA: Five Years Later," in *Congressional Record*, U.S., Congress, House, September 9, 1970, pp. 8492–8494.

60. Bailey and Mosher, *ESEA*, p. 222. The evidence they cite in footnote 16, all from 1967, includes the critical study *Racial Isolation in the Public Schools* (Washington, D.C.: U.S. Commission on Civil Rights, 1967).

61. Joel S. Berke and Michael W. Kirst, *Federal Aid to Education* (Lexington, Mass.: Heath, 1972).

62. Federal aid averaged 8 percent of per-pupil expenditure in the sam-

ple districts, with local taxes accounting for approximately half and state equalization-formula aid for the remainder.

63. Berke and Kirst, *Federal Aid*, p. 45.

64. Milbrey Wallin McLaughlin, *Evaluation and Reform: The Elementary and Secondary Education Act of 1965, Title I* (Cambridge, Mass.: Ballinger, 1975).

65. Thomas, *Education*, p. 230. The reference to Theodore Lowi was to his *The End of Liberalism* (New York: Norton, 1969).

66. Julie Roy Jeffrey, *Education for the Children of the Poor: A Study of the Origins and Implementation of the Elementary and Secondary Education Act of 1965* (Columbus: Ohio State University Press, 1976). For a defense of the goals and achievements of the Great Society (but not of its inflated expectations and naïveté), see Sar Levitan and Robert Taggart, *The Promise of Greatness* (Cambridge, Mass.: Harvard University Press, 1976), ch. 6.

67. For a sampler of these debates, see Donald M. Levine and Mary Jo Bane, *The "Inequality" Controversy: Schooling and Distributive Justice* (New York: Basic Books, 1975). For an excellent critical assessment of the role of social science and social scientists in both the construction and the subsequent criticism of the Great Society, see Henry J. Aaron, *Politics and the Professors: The Great Society in Perspective* (Washington, D.C.: Brookings Institution, 1978), especially ch. 3 on education.

68. See for example the politics-of-education credo in Frederick M. Wirt and Michael W. Kirst, *The Political Web of American Schools* (Boston: Little, Brown, and Co., 1972); and Michael W. Kirst, *State, School, and Politics: Research Directions* (Lexington, Mass.: Heath, 1972).

Part 3 | The White House

6 | Johnson and the White House Staff

by Larry Berman

IN JANUARY 1971 THE *New York Times Magazine* featured an article by John Roche entitled "The Jigsaw Puzzle of History," in which the former special assistant to President Johnson argued that no "historically valid" treatment of the Johnson presidency would emerge for at least another decade. The problem, in Roche's view, was the current unavailability of primary-source documentation as a data base for rigorous empirical analysis. Many participant-observer accounts which purportedly depicted life within the walls of the White House were actually little more than "disguised autobiography and/or therapy."[1] Roche was particularly disdainful of reports which reduced the performance of Johnson's White House staff to a variant of "Caligula's Court."[2] Moreover the stereotyped picture of Johnson berating his younger aides, surrounding himself with adoring sycophants, demanding loyalty of the Macy's window variety, and forcing consensus rather than debate among his advisers dramatically oversimplified the advising process. According to Roche, "This is the crux of the matter for the historian—not only was there verbal argument, respectful but nonetheless sharp, but there were pieces of paper: 'Secret–Eyes Only' memos to the President from his staff. There were full transcriptions of various crucial meetings. Each of us has a set of our memos, but only the presidential archives in Austin contain the whole range . . . The net result is that most White House 'revelations' would be thrown out of a court of law in about thirty seconds; they simply lack any probative substance."[3] Henceforth, objective analysis of the Johnson presidency would have to be intricately linked with archival documentation from the Johnson Library. Then, and only then, could we "poor souls," as Roche called us, "try to put the jigsaw [puzzle] together when all the precincts reported."[4]

While all of these empirical precincts may never report, students of the Johnson presidency must certainly be prepared to undertake the type of "historically valid" analysis demanded by Roche. The purpose of this essay is to illustrate how systematic archival research in the Johnson Library can yield detailed knowledge on the functioning of the Johnson presidency, especially in the areas of White House staffing and political campaigns. I perceive my task as somewhat akin to that of a guide in a national park—leading my readers through part of the landscape, and identifying key relationships, personalities, and trends. I offer a basic map of the terrain, but explorers know that real knowledge of the environment occurs as one leaves the tourist trail of "basics" for the forest of deeper research. In charting this course for future researchers, I will interweave bibliographical materials with an analysis of available archival documentation.[5]

White House Staffing: Perception vs. Evidence

The lack of original empirical research on the presidency has resulted in a situation where, according to Professor Hugh Heclo, there is "remarkably little substantiated information on how the modern office of the President actually works."[6] The area of presidential advising is a case in point. All of us would agree that president-adviser relations constitute an integral component of the presidential decision-making process. How a President seeks advice, how expert knowledge is used, how advisers are recruited for specific or general-role tasks, the motivation of advisers, and the modes of interaction are key factors in determining the success or failure of a presidency.

Yet, as an area for systematic inquiry, presidential advising is a rather nebulous subject.[7] While all Presidents seek good advice, no two go about it the same way. The literature abounds with truisms, beginning with the "most true" observation that a President's personal style accounts for most of the variation in use of staff. Most purported analyses of White House staffing during the Johnson administration, for example, concentrate on the impact of Johnson's personality on the quality of advice received. The most commonly evoked comparison is between a too scared, too young, too Texan Johnson staff and a Kennedy band of enterprising brothers whose Irish descendancy provided more formidable attributes than the Texas inheritance. It is difficult to find a historian or political scientist who rates Johnson's use of White House staff over Kennedy's. Yet such perceptions rest not so much on the actual performance of each staff as on the shadow which presidential personality or style casts over the surface level of staff operations. I believe Lyndon Johnson's personality dominated his administration to such a degree that political scientists have reduced analysis of White House advising to the impact of his personality on the process itself—grossly over-simplifying the complex and highly interdependent variables of presidential advising. In this essay I want to show how materials from the Johnson Library can be used to study the advising process rather than Johnson's personality.[8]

In mid-1965 Harry C. McPherson, special counsel to the President, wrote to President Johnson about a significant problem confronting the White House staff (to illustrate the richness of the data, I will quote extensively from this and several subsequent memoranda relating to the staff's "image" problem):

> You said you wanted us to (1) praise each other to outsiders and (2) have a passion for anonymity. I realize these are not absolutely incompatible, and they are attributes every strong President has desired in his staff. But coupled with the power and dominance of your personality the prescription does not appear to welcome the emergence of your staff as a distinguished collection of individuals. The public, if it thinks of us at all, thinks of docile calves hustling around at the will of a singular bull. . . .
>
> There was a mystique about the Kennedy staff, that it was a free-swinging, free spirited collection of brilliant and independent intellects; each man became a personality, and oh what a good time they had running the government. On the other hand, we are rather bright, nice young men who lost our independence of mind the day we signed on. It wasn't true about the Kennedy staff, and it's not true about us, but it is a myth that dies hard.[9]

Less than a year later, McPherson was still troubled by outside perceptions of the staff's image; he wrote to Press Secretary Bill Moyers that "the press considers us humorless. The press believes the President is unable to laugh at himself, and that his staff is too frightened to laugh at anything that goes on around the White House. The press believes we lack 'gaiety,' and are a bunch of drones who are afraid ever to step out of line. We don't go to lunch; we don't play touch football or softball; we just work. Our only relaxation is complaining about the hours." McPherson added that such perceptions were "directly related to the image of the Kennedy staff —young, vibrant, light-hearted, Finding Government Fun." McPherson believed that the solution involved changing the perceptions held by the press—"a cynical crowd who had rather destroy a stuffed shirt than eat."[10]

Then in February 1967, Alan Otten reported in the *Wall Street Journal* on the "degeneration in the quality of advice [Johnson] was getting from within his official family." The departure of such "brilliant and independent-minded advisors" as George Ball, McGeorge Bundy, and Bill Moyers left the President with a new group "not quite as sharp or as willing to argue." Otten observed that most of the top staff were tired, overworked, and stretched thin by their boss. What Johnson needed were aides with "judgement and independence, a willingness to ask questions and argue."[11] (McPherson would later tell Otten that he had lost all objectivity in reporting White House activities.)[12]

The Otten article prompted McPherson to send Press Secretary George Christian "two recommendations for stiffening the sycophantic spines of our staff and improving its image in the public prints":

1. Stage a fist-fight between the staff and the President with full Rose Garden TV coverage. Special Assistants should background the columnists on the tactics they intend to use. The President's military aides, Cross and Robinson, together with Chief Rowley, can be expected to fight on his side. During the one-month training period preceding the fight, Watson, Jacobsen, Kintner, Rostow, and Califano will give up smoking cigarettes, Cater and McPherson cigars. Smoking is fatiguing, and as Otten says, the staff is fatigued enough as it is.

2. Ask several former staff assistants to President Kennedy to come in and instruct our men on how to fight against a President. O'Donnell, Sorensen, Schlesinger, and Powers should describe their many vituperative encounters with President Kennedy, particularly during and after the Bay of Pigs affair. Their example should serve to strengthen our will, and give us a better understanding of the ways in which independent-minded assertive assistants can promote the national interest by standing their ground against the temporary occupant of the White House.[13]

How did these perceptions of Johnson's staff arise? Lyndon Johnson was not (despite his assertions to the contrary) an innocent victim of the magic word. Nowhere were Johnson's weaknesses more apparent than in his relationship with the press. Douglass Cater notes that "this was a man who in the legislative experience had found total mastery of the communication system in a confined environment of Congress was essential to the kind of job he was capable of doing. When he got to the presidential level, it was no longer possible."[14] Johnson tried to control the flow of information both to and from the White House—an operating principle which permeated virtually all functional staff responsibilities. He often insisted that important announcements originate from the White House, not the departments. Johnson's subsequent refusal to use Cabinet officers as lightning rods meant that the President, not his staff, caught flack on many issues. From a staffing perspective this approach had serious flaws. Bob Hardesty wrote to Robert Kintner that while "the President is fond of saying that you never hear of a Harold Ickes and Harry Hopkins fist-fighting in the Rose Garden in *this* Administration . . . you never hear of an Ickes or Hopkins taking the *heat* off of the President, either. It seems to me that the President needs some lightning rods in his cabinet: men to do some of the dirty work, and men to share some of the blame when things go wrong."[15] Tom Johnson similarly informed the President, "It is my view that you have become so closely associated with all the major issues which face this country that you are suffering from it . . . I believe a better course would be to have your decisions and feeling on a particular matter voiced through the Cabinet and through the agency heads who are most directly concerned with the issue. Let them shoulder more of the burden for the faults of their programs. Rather than the President losing popularity for weaknesses, it seems more appropriate for the department head to receive the criticism."[16]

An illustration of Johnson's need to control information was his explicit insistence that staff members talk to the press only when instructed by the press secretary. George Christian, then press secretary, recalls that the President "did not like for a fellow who wasn't the press secretary to be saying much to the press—saying anything to the press for that matter—unless the press secretary asked him to do it or unless he asked him to do it."[17] In December 1968, for example, Joseph Califano wrote to President Johnson that he and Larry Levinson had just met with journalist Joseph Kraft to discuss new issues facing Congress, especially Medicare-Medicaid and tax credits for social programs. Johnson was furious and wrote at the bottom of the memorandum: "Joe—may I *again*—*again* ask you and *all* your *associates* to please meet with press members during your association with my administration upon request of Press Secretary Christian only. This request has been made before and will not be made again."[18]

When Robert Kintner informed Johnson that Robert Donovan,

chief correspondent for the Los Angeles *Times*, wanted an interview, Johnson wrote across the memorandum: "No. I don't trust him or the Times."[19] When Hugh Sidey requested an interview with White House staff member Ben Wattenberg on "The White House Staff after Moyers," Johnson, in writing, urged Wattenberg to *"measure each word."*[20] When Harry McPherson informed Johnson that journalist Tony Lewis had called from London to congratulate Johnson on selecting Arthur Goldberg for the Supreme Court and to recommend either Paul Freund or Burke Marshall to succeed Goldberg, Johnson wrote at the bottom of the memorandum: "I don't think correspondents ought to be advocates, lest it interfere with their 1st amendment objectivity."[21]

Reporters were shunned as if they carried bubonic plague, shown minimum respect, and told nothing unless authorized by the President. Following a presidential reprimand, for example, Douglass Cater wrote to Johnson, "My policy in dealing with reporters has been as follows: When called upon by them, to treat them courteously but tell them nothing (pursuant to your instructions). Those known to be treacherous, I give a swift brush-off. Many of my former colleagues I avoid altogether. Those whom I consider reliable, I have provided a minimal amount of backgrounding on subjects I judged to be within your guidelines." The memorandum concluded that henceforth Cater would "see and talk to no reporters unless specifically requested by you or Moyers. This will make my job a great deal easier but *I respectfully suggest that it will contribute to making the press stories about you and your Administration a great deal more snide.* Needless to say, if at any time you have reason to doubt either my credibility or my judgment, I would like to make my departure as swift and silent as possible."[22]

When Drew Pearson called the White House to find out why Johnson had not kept his promise to see Henry Nennen of the German magazine *Stern* (a strong supporter of the President), Johnson wrote to Kintner, referring to Pearson, "He's lying. Bill Moyers told him earlier that I wasn't prepared to do this now but that we would keep it under advisement. You tell him now that I'm not going to do it. I'm not in the business of selling interviews."[23]

The record also shows that Johnson believed his failing popularity resulted from a mishandling of information by his press secretaries. In a December 1968 interview with Helen Thomas, Johnson implied that "some of his early press secretaries were responsible for the credibility gap."[24] This remark prompted George Reedy to write Johnson that "a couple of people have told me that they thought you were referring to me." Johnson scribbled a message across the memorandum: "Last man in world would be him and he knows it."[25] (Johnson had, however, already asked Fred Panzer to prepare a detailed study of presidential popularity ratings under Reedy and Moyers.)[26]

Many former White House members blame Bill Moyers for the credibility gap. Moyers, according to Jake Jacobsen, answered too many questions and never said "I don't know . . . Whether it was the President's answer or him, you never did know that."[27] Johnson's first press secretary, George Reedy, also blames Moyers (for understandable reasons): "It was no accident that the President's popularity started to fall abruptly as soon as Bill took over . . . What Bill did was pin responsibility upon the President in private conversations with the press. Of course, he disliked the President intensely and he had for many years, and made no secret about it from anybody but the President. And since Bill was never overly scrupulous about the truth, the phrase credibility gap I think was attached to the operations of this administration."[28] Johnson's last press secretary, George Christian, believed that "many members of the press, in retrospect, thought that Bill [Moyers] went beyond what the President's policies or thinking were on certain subjects—that sometimes it was Moyers' thinking rather than the President's . . . Now in Bill's conversations with reporters, his overview of the situation might conform to the President's and might not, frankly."[29]

Following Walter Lippmann's credibility-gap series in March 1967, that journalist and former friend of Lyndon Johnson became a personal target of the administration. Fred Panzer wrote to the President that Lippmann had supported Alfred Landon in 1936, Thomas Dewey in 1948, and Dwight D. Eisenhower in 1952. Panzer attached a "catalogue of Lippmannisms" which sought to discredit Lippmann: "Granted that nobody is perfect, granted that consistency is the Hobgoblin of little minds, a review of some of Lippmann's shifting statements puts one in the mind of Dryden's 'man's so various that he seemed to be not one, but all mankind's epitome.' During his half century or so of political punditry, he has made statements that lead one to ask: 'Will the real Walter Lippmann please stand up?'"[30]

As Senator William Fulbright increased his vocal opposition to the war, the Johnson staff was instructed to research all "contacts" between Johnson and the senator. The staff found 119 such contacts as of July 22, 1966, including 6 private visits, 27 telephone conversations (21 initiated by the President), 3 trips with the President, 16 congressional leadership meetings, 4 ceremonies, 18 group meetings, 12 dinners, 12 luncheons, 11 receptions, 8 informal social meetings (swim and lunch, family dinners) and 2 boat rides. When Fulbright, chairman of the Senate Committee on Foreign Relations, demanded televised hearings on the capture of the *Pueblo* (and the conduct of American foreign policy in general), Johnson had his staff dig up a 1961 article in which the senator argued that presidential power in foreign affairs was too constricted by congressional power. Johnson thought the effort so good that he instructed McPherson to "make copies for Rusk, Clifford, McNamara, McGeorge [Bundy], et al."[31]

The preceding material suggests that Lyndon Johnson's personal style may have influenced outside perceptions of staff performance as well as role expectations of staff members. Johnson's preoccupation with secrecy, his need for controlling information both to and from the White House, his failure to schedule regular press conferences, his extreme sensitivity and tendency to overreact to written criticism, and his tight rein on the White House staff—all contributed to negative perceptions of what people were doing in the White House. Moreover, some of the most significant White House staff responsibilities have escaped analysis precisely because of Johnson's operating style.

One of the general difficulties in analyzing White House staffing patterns is that President Johnson constantly shifted assignments and preferred his special assistants to be generalists rather than specialists. In May 1966, for example, Johnson asked Robert Kintner, Cabinet secretary and White House special assistant, to develop an organization chart of the White House. Kintner sought the advice of a more seasoned special assistant, Bill Moyers, who warned Kintner that "advising the President of the United States is an intangible assignment, and thus sometimes a frustrating one . . . It will take time for you to adjust to the completely different environment of the White House, to the nebulous state of affairs here, to the personality of the President, to the other advisors, to the bureaucracy, to the pace of everything in this *unnatural world*."[32] Moyers then explained to Kintner that in the Johnson White House, an organization chart "is a gross misuse of a good man's time; nothing useful can come from it since the White House staff reflects the personal needs of the President rather than a structural design. If there is a design, it is radial—like the spokes of a wheel radiating out from the hub . . . In his own mind the President knows what each man does; he doesn't need an organization chart to show him. In our minds, we know what the President expects of us; a chart is irrelevant." [33]

Irrelevant or not, Bill Moyers, Marvin Watson, Jack Valenti, and Joseph Califano all tried their hands at drawing an organization chart. And in August 1966 John Macy, chairman of the Civil Service Commission, compiled a confidential catalog of functional "White House Staff Assignments." [34] Macy's list included job descriptions for such well-publicized aides as Bill Moyers, Joseph Califano, Harry McPherson, Walt Rostow, Douglass Cater, Marvin Watson, Jake Jacobsen, and Robert Komer. One name on the list, Robert Kintner, stands out because Kintner was identified as Cabinet secretary, chairman of White House staff meetings, principal liaison with Cabinet officers and agency heads, and assistant to the President on special projects. To the uninformed observer this sounds impressive; the informed analyst can only wonder who this man was. The answer serves to illustrate, I believe, both the usefulness and the complexity of archival materials.

Robert Kintner, a former Washington columnist, later president of ABC and NBC, and a close personal friend of Lyndon Johnson, joined the administration in March 1966 as secretary of the Cabinet and special assistant to the President. [35] Kintner was expected to advise the President on top-level presidential appointments, cultivate media contacts, formulate election strategies for 1966, and help improve the President's image. In a rare interview with Kintner after his appointment, journalist Catherine Mackin wrote, "At 56, Kintner is the oldest of the White House Special Assistants and has a warm friendship with the President that pre-dates Mr. Johnson's election to Congress in 1937. Furthermore, he is probably better geared psychologically to serve the President than any member of the White House inner circle . . . He has no political ambition, no need for money and no desire for publicity. If asked, he will say his ambition is only to be of help to the President." [36]

There are few references to Kintner in the secondary literature. Eric Goldman writes that after deciding to resign, he sought Kintner's advice because Kintner was "a long-time friend of the President's with no ambitions within the White House. Kintner, I felt, would give me answers I could trust." [37] In his oral history, however, John Roche recalls:

> When I arrived in the White House there was a guy sitting in the basement in the corner room whom I took to be the White

House bookmaker. His name was Kintner, and he sort of sat in there. I figured he was taking bets. I didn't know what else he did. He looked like a bookie.

He was in my judgment a thoroughly unpleasant man . . . He used to write his memos in third person. "If the President feels . . . I think the President should do the following". . .

He had one staff meeting or two. Every so often he'd call a staff meeting to assert his baronial standing.[38]

Certainly the archives dispel Roche's account of a man who did little more than run a few staff meetings and supervise the speech operation. Kintner advised the President on a wide range of issues, and his written recommendations were not sycophantic. For example, in March 1967, Kintner wrote to the President: "I am making this 'Eyes Only' because it is rather personal and, to be frank, I don't think you will like what I am about to say; however, as I have told you many times, . . . as long as I am in the White House I intend to give you what I think is the right advice."[39] In a confidential memorandum to Moyers, which Kintner asked be kept between Moyers and the President "because such effectiveness as I have outside the White House can be diminished if the correspondents do not speak to me as freely as they do now," Kintner observed that he planned to carry out his tasks "anonymously" and felt obligated to report the truth, however unpleasant that might be for the President. Kintner began by pointing out the President's liabilities, including his sensitivity to what was printed about him, the shutting out of individuals who didn't agree with him, the lack of preplanned press conferences, and a poorly organized White House staff.[40] In another confidential memorandum to the President, Kintner prefaced his remarks by noting that "at least you are getting honest opinions from one in support and no axe to grind." Kintner then discussed such topics as Johnson's overexposure in the media, his need to talk with people he respected (Dean Rusk, Robert McNamara, Alvin Wirtz, John Gardner, Marvin Watson, Jake Jacobsen, George Christian, Harry McPherson, Abe Fortas, and Clark Clifford) and problems in Johnson's style: "I am bothered about the possibility of your return to a technique where the White House Press Secretary announces too much (he should have good news) and where the President appears too often . . . I realize it is not too pleasant to tell someone this as I have told you several times."[41]

Kintner was a constant source of advice on ways to improve the President's image. He attended meetings at which Johnson delivered semiformal and informal remarks so that Kintner could develop "the best method to handle meetings with the press, taking into account that you do not want a televised press conference."[42] In a confidential memorandum to the President on the subject of "Suggestions to Counteract the Public Attitude toward Administration Policies," Kintner argued that the President, for his own good, should have regularly scheduled press conferences (every ten days) because "there is something wrong with the flow of information from the administration to the public."[43]

Kintner soon received Johnson's authorization to hold weekly meetings for all special assistants. He kept detailed records of these meetings and reported the results immediately to Johnson. The staff meetings did not carry decision-making responsibility but provided a forum for the basic exchange of ideas.[44] The meeting agendas offer hitherto unavailable insight into the everyday operation of the White House for a period of one year, though they do not show how the advisers operated during crises. A variety of problems was discussed during these meetings—attracting bright people to government (June 10, 1966); dealing with press criticisms (June 17, 1966); answering presidential mail (June 24, 1966); improving polling procedures and dissemination of information (June 24, 1966); restructuring the speech-writing operation (June 24, 1966); improving social relationships with senators (June 24, 1966); foreign policy briefings (July 8, 1966); and leaves of absence for assistants (November 21, 1966), to give a few examples. By February 1967, however, Johnson was upset at the number of leaks emanating from the staff meetings and instructed Kintner to reduce membership to Marvin Watson, Jake Jacobsen, Walt Rostow, Harry McPherson, Douglass Cater, Joseph Califano, George Christian, Henry Wilson, and Mike Manatos. Kintner pleaded with the President to reconsider his decision because:

1. I am sure that [the meetings] are bettering the morale of the staff within the White House and giving a spirit of unity.

2. The great majority of the people attending rarely have a chance to hear discussion of White House matters in fields other than the ones with which they are directly affected.

3. It is an excellent vehicle for word of mouth, in behalf of the President, because everyone there has some kind of business and social contact, whether they are press people, government people or merely friends.

4. Over the months in press conferences many misapprehensions on White House operations have been corrected.

5. Immodestly, I have had a great deal of experience with staff meetings at ABC and NBC, and I know their method of increasing loyalty, efficiency and understanding of personnel.[45]

Nevertheless, the staff meetings were soon discontinued. By mid-May 1967, Jim Jones wrote to Marvin Watson recommending that the Friday afternoon staff meetings be reinstituted: "I am afraid that too many of our well-meaning staff are trying to churn out ideas and recommendations as to how the President can 'improve image' or 'affect public opinion' without giving sufficient thought. For example, Doug Cater has made two recommendations in the last month which the President has approved, and after they came out of night reading I called certain problems to Cater's attention and changed his mind and felt the President should not do either of his recommendations. Ben Wattenberg, Joe Califano and others have also meant well with such suggestions that were not feasible or were objected to by another staff member such as George Christian after the President had approved."[46] However, these meetings had lost their usefulness to Johnson. Most interview respondents formerly on the Johnson staff told me that Kintner had been brought to the White House because Johnson was in an "organizational mood." One respondent said that "while Kintner did have a mandate from LBJ, those who knew LBJ knew it would not last." The master technician and coordinator from NBC was appointed to be Johnson's liaison with the media world and was given vast responsibilities over the "second tier" of advisers, but the President never told McPherson, Rostow, Califano, Moyers, and Christian to coordinate with Kintner.[47]

The Kintner materials establish a new context for empirical research and must be incorporated into future analysis of White House staffing during the Johnson administration. Together with the papers of Harry McPherson, Douglass Cater, Joseph Califano, and Marvin Watson, they provide information unavailable in the secondary literature for an analysis of the advising process and structure in the Johnson White House. I am convinced that further analysis of staffing patterns will reveal just how much Lyndon Johnson's personality distorted perceptions of the operation of his presidency. Insiders as well as outsiders were affected by the force of Johnson's personality. For instance, Bill Moyers told Harry McPherson that only after leaving the White House was he able "to see the value and skill" of Johnson's leadership. Moyers believed that Johnson was not a "'reasonable man,' in the sense of judging everybody coolly. Kennedy was, and his performance indicates that 'reasonable' men can't control 'unreasonable' forces. You have to have a gut reaction. You have to be 'unreasonable' to some extent. It's easier for me to see that now than it was when I was working there—when my own feelings got tied up in [Johnson's] 'unreasonableness.'"[48] This candid reappraisal of the impact of Johnson's style upon Moyers' perception reveals how important it is to separate the effects of Johnson's personality from other analytically independent elements of White House staffing and advising. The Johnson Library offers a great deal of material for systematic research on these other elements.

The 1968 Presidential Election: Advisers at Work

The 1968 presidential campaign provides a fascinating opportunity to assess the response of advisers to the volatile and highly politicized environment of American politics. Johnson faced challenges from a full range of White House aspirants including George Wallace, Richard Nixon, Nelson Rockefeller, Eugene McCarthy, and Robert Kennedy. Harry McPherson wrote to Johnson just thirteen days before the President's March 31, 1968, withdrawal, "As the incumbent President you are (to some degree, at least) the natural defender of the status quo. You represent things as they are—the course we are following, the policies and programs we have chosen. Therefore, you are the most conservative of the six—the man who is not calling for change, but resisting it. That is a tough position today."[49] Subsequently, when Johnson asked for continuing support of his administration, what he was really requesting was support for a presidency during which the Vietnam War claimed tens of thousands of American lives and $30 billion a year in resources—and was no closer to completion in 1968 than in 1964; a faltering butter-and-guns economy; racial and civil unrest documented by the Kerner Commission report; alienation of youth from government; a growing crime rate soon to become the number one public problem; diminishing American power abroad; and a general credibility gap between the government and its client, the people.

The holdings of the Johnson Library are particularly useful for gaining a finer appreciation of events during the 1968 campaign.[50] Johnson's March 31 decision not to seek reelection occurred well into the campaign-preparation process. A great deal of political groundwork had been completed, the early primaries were a matter of record, and the President's political advisers (especially James Rowe, Lawrence O'Brien, John Roche, and Marvin Watson) were recharting the President's campaign strategy. Moreover, to fully understand the problems of 1968, one should begin with the 1966 midterm election. In this area also, the holdings of the library are quite extensive. The election, characterized as a "surge and decline" phenomenon, negated most of the Democrats' 1964 electoral gains.[51] The Republicans fractured the Democratic power base in big-city states by winning twelve of thirteen elections for senator or governor in the ten largest states and sixteen of nineteen elections for senator and governor in cities of 750,000 or more. Several factors contributed to the Democratic defeat: lack of money, drop in turnout, a disorganized campaign, limited use of the media, and poor party discipline.

Most political experts agreed that Johnson had plenty of time to head the Democratic National Committee (DNC). Yet Theodore White reported that "in 1966 [Johnson] had slashed the budget of the Democratic National Committee to the bone, eliminating even the vital voter-registration division, a decision the Party was bitterly to regret in 1968. His callous humiliation of John Bailey, the nominal National Chairman, a veteran of great experience in the political wars, was a matter of Washington gossip."[52] According to Rowland Evans and Robert Novak, Johnson was "afraid that if he replaced Bailey with a tough-nosed political manager, the National Committee might be built into a power center capable of challenging the White House. This is, of course, preposterous, but to non-northern Democrats the National Committee has always represented a center of big-city power politics. And with the Johnson and Kennedy wings of the party more suspicious than ever of each other, Mr. Johnson apparently does not want to give the committee any independent power of its own."[53] A revitalized DNC would have served as a source of patronage for party leaders throughout the country, helped to reestablish party structures in the states, and provided efficient and well-organized voter-registration drives. But Johnson evidently ignored all recommendations and did very little to support the party's formal organization.[54]

In many ways the Republican candidates were the least of Johnson's worries. The President faced serious challenges from within his party, first from Eugene McCarthy and George Wallace and later from Robert Kennedy. The holdings in the Johnson Library show how the Johnson camp responded to these challenges, sought to use the incumbency, and ironically misjudged their opponents' strengths and Johnson's own weaknesses. Documents show that as early as April 1967, eleven months preceding the New Hampshire primary, the Johnson White House staff was hard at work developing election scenarios for 1968. Of particular concern were the motives and strategy of Robert Kennedy. This is especially apparent in John Roche's memoranda. Roche believed that Robert Kennedy's strategy was being dictated by two opposing teams: the "more militant in Bobby's following want a positive assault on the Administration—e.g., a 'spontaneous' write in in the New Hampshire primary," while others like Edward Kennedy, Joe Dolan, and Kenny O'Donnell did not want to be drawn into an intraparty fight. According to Roche, "They will urge Bobby to make the right act of fealty—and stand aside as the temple comes crashing down, ready to pick up the pieces for 1972. Bobby, in short, has a vested interest in the defeat of the national ticket in 1968." Roche advised Johnson that "the Kennedy corporation" should be told that if Johnson went down, "they will go down with us." If they "shaft the ticket in 1968, a number of us will be on world tours in 1972. The Republicans we can beat—if we find the time to go after them."[55]

In January 1968 James Rowe wrote a memorandum to Johnson with a different view about Kennedy's possible candidacy: "I am convinced that Bobby Kennedy has made a political judgement that he cannot take the nomination away from you in 1968, or, that if he could, it would inevitably result in a shattered Democratic party which would go down to defeat before the Republican candidate— and destroy Bobby forever." Rowe suggested that someone go to Kennedy and say:

> Bobby, you are ambitious and you want to be President. I want to speak to you in your own *self-interest . . .*
>
> You cannot defeat [Johnson] in the convention. Even if you could you would defeat yourself at the same time, and you would be responsible for the election of a Republican President . . .
>
> Of course you are frustrated, but if you want to be President in 1972, there is in 1968 only one way you can help yourself. That is to support Johnson actively as far as your integrity will allow.[56]

By late January Roche was able to write that if Kennedy challenged the party, "he risks total *obliteration*" because "if he goes in 1968, he will split the Democratic Party hopelessly, virtually guaranteeing a G.O.P. victory. And he will never be able to put the pieces

together for 1972—a *significant number of us would dedicate ourselves wholeheartedly to his political destruction* . . . And if Kennedy split the party in 1968, the Democrats would devote the next
four years to civil war, with Bobby as the wrecker. The nomination
would again be worthless." Roche concluded with a question:

> Does he realize this? Of course, he does. He is an arrogant little
> *schmuck* (as we say in Brooklyn), but nobody should underesti-
> mate his intelligence.
>
> He must also realize that the "new Bobby" image he has
> worked so hard to create these last five years would go up in
> smoke in five minutes if he went after the nomination—back
> would be the *"old Bobby," the ruthless, unscrupulous schemer
> who will stop at nothing in his drive for power.*[57]

The Kennedy challenge was but one of several hurdles facing
the President's reelection. As early as September 1967, Roche wrote
to the President with a warning that "the voter does not live in the
perspective of history—*unless you can put him there.*" Roche provided a list of do's and don't's: Johnson should not assume that the
1968 election would be as easy as 1964; he should expect that the
Vietnam War would create general dissatisfaction among the electorate, as did Kennedy's Catholicism; he should avoid defensive ex
planations by breaking out of the current "siege" mentality; and perhaps most important, he should build an effective national political
organization. "You didn't need one in 1964, but in 1968 organization
will be crucial. Bailey is out of his depth."[68]

Roche's memorandum was soon followed by Lawrence O'Brien's
lengthy "White Paper for the President on the 1968 Presidential
Campaign," which offered an astute assessment of the President's
options:

> We must put ourselves in the position of the voter who will ask
> the question: "why would I vote for four more years of LBJ? . . ."
>
> It would be patently unwise to underestimate the difficulties
> of winning re-election in 1968. Obviously, the problem is sub-
> stantially different this year than it was in 1964 . . . In 1968, like
> it or not, we will be on the defensive to a much greater degree
> than we were in 1964 . . . And while there was no anti-Johnson
> vote in 1964, it would be blindness on our part not to recognize
> the fact that there will be such a vote in 1968. We need to know,
> and soon, the extent of the vote on a state-by-state basis . . . we

need to know the attitudes voters hold, the depth of these attitudes, and how they can be changed.

Nationally, the Democratic party faces serious organizational problems. Most of the state organizations are flabby and wedded to techniques which are conventional and outmoded . . . The DNC is not staffed or equipped to conduct a successful Presidential election. The Democratic party, to a greater or lesser extent, has lost contact with the voters.[59]

O'Brien predicted that the Republicans would present themselves as the party of peace, in contrast with the party of war, lies, and credibility gaps. The Republicans would argue that only they could end the war, stop rioting in the streets, restore America's prestige, and curtail spending. O'Brien had no doubt that Johnson would be the Democratic candidate. Moreover, Johnson had to prepare both a defense to these charges and an offense of his own. The task involved lengthy planning and strategy.

In retrospect it seems that Johnson's political advisers served him well in the quality of their recommendations, and Johnson served himself poorly in rejecting expert advice. The President's failure to upgrade the DNC or to replace its director precipitated many of the 1968 problems later inherited by Humphrey. Future analysis can focus fruitfully on the relationship between these advisory recommendations and Johnson's own judgments.

The New Hampshire primary became, in retrospect, the loose thread which, when pulled, unraveled the Johnson presidency. The Marvin Watson files at the Johnson Library provide detailed information on state-by-state primary organization and are especially useful for assessing what happened in New Hampshire and other primary states. I will utilize the New Hampshire case to illustrate the type of analysis researchers may undertake at the library. John Bailey of the DNC believed that Johnson faced serious problems in New Hampshire. The President's name was not on the ballot; he was not a declared candidate; and delegates could not pledge themselves to a noncandidate. Eugene McCarthy had just announced his intent to run in New Hampshire. Johnson was banking on a heavy write-in campaign.[60] Johnson's advisers did not view McCarthy as a serious candidate. To Richard Scammon, McCarthy's candidacy was "no real threat," and John Roche wrote of "politically obliterating McCarthyism in Wisconsin."[61] Yet, when New Hampshire voted on March 13, 1968, Johnson received 49.5 percent (27,243 votes) to McCarthy's 42.4 percent (23,280 votes). When all write-ins were tabulated, the President of the United States had won the primary by all of 230 votes, and McCarthy had captured twenty of twenty-six delegate votes.

The McCarthy vote was, of course, deceptive—not *for* peace but in protest, many self-proclaimed hawks voting for McCarthy to protest Johnson's handling of the war. As Philip Converse et al. note in their seminal analysis of the 1968 campaign, "The McCarthy vote in New Hampshire certainly reflected a groundswell of anger at the Johnson administration, and an expression of desire for a change . . . Among his supporters in the primary, however, those who were unhappy with the Johnson administration for not pursuing a harder line against Hanoi outnumbered those advocating a withdrawal from Vietnam by nearly a three to two margin! Thus the McCarthy tide in New Hampshire was, to say the least, quite heterogeneous in its policy preferences: the only common denominator seems to have been a deep dissatisfaction with the Johnson administration."[62] A postmortem report done for Johnson on the New Hampshire primary echoed what survey research later proved: "It would be a mistake to tag the McCarthy vote as a measure of dove sentiment (a private pre-election poll is said to have reported that 40% of those declaring for McCarthy also favored escalation)."[63]

This interpretation of McCarthy's support is not novel, but documents in the Watson files show that Johnson received advance polling information about how New Hampshire might vote but did little to offset the appearance of a McCarthy victory. Three months before the primary the White House authorized a survey of 1,115 registered New Hampshire voters which showed Johnson running well ahead of McCarthy (76 to 6 percent). An analysis of attitudes revealed, however, that "New Hampshire is a hawk's nest . . . voters are the most militant on Vietnam than voters in any other state we surveyed during 1967."[64] What followed was, in retrospect, a misreading of the implications: "This means, of course, that candidates who take a hard line in Vietnam are going to do better in New Hampshire than candidates who preach a softer position. It also indicates clearly why Senator McCarthy shows up so poorly in New Hampshire: he simply does not speak their language." By February 1968 another opinion survey pointed to "an increase in the percentage who intend to vote for Eugene McCarthy in the New Hampshire Democratic Primary" and warned, "We believe McCarthy is rapidly building the support *which will lead to a press interpreted victory in the state.*" The pollsters predicted a 30 percent or more vote for McCarthy. This conclusion is remarkable considering that both the

Roper and Quayle public-opinion polls conducted during the same period showed Johnson defeating McCarthy 63 to 12 percent and 74 to 20 percent, respectively.[65]

Within the White House, assessments of the New Hampshire results and McCarthy's chances differed. To John Roche, New Hampshire demonstrated the necessity of getting Johnson's name on the ballot: "Campaigns can't be won by proxy, and the longer you put off announcing your intentions for 1968, the worse the moral situation gets, and the more the opportunists start canvassing their options."[66] Roche's advice was to "announce your candidacy after the April 4 Wisconsin primary—let your supporters see you in the flesh." Richard Scammon also believed that "the option for the President to run or not to run may not be in August as is now assumed—it may be now."[67] Scammon believed McCarthy would not get the nomination but would hurt Johnson in November. The real problem was that by August "the President may have picked up the image of 'a loser' which could be an albatross around his neck, and get the local politicians around the country very disturbed and restless." To Scammon, Johnson's loss of New Hampshire was due primarily to lack of leadership and secondarily for not being on the ticket, poor organization at the polls, poor delegate selection, and a poorly run campaign. Louis Harris believed that Johnson lost ten points for not being on the ballot and that 15 percent of McCarthy's vote was strictly anti-Johnson.[68]

Following New Hampshire, Robert Kennedy announced that he was "reassessing" his options. According to Arthur Schlesinger, "Robert Kennedy felt that McCarthy's success had boxed him in. Obviously, he could not now expect Gene to withdraw."[69] As Roche wrote to Marvin Watson, Kennedy "can't turn Gene McCarthy off. Gene has the taste in his mouth and has gone over the brink of total commitment. Besides, if Gene were to pull out, the whole affair would be like shabby Machiavellianism . . . Bobby is playing a *convention*, not a primary strategy."[70] Roche believed that some Kennedy supporters would actually do all they could to support McCarthy in order to lock the convention.

By March 16, Kennedy announced his candidacy and many insiders began questioning Johnson's own plans. In a March 28 memorandum to Johnson, for example, political adviser James Rowe commented that if the President was not running, "I [am] certainly wasting alot of my time." Rowe concluded by saying that whatever doubts he had about Johnson's plans were put away the day Kennedy announced his candidacy: Johnson "is not about to turn the country over to Bobby."[71] Campaign adviser John Roche expressed similar misgivings, writing to Johnson that "should you decide not to run, I hope you will give a few of us enough advance notice so we can escape the country."[72] On March 31, 1968, Johnson announced his decision not to seek reelection.[73]

The Watson election materials together with the oral histories provide a clearer perspective on personalities and events in the 1968 election. These materials are located in the Marvin Watson files, part of the subject file (PL and PR) of the White House Central Files in the Johnson Library. The holdings include details on campaign organization, advance planning, delegate selection strategy, grass roots organizing within key primary states, tactics and problems in raising money, the relationship between the Democratic National Committee and the White House, campaign scheduling, state-by-state polls of political climate, relationships with the media, and the daily interaction of campaign advisers with the incumbent. This rich data base supplements the 1968 election literature. The research materials will answer questions such as these: (1) How was the campaign organized on a state-by-state basis? (2) What role did the White House staff play in organizing and disseminating political information? (3) What criteria determined whether the President's name would be placed on primary ballots? (4) What strategies were employed to offset threats from within the party (McCarthy, Kennedy, Wallace) and from outside (Nixon, Romney, Rockefeller)? (5) How was information about Johnson's standing in the polls vis-à-vis these challenges (individually or collectively) presented to the President? (6) When should Johnson officially declare his candidacy? (7) How did political strategists give advice to the best politician of them all? (8) Should the White House, based on the information it possessed, have anticipated the problems encountered in the primary states? (9) How did the Johnson camp assess its efforts in retrospect, and are these lessons here for future incumbent candidates?

I began this essay by agreeing with John Roche that only the presidential archives of the Johnson Library in Austin provide the data necessary for systematic analysis of the Johnson presidency. I have tried to show how this valuable primary-source evidence can be used to gain a finer understanding of the Johnson presidency. Archival research will not yield a "new" Lyndon Johnson but rather a new perspective on aspects of his presidency other than personality. The evidence shows, I believe, that Johnson's advisers served him rather well, not as sycophants but as capable individuals struggling to operate within an environment shaped by a failure in public relations. The staff recommendations were often harsh and to the point. Johnson's March 31, 1968, decision was not made in a political vacuum. Harry McPherson, for example, was willing and able to tell the President thirteen days before the withdrawal, "I think this course we seem to be taking now will lead either to Kennedy's nomination or Nixon's election, or both . . . I have sensed a progressive narrowing of tolerance toward those who don't stand at attention for us when we say 'pop to.' *This is wrong.*"[74] Researchers will learn a great deal more about how Lyndon Johnson's staff worked with the President from studying the materials deposited in the Johnson Library. All of the precincts will never report, but available information can be used to understand the Johnson presidency as it operated under the constant strains and demands of American government. In-depth empirical analysis of the problems, issues, and procedures of the Johnson presidency may also help future presidents adopt better operational strategies and organize better staff-support structures. That, in the final analysis, would be a fine legacy from the Johnson papers.

Notes

1. John Roche, "The Jigsaw Puzzle of History," *New York Times Magazine* (January 24, 1971), pp. 14–15, in *Sentenced to Life* by John Roche (New York: Macmillan, 1974), p. 86.

2. See Patrick Anderson, *The President's Men* (Garden City, N.Y.: Doubleday, 1968); David Halberstam, *The Best and the Brightest* (New York: Random House, 1969); Richard Tanner Johnson, *Managing the White House* (New York: Harper and Row, 1974); Robert Sherrill, *The Accidental President* (New York: Grossman, 1967). On the other hand, it is doubtful that Gene Latimer's letter to the President is universal in its applicability: "My dear chief: when anyone discusses 'alleged cruelty' to staff I hasten to set the record straight. I have yet to hear of another boss who would lend you his money, keep your accounts, pay your bills, trust you with his children, and generally supervise your well being. Nor have I ever heard any other ex-employees say anything except that he loves you. And so do I" (Gene Latimer to the President, July 12, 1965, FG 11-8, box 67, April 25, 1965–February 4, 1966 folder, Executive File, White House Central Files, Johnson Library).

3. Roche, "Jigsaw Puzzle," p. 87.

4. Ibid., p. 99.

5. For an extensive bibliographic review see Fred Greenstein, Larry Berman, and Alvin Felzenberg, *Evolution of the Modern Presidency: A Bibliographic Survey* (Washington, D.C.: American Enterprise, 1973), ch. 11.

6. Hugh Heclo, *Studying the Presidency: A Report to the Ford Foundation* (New York: Ford Foundation Press, 1977), pp. 30–45.

7. For a recent exception see Alexander George, *Presidential Decision-Making in Foreign Policy: The Effective Use of Information and Advice* (Boulder, Colo.: Westview Press, 1980).

8. The White House staff certainly understood this problem. In December, 1966 staff member Bob Hardesty wrote to Robert Kintner, "Joseph Kraft lamented in his column one day last week that Johnson-watching and Johnson-analyzing has almost become an obsession with the Press, but the problem is that there's no one else around for them to focus on. I submit that if the Cabinet officers were encouraged to come into their own a little more, the LBJ obsession would begin to diminish" (Bob Hardesty to Robert Kintner, December 20, 1966, FG 11-1, box 21, Confidential File, White House Central Files, Johnson Library).

9. Harry McPherson to the President, July 13, 1965, McPherson memoranda to the President, box 52, Harry McPherson Files, Johnson Library.

10. Harry McPherson to Bill Moyers, March 8, 1966, FG 11-8, February 5, 1966–July 20, 1966 folder, Executive File, White House Central Files, Johnson Library.

11. Alan Otten, "The Consenting Advisors," *Wall Street Journal*, February 27, 1967.

12. Otten was viewed as a real problem by the staff, as seen in Joseph Califano's memorandum to Bill Moyers of May 27, 1966 (FG 11-8, February 5, 1966–July 20, 1966 folder, Executive File, White House Central Files, Johnson Library). By January 9, 1967 McPherson wrote to the President, "Al Otten came to see me today—the first time since two months ago, when I told him he ought to quit the White House because his deep antipathy to your administration was destroying his objectivity and balance as a reporter" (Harry McPherson to the President, January 9, 1967, Memoranda to the President, 1967, box 53, Harry McPherson Files, Johnson Library).

13. Harry McPherson to George Christian, February 28, 1967, box 19, White House staff folder, Harry McPherson Papers, Johnson Library.

14. Douglass Cater Oral History Interview, tape 2, p. 31, Johnson Library.

15. Bob Hardesty to Robert Kintner, December 20, 1966, FG 11-1, box 21, Confidential File, White House Central Files, Johnson Library.

16. Tom Johnson to the President, December 9, 1966, FG 1, Ibid.

17. George Christian Oral History Interview, p. 12, Johnson Library.

18. Joseph Califano to the President, December 6, 1968, FG 11-8-1, Califano, Executive File, White House Central Files, Johnson Library. See also Califano memoranda to the President, 1968, Joseph Califano Files, Johnson Library.

19. Robert Kintner to the President, February 9, 1967, FG 1, box 16, Confidential File, White House Central Files, Johnson Library. The staff later prepared a lengthy analysis of Robert Donovan's article, "LBJ Pollster Raps 'Misleading' Leaks" (*Washington Post*, November 26, 1967). The ten-page memorandum identified sixteen misleading statements made by pollster Archibald M. Crossley to Donovan.

20. Ben Wattenberg to the President, January 17, 1967, FG 11-8, July 21, 1966–October 31, 1966 folder, box 68, Executive File, White House Central Files, Johnson Library.

21. Harry McPherson to the President, July 20, 1965. Memoranda to the President, 1965, box 52, Harry McPherson Files, Johnson Library.

22. Douglass Cater to the President, "Relations With the Press," September 29, 1965, September 1965 folder, box 14, Douglass Cater Files, Johnson Library.

23. See Robert Kintner to the President, December 8, 1966, attachment with President's response, December 1966 folder, box 4, Robert Kintner Files, Johnson Library.

24. George Reedy to the President, December 3, 1968, December 1, 1968 folder, FG 1, Executive File, White House Central Files, Johnson Library. In his oral history interview George Reedy recalled that "somebody one day took . . . the polls and showed [Johnson] how his own popularity had been dropping off rapidly during the same period that Bill's popularity was building up so rapidly and I think that opened up the light to him" (George Reedy Oral History Interview, Johnson Library).

25. George Reedy to the President, December 3, 1968, December 1, 1968 folder, FG 1, Executive File, White House Central Files, Johnson Library.

26. Fred Panzer to the President, "Background on Presidential Press Relations," February 21, 1967, February 11, 1967–February 24, 1967 folder, FG 1 (14), Ibid.

27. Jake Jacobsen Oral History Interview, pp. 33–35, Johnson Library.

28. George Reedy Oral History Interview, tape 4, pp. 11–14, Johnson Library. Reedy recalled an occasion when a group of singers had just returned from Vietnam for a ceremony in the east wing, "and these boys sang a couple of songs while the President was standing there. The President doesn't particularly understand modern music. I'll never forget Bill running around tugging reporters at the arm and laughing, saying 'Ha, ha, ha, ha! It doesn't mean anything to the stupid son-of-a-bitch, does it?'. . . [Moyers] used to give excellent imitations of the President's Texas drawl and Mrs. Johnson's Texas drawl at parties around town. He disliked the President intensely" (tape 4, p. 13).

29. George Christian Oral History Interview, pp. 12–15, Johnson Library.

30. Fred Panzer to the President, March 31, 1967, March 12, 1967–March 31, 1967 folder, FG 1 (14), Executive File, White House Central Files, Johnson Library.

31. See Harry McPherson to the President, February 7, 1968, with attachment, "Excerpts from article by Senator Fulbright," Memoranda to President, 1968, box 53, Harry McPherson Files, Johnson Library.

32. Bill Moyers to Robert Kintner, April 8, 1966, FG 11-8-1, Confidential File, White House Central Files, Johnson Library.

33. Bill Moyers to Robert Kintner, May 5, 1966, FG 11-8, Ibid. Moyers

compared Johnson's staff "to a basketball team where the ball was passed back and forth in a comparison with President Eisenhower's organization which was patterned after a football team with Sherman Adams as the Quarterback." See also Robert Kintner to the President, May 6, 1966, WH 10, FG 11-8-1, Confidential File, White House Central Files, Johnson Library.

34. White House Staff Assignments, August 8, 1966, FG 11-8-1, Ibid.

35. On August 12, 1966 Kintner notified the President that Macy had completed his list. Johnson asked Kintner to check with all staff members "so that they might make any changes in their descriptions." Kintner later informed Johnson that "Bill Moyers, Marvin Watson, Jake Jacobsen, Mike Manatos, Henry Wilson, Barefoot Sanders, Milt Semer and I made no changes" (Robert Kintner to the President, August 12, 1966 and September 10, 1966, box 3, Robert Kintner Files, Johnson Library).

36. Catherine Mackin, Hearst Headline Service special, Sunday, June 19, 1966, attached to Robert Kintner to the President, June 20, 1966, FG 11-8-1/Kintner, Executive File, White House Central Files, Johnson Library. Kintner wrote to Johnson that "I saw Miss Mackin, reluctantly and urged her not to write any story. I told her I wanted to remain anonymous, and that I had had more than my share of publicity in my day. . . . I want to be sure that I have made my attitude on personal publicity clear. Practically every reporter that I have known in Washington has wanted to write an article about me, and I have completely discouraged them. I would rather spend my time building up other members of your staff, particularly Marvin Watson, whom I think is greatly underestimated and Jake Jacobsen, to my mind, represent a real affirmative asset for you." Interestingly, Johnson scribbled across the bottom of the memorandum, "I understand and agree that this is good."

37. Eric Goldman, *The Tragedy of Lyndon Johnson* (New York: Knopf, 1969), p. 565.

38. John Roche Oral History Interview, p. 38, Johnson Library. It *is* curious that Kintner has received such little attention in the secondary literature, particularly because he was not as anonymous as he wished. On June 19, 1966, for example, *The Sunday Bulletin* featured an article by Anthony Day entitled "Around the Center of Power: Bond of Service Links President's Eight Assistants." The eight assistants were Walt Rostow, Harry McPherson, Douglass Cater, Bill Moyers, Marvin Watson, Jake Jacobsen, Joseph Califano, and Robert Kintner.

39. Robert Kintner to the President, March 2, 1967, FG 1 (1967), box 16, Confidential File, White House Central Files, Johnson Library.

40. Robert Kintner to Bill Moyers, April 30, 1966, PR 18, box 83, Ibid.

41. Robert Kintner to the President, August 1, 1967, FG 1 (1967), Ibid.

42. Robert Kintner to the President, June 3, 1966, PR 18, Ibid.

43. Robert Kintner to the President, June 14, 1966, FG 1, Ibid.

44. In May 1964 the President had instructed Bill Moyers to organize weekly staff meetings for McGeorge Bundy, Horace Busby, Ralph Dungan,

Myer Feldman, Richard Goodwin, George Reedy, Jack Valenti, and Lee White. "He wants us to talk about his activities already on the calendar and what others might be added, statements he might make during the week, last-minute ideas for speeches he will be making that week, etc." (Bill Moyers to McGeorge Bundy, et al., May 1, 1964, WH 10, Executive File, White House Central Files, Johnson Library). The Kintner files show the inaccuracies of Roche's observation about holding "one staff meeting on two" (Robert Kintner Files, Johnson Library).

45. Robert Kintner to the President, February 18, 1967, WH 10, FG 11-8-1, Confidential File, White House Central Files, Johnson Library. By February 17, 1967 thirty-eight people were attending staff meetings: Clifford Alexander, Francis Bator, Farris Bryant, Joseph Califano, Liz Carpenter, Douglass Cater, George Christian, Walter Coyne, James Cross, Ervin Duggan, Bob Fleming, Bob Hardesty, Bill Hopkins, Jake Jacobsen, Jim Jones, Tom Johnson, Robert Komer, Larry Levinson, Henry Wilson, Jack McNulty, Harry McPherson, John Macy, Charles Maguire, Mike Manatos, Sherwin Markman, Lawrence O'Brien, Fred Panzer, Paul Popple, Juanita Roberts, Chuck Roche, John Roche, Walt Rostow, Bill Schoen, Whitney Shoemaker, Irvine Sprague, Will Sparks, Ben Wattenberg, and Marvin Watson. Compare this with the President's June 21, 1966 directive that the meetings be reduced to sixteen: Bill Moyers, Marvin Watson, Jake Jacobsen, Douglass Cater, Joseph Califano, Walt Rostow, Robert Komer, Harry McPherson, Milt Semer, Governor Bryant, Barefoot Sanders, Lawrence O'Brien, James Moyers, George Christian, Francis Bator, and Robert Kintner.

46. Jim Jones to Marvin Watson, May 17, 1967, March 1, 1967, folder, WH 10, box 20, Executive File, White House Central Files, Johnson Library.

47. John Roche believed that "Kintner had been out to kill Califano and didn't succeed, obviously" (John Roche Oral History Interview, p. 45, Johnson Library). One of my anonymous interview respondents told me Moyers viewed Kintner as an empire builder who wanted Moyers' empire. This fits with Catherine Mackin's conjecture "whether Kintner is being groomed as Mr. Johnson's first official chief of staff, . . . [which] raises the question of whether Kintner might replace Bill Moyers as the 'first among equals' on the White House staff" (Hearst Headline Service special).

48. Harry McPherson to the President, June 20, 1967, box 53, McPherson memoranda to the President, Harry McPherson Files, Johnson Library.

49. Harry McPherson to the President, March 18, 1968, box 53, Ibid.

50. The Johnson Library holds 257 linear feet of DNC records available to researchers who have obtained written permission from the DNC.

51. Philip Converse et al., "Continuity and Change in American Politics: Parties and Issues in the 1968 Election," *American Political Science Review* 63 (December 1969): 1083–1105; V. O. Key, "A Theory of Critical Elections," *Journal of Politics* (February 1955), p. 318; Douglass Cater to the President, November 29, 1965, November 1965 folder, box 14, Douglass Cater Files, Johnson Library; Fred Panzer to Jake Jacobsen, January 5, 1967,

PL 2, box 71, Confidential File, White House Central Files, Johnson Library.

52. Theodore White, *The Making of the President 1968* (New York: Atheneum, 1969), p. 129.

53. Rowland Evans and Robert Novak, "Inside Report: Later Than LBJ Thinks," *Washington Post*, December 21, 1966.

54. Johnson did receive several recommendations for DNC director. Robert Kintner recommended Bill Wirtz; Bill Moyers recommended Richard Scammon; and Harry McPherson recommended Larry Levinson and John Gilligan.

55. John Roche to the President, April 18, 1967, box 29 (1375 B), Marvin Watson Files, Johnson Library.

56. James Rowe to the President, January 16, 1968, Ibid. Rowe added that "Bobby is an emotional fellow. He is quite capable of jumping off the deep end."

57. John Roche to the President, January 26, 1968, John Roche Memoranda folder, Ibid.

58. John Roche to the President, September 16, 1967, John Roche Memoranda folder, Ibid.

59. Lawrence F. O'Brien, "A White Paper for the President on the 1968 Presidential Campaign," September 29, 1967, Confidential File, White House Central Files, Johnson Library. See James Rowe's response to O'Brien's white paper and Rowe's response to O'Brien's critique, box 29 (1375 B), Marvin Watson Files, Johnson Library.

60. John Bailey to Marvin Watson, January 5, 1968, New Hampshire Primary folder, box 10, Ibid.

61. Richard Scammon to the President, November 21, 1967, Politics folder, box 31 (1753), Harry McPherson Papers, Johnson Library; John Roche to the President, December 11, 1967, box 29, Marvin Watson Files, Johnson Library.

62. Converse et al., "Continuity and Change in American Politics," p. 1092.

63. Bernard Boutin to (unknown), March 14, 1968, New Hampshire Wrap-up folder, box 10, Marvin Watson Files, Johnson Library.

64. "Survey of Political Attitudes in New Hampshire," box 11, Ibid.

65. "Survey of Opinion among Democratic Primary Voters in New Hampshire," February 1968, box 11, Ibid.

66. John Roche to the President, March 14, 1968, box 11, Ibid.

67. Ben Wattenberg to the President, March 13, 1968, New Hampshire Primary folder, box 11, Ibid.

68. Fred Panzer to the President, March 13, 1968, Ibid.

69. Arthur M. Schlesinger, Jr., *Robert Kennedy and His Times* (Boston: Houghton Mifflin, 1978), p. 849.

70. John Roche to Marvin Watson, March 13, 1968, New Hampshire Primary folder, box 11, Marvin Watson Files, Johnson Library. In a fascinating memorandum, McPherson wrote to the President that according to Mc-

Carthy's friends, McCarthy might be willing to do two things to get the nomination: "First, if elected, he is willing to re-submit Fortas and Thornberry to the Senate next year. Second, he is willing to permit President Johnson to name his Vice-Presidential running mate—within reasonable limits" (Harry McPherson to the President, August 12, 1968, Memoranda to the President, 1968, box 53, Harry McPherson Files, Johnson Library).

71. James Rowe to the President, March 28, 1968, box 29, Marvin Watson Files, Johnson Library.

72. John Roche to the President, March 28, 1968, John Roche Memoranda folder, Ibid.

73. See Lyndon Baines Johnson, *The Vantage Point* (New York: Holt, Rinehart, and Winston, 1971) for an interesting discussion on events leading to this announcement.

74. Harry McPherson to the President, March 18, 1968, Memoranda to the President, box 53, Harry McPherson Files, Johnson Library.

7 | Johnson and the Media
by David Culbert

LYNDON JOHNSON WAS NOT just interested in mass media, he was obsessed. "You guys," he told a network producer shortly before his death, "all you guys in the media. All of politics has changed because of you. You've broken all the machines and the ties between us in Congress and the city machines." The President recognized the agenda-setting function of network news; he listened around the clock to know what the public was being told. "Television and radio were his constant companions," biographer Doris Kearns declares. "Hugging a transistor radio to his ear as he walked through the fields of his ranch or around the grounds of the White House, Johnson was a presidential teenager, listening not for music but for news." And Johnson insisted that his aides share his enthusiasm. "We were just constantly being peppered with news," Press Secretary George Christian recalls. "He read all the available daily papers . . . before anybody else even got to stirring and he watched the network morning shows. . . . Then he would turn on the hourly newscasts and then he had of course AP and UPI in his office."[1]

Johnson's obsession with what others said was the result of an inordinate concern with his own image, both aural and visual. He was a modern Narcissus, looking into the media pool for confirmation of his presidential stature. He never sounded convincing in public. Senator Paul Douglas once said that he "never saw Lyndon Johnson win a debate conclusively on the Senate floor, and he never heard him lose one in the cloak room." Doris Kearns has an elaborate, unconvincing explanation that Johnson's mother withheld her love unless he sounded "as solemn as an owl" in public.[2] Actually Johnson felt uncomfortable before the camera because it allowed viewers to focus on form rather than substance; it froze his awkward physical appearance in time.

Television also emphasized the way he spoke. Johnson's national importance coincided with the emergence of civil rights as a major issue. To talk "corn pone" ruined his attempt to sound credible to Northerners. No gimmick, whether new glasses, a new Tele-Prompter, a different color shirt, or a new backdrop, could turn Johnson into a winsome performer on television. Such efforts, Press

Figure 1. A staged photograph of Johnson and two unidentified persons listening to a floor-length radio, probably 1941. Johnson wanted his constituents to know that he got his information from a modern medium of communication.

Secretary George Reedy claims, were wide of the mark: "They are effective only in regard to adjectives, not to the hard substantive news that is the ultimate shaper of public opinion."[3]

Reedy's assertion has resonance, even if it is not quite true. Johnson's skills in wheedling and conniving, however important in getting legislation through Congress, failed to inspire confidence in the office of the presidency. Johnson was the old dog who just could not learn new tricks. His accent and garbled syntax betrayed him when he talked in public in the same manner he talked on the telephone or in private. He did not look or sound heroic—he looked like a politician.

Johnson had particular problems with his image owing to endless unflattering comparisons with his handsome predecessor, John Kennedy. A New England accent, youthful good looks, and playful banter in public went a long way toward creating Kennedy's image of heroic leadership. Kennedy looked and sounded as though he could get results even if reality was something else. Johnson had none of these media assets, though he did bring change through his mastery of the legislative process. It was also Johnson's fate to serve as President during a period when the pragmatic skills of the politi-

Figure 2. Johnson giving the kick-off speech for his Senate race, San Marcos, Texas, May 3, 1941. Johnson's mother, wife, and three sisters are seated on the stage. The band members sit in front, helping to swell the audience. The painted figures of Roosevelt and Johnson on the backdrop resemble folk art. The stage is almost overwhelmed by the battery of microphones, each with the large-sized station call letters typical of the era. Candidate Johnson is giving his all, perhaps hoping that listeners will imagine a grander setting.

Figure 3. In May 1937 Franklin Roosevelt visited Texas and posed with Congressman Johnson and Governor James Allred. Johnson admired Roosevelt's political skills, including his mastery of the medium of radio. Paintings based on this photograph—but with Allred left out—were used in the 1941 campaign (see Figs. 2 and 4).

Figure 4. A visual icon from the 1941 campaign. In this campaign Johnson used a musical group which toured the state singing "God Bless America." The female lead even resembled Kate Smith, whose figure distinguished her from most popular singers of the day.

cian were held in low esteem. In American society during the 1960s, many called for ideological crusades in which the physical appearance of the leaders played a major role.

A Background in Publicity

Lyndon Johnson had a lifelong interest in the mass media; to him politics and publicity were virtual synonyms. At Southwest Texas State Teachers College he edited the school newspaper, *The College Star*. His wife, Claudia Taylor, was a journalism major. From the time he arrived in Washington in 1931, he read all the Washington papers in addition to those from New York and the *Congressional Record*. According to Doris Kearns, Johnson "relaxed in bed with a sheaf of government documents as others relax with a good mystery."[4]

Johnson recognized early the value of radio, the central medium of communication for America in the 1930s. His wife reports that her husband first broadcast over radio in Houston in late 1931, just before leaving for Washington, and "there was a radio in his car as far back as I can remember." There was also a radio in their home and another in his office, and he made "extensive use of radio in his campaigns from 1937 on." Radio enabled him to get his message across directly to voters as well as to reach an audience that might not see him in person (see Figures 1 and 2).[5] The Johnson personal fortune was also based on media. Thanks in part to the advice of CBS President Frank Stanton, the Johnsons purchased the CBS radio affiliate in Austin in 1943.[6]

Johnson remained an avid radio fan the rest of his life. In the White House he listened in the early morning, randomly switching from station to station, never sure which station he had tuned in. He would order staff members to track down who had said what, no mean feat considering the number of Washington, D.C., stations to choose from.[7]

The Importance of Television

Staff members recall that Johnson had a television set in his Senate office during the late 1950s, but his fascination with the medium intensified when he became President in November 1963. Such interest was natural for a media enthusiast, since the 1960s saw the demise of the newsreel and the emergence of thirty-minute network news shows. Frank Stanton suggested installing a unit with three television monitors and a remote control switch in the President's bedroom so Johnson could watch all three evening news shows at once.[8] One of the best-known images of Johnson's presidency is this bank of monitors, which was duplicated in the Oval Office, at the LBJ ranch, and on one occasion in a hospital room (see Figures 5–7).

The President loved any technological innovation which enabled him to get more information faster. In July 1966 the White House Communications Agency (part of the Army Signal Corps) set up a videotape playback machine which enabled Johnson to see television programs at his convenience (Figure 8).

Johnson relied on television newsfilm to make vivid the reality of civil rights confrontations, as David Garrow points out in his excellent *Protest at Selma*.[9] Television covered the Alabama troopers who beat up peaceful marchers on March 7, 1965. Johnson says in his memoir that he "felt a deep outrage" as he "watched the reruns of the Selma confrontation on television." He indicates that not just the event itself but the experience of seeing the violence moved him and millions of other Americans to seek guarantees embodied in the Voting Rights Act of 1965.[10]

Figure 5. There were three screens in the White House bedroom and at the ranch in Texas. This January 1968 photograph shows the President holding the remote control switch.

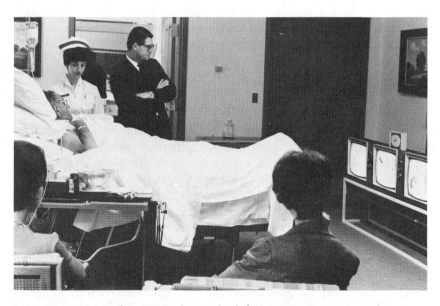

Figure 6. In November 1966 Johnson had three monitors set up in his room at Bethesda Naval Hospital so he could watch television even while hospitalized. Notice the transistor radio at his side.

Figure 7. Johnson's most publicized console in the Oval Office. The UPI and AP teletype machines are to the left of the screens. On the desk is a telephone with twelve outside lines. The President is watching the Senate Foreign Relations Committee Hearings, March 12, 1968. That same evening he told a group, "So, I will return home now to watch another television replay—I am going home to look at the 'Dean Rusk Show.' That's the show, you know, that was two years in production. We had a great cast but no plot" (Remarks to Veterans of Foreign Wars dinner, in *Public Papers of the Presidents: Lyndon B. Johnson, 1968–69* [Washington, D.C., 1970], 1:383).

The President also watched television in the summer of 1967 to learn about conditions in downtown Detroit during the riots. Just before midnight on July 24 he announced on national television that he was sending federal troops. Returning to the White House with several of his assistants, he "watched the latest network reports of the riot conditions."[11] The President sought verification for his controversial decision in the scenes of violence which the media provided. Johnson felt the need to confirm his numerous other sources of information in the "actuality" of television images.

There is another side to Johnson's obsession with what was being reported. According to the mythology of the Johnson years, the President made a daily practice of calling journalists himself and angrily demanding corrections to stories just broadcast or published. For example CBS reporter Dan Rather claims that "More often what I got was a phone call from the President himself, moments after the Eve-

Figure 8. The President studies his own performance immediately following the televised November 17, 1967, press conference in which he emphasized the progress being made in Vietnam. Virtually all photographs taken
by a White House photographer from 1963 to 1969 are arranged by date in
contact books at the Johnson Library. These books can mislead the researcher, since a small print may obscure faults in the negative. The
audiovisual archives staff recommends that whenever possible researchers
use the cross-indexed files of edited photographs. This image of the playback machine comes from the contact books, and its poor composition is
obvious. It is, however, an excellent photograph of the machine.

ning News, demanding, as only he could, 'Rather, are you trying to fuck me?'"[12]

How much evidence is there that Johnson monitored the three networks each evening, telephone in hand? The massive White House card index in the Johnson Library supposedly records the names, dates, times, and durations of all telephone calls to and from the Oval Office and the names of all individuals who visited the President or dined with him. There are surprisingly few cards for even the most prominent journalists of the 1960s. Dan Rather, for example, has nineteen entries from July 1964 to December 1968 but not a single reference to a telephone call. Other prominent commentators and editors appear considerably less often.[13]

Johnson clearly loved to use the telephone, however. Earle Wheeler, then Chairman of the Joint Chiefs of Staff, recalls Johnson's use of long distance calls to test public sentiment. At Tuesday luncheons of the National Security Council, Wheeler remembers, "There was nothing unusual at all for him to say, 'Well, now, I called so-and-so, and so-and-so, and so-and-so last night.' They would be people all around the country. [He was] just taking their pulse."[14]

The scholar who wants to use the central card index to gauge influence or to document something the President may have done on a particular day will be disappointed to learn that the index does not record calls Johnson made from a special private line in the Oval Office. Nor did staff prepare cards for days when Johnson was traveling. (The President could place direct calls while flying in Air Force One.) However, Johnson's personal secretary, Juanita Roberts, believes that the President rarely used the private line in the Oval Office, since it required his making an additional effort. Johnson had twelve outside lines; with these he pushed a button and told a White House operator to contact someone for him. To use the private line he had to dial the number himself, which meant either looking up the number, having it memorized, or carrying a list of often-dialed numbers. Roberts never saw such a list and does not think it was Johnson's style to dial a number himself.[15] Robert Fleming, then deputy press secretary in charge of television, believes stories about Johnson's calling reporters were greatly exaggerated. The President did make such calls, he believes, but not often, since he could not watch the evening news every night. More often, Fleming thinks, Johnson would call George Christian and blow off steam.[16]

Johnson, Juanita Roberts recalls, would often work at his desk with the television on, but her doubts about how regularly Johnson watched the evening news—traditionally the programs considered

Figure 9. The Johnson Library's photographic index can help identify those who dined at the President's table—persons Johnson particularly sought to influence. In this 1967 dinner honoring over one hundred members of the press, Walter Cronkite sits two seats to Johnson's left.

most influential in terms of audience size—are confirmed by daily memoranda describing the contents of network television programs which the President had staff members Peter Benchley and Robert Fleming prepare from the summer of 1967 through April 1968. It is hard to see why such documents would have been necessary if Johnson had been watching each evening himself. Check marks here and there indicate that the President actually read these reports, supporting the conclusion that he simply did not have time to watch the news every night, no matter what was being said.[17]

Quite possibly the most significant instance of media influence on Johnson was a CBS special television report by Walter Cronkite, broadcast nationwide on February 27, 1968. Concerned by the Tet Offensive and allegations of military disaster, Cronkite decided to go to Vietnam himself to find out what was happening. He was shocked by what he saw, and in his commentary and the images he selected, he publicly turned against further escalation. "It seems now more certain than ever," he concluded, "that the bloody experience of Vietnam is to end in a stalemate."[18] According to David Halberstam, Johnson watched this broadcast "in Washington" and told his press secretary, George Christian, that "it was a turning point, that

Figure 10. National Youth Administration Director Johnson walks with his assistant, Willard Deason, probably in downtown Austin. The image of New Deal youthful energy, Johnson exudes a wonderful self-confidence, but his ill-fitting suit produces a slightly comic effect.

if he had lost Walter Cronkite he had lost Mr. Average Citizen. It solidified his decision not to run again."[19] The implication of such a statement is extraordinary—it is a documented instance of a television newscast affecting a major policy decision of a president. As such it compares with CBS commentator Edward R. Murrow's attack on Senator Joseph McCarthy in March 1954, which media enthusiasts have cited as evidence that television news destroyed McCarthyism.[20]

What evidence does the Johnson Library have regarding the Cronkite broadcast? The White House Diary and Diary Backup Files show that the President was in Texas, not Washington, on February

Figure 11. In this unidentified Texas town, the central business district features order offices for Montgomery Ward and Sears, a barber shop, and a land office. The local citizens stand on the courthouse square awaiting Johnson's drop from the sky. Such showmanship—creating an image of modernity—helped Johnson win a close race.

27, 1968. He spoke in Dallas in the morning. His evening schedule was full, even for someone with an enormous amount of energy:

8:30 p.m.	Dinner
8:50 p.m.	Changed to black tie
9:05 p.m.	Out of house—to Jetstar walking
9:10 p.m.	Plane departed LBJ ranch
9:25 p.m.	Wheels down—Bergstrom AFB, Texas
9:50 p.m.	President arrived Gregory Gym [University of Texas]
10:06 p.m.	Started speech honoring John Connally on 51st birthday.[21]

Meanwhile, Cronkite's special went on the air at 10:00 P.M. EST (9:00 P.M. CST). Johnson traveled from the ranch to Austin as Cronkite spoke. He later boarded Air Force One for Washington, D.C., arriving home at 2:11 A.M. In the morning he saw Robert McNamara at 8:04 A.M. and breakfasted with his key foreign-policy advisers at 8:35 A.M. He did not have time to watch NBC's *Today Show*, which he often viewed in the morning.

Johnson could not have seen the broadcast as originally aired,

REVEILLE

Figure 12. In this 1965 cartoon Johnson, attired in a trim business suit, tries to awaken fat, apathetic Americans to the importance of Vietnam. © The Washington Star.

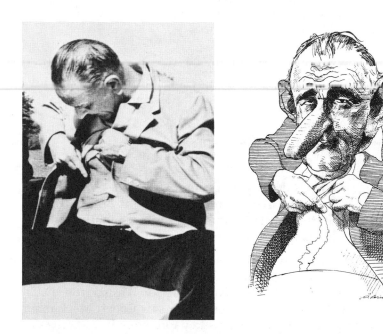

Figure 13 (*left*). Johnson showing his scar, October 20, 1965. Photo © UPI.
Figure 14 (*right*). Drawing by David Levine. Reprinted with permission from *The New York Review of Books*. Copyright © 1968 Nyrev, Inc.

but he could have watched a videotaped playback. The log sheets in the Johnson Library's audiovisual archives show that the Cronkite special was taped. In December 1967 it had become possible for the President to see videotaped programming in his own bedroom on one of the monitors. The log sheets do not indicate whether the President saw a recorded program.[22]

I talked with George Christian to see if he remembered watching the broadcast with Johnson on videotape. Christian was confused to hear that Johnson had been in Austin giving a speech on the night of February 27, for he clearly remembered that he and the President sat and watched the program together. "Johnson did talk about [Cronkite's] going to Vietnam and in effect turning against the war," he insisted, "and it did worry him immensely that Cronkite had in effect become dovish, because he saw the impact was going to be tremendous on the country. . . . I know we talked about the Cronkite program."[23]

Did Johnson actually see the program or just hear about it from a staff memorandum, a newspaper account, or network radio? There is no way to be certain, but since this was one of a very few news broadcasts videotaped by the White House in February 1968, it seems quite possible that Johnson did see the taped program. Harry McPherson, counsel to the President and one of his most effective speechwriters, also believes the Cronkite special "had a huge impact on Johnson and his sense of crumbling public support for the war." McPherson feels that Johnson "liked and trusted" Cronkite, a fellow Texan, though he considered David Brinkley of NBC's *Huntley-Brinkley Report* to be "a smart ass." In McPherson's view, Johnson generally watched television not so much for information as to "gauge what its impact on the public would be."[24]

The agenda-setting function seems a logical explanation for Johnson's concern with television news. Network coverage is brief, larded with advertisements, and tends to be cautious. The experienced politician uses television news as another informal device for gauging changing public opinion about selected issues. While Cronkite did not force Johnson to change his Vietnam strategy, Cronkite's special program did more to persuade Johnson that optimistic promises of light at the end of the tunnel were no longer acceptable than a whole series of reports in the *New York Times* or the *Washington Post*. It mattered to Johnson and millions of other viewers that Walter Cronkite had personally gone to Vietnam before preparing his special report; actually seeing him in Vietnam added a credibility hard to ignore.

Figure 15. Johnson loved this photograph because it exudes integrity and credibility. This is the image of a man who comes from the land—tough, grizzled, dependable, not given to boasting—the heroic figure John Wayne played in so many Hollywood productions.

The Johnson Image

Johnson spent his entire life trying to improve his image, that combination of physical appearance and personality which, among other criteria, enables individuals to appraise the credibility of elected officials. When Johnson became Texas state director of Roosevelt's National Youth Administration in 1935, he naturally sought to overcome his rural origin by outfitting himself in such a way as to emphasize his urbanity (see Figure 10).

Johnson also recognized the value of publicity in shaping one's image and employed unusual devices to build support. In his 1948 senate race, he used a helicopter to reach remote parts of the state (Figure 11).

During the 1950s Johnson's image was that of the Texan in Washington. Cartoonists pictured the Senate majority leader in a cowboy hat and boots. He gained a suit only after becoming President.[26]

As President, Johnson quickly became a handy target for caricature, as he admitted in May 1965 when he spoke to members of the Association of American Editorial Cartoonists about the need to increase American concern about Vietnam. "After looking at some of the cartoons you have drawn," he declared, "I thought I'd invite you over to see me in person. After all, I had nothing to lose." He added, "What you draw remains in the public memory long after these other words are forgotten."[27]

Johnson's presidential image converged in photographs and cartoons. The notorious scar photograph of October 20, 1965 (Figure 13) fixed a public image of Johnson as a person lacking Kennedy's class and presidential stature. The UPI caption reads, "President Johnson, in good spirits after a walk around the hospital grounds and buoyed by the thought of leaving the hospital, pulls up the tails of his sport shirt to show his surgical bandage and to illustrate just where it was that the surgeons 'messed around' in his abdomen." The photograph appeared the next day in newspapers throughout the world, in some instances with an enlargement of the scar "transmitted in answer to requests." Thousands wrote to protest the photograph's poor taste. A few, fancying themselves wits, "thanked God the President had not suffered from hemorrhoids."[28] What possessed Johnson to pull up his shirttail remains a mystery, but the media succeeded in making him look ridiculous. The scar remained part of his presidential image.

The photograph later inspired David Levine's cartoon of Johnson's Vietnam scar, one of the best-known anti-Johnson images (Figure 14). Levine exaggerated the size of the President's ears, the length of his nose, and the thinness of his hair and gave him a pronounced double chin, along with the eyes of a dishonest speculator. Levine's cartoon presumed a collective memory of the scar photograph and made the scar into a symbol of Johnson's Vietnam policies and the credibility gap plaguing his administration. These two images remain significant visual documents of the way Americans in the 1960s saw their President.

A vain man, Johnson decided to shape his own visual image. Staff photographers took over 500,000 photographs during the White

House years.[29] The President regularly gave away inscribed pictures and had albums prepared for dignitaries. He studied himself in image after image, looking for indications of veracity and Eastern urbanity. Harry McPherson tells of a conversation with the President about one photograph. "God, look at that photograph," Johnson said.

> It had what I call his John Wayne look—you know, the smile as we look into the Western sunset with Old Paint. It's the inverted "V's" in the brows and smile on the face: weathered, troubled, but still philosophical, Uncle Lyndon looks to the West. And he said, "Have you ever seen anything phonier in your life?" And I said, "No, I haven't."
>
> He had one of those smiles on, standing next to somebody, and he said, "I didn't want to be there with that guy. I don't care anything about him; I didn't want to be there with the picture, and I knew that would show. So I tried to put on a smile. And every time I try to do that, I look phonier. It all comes through and I can't break it."[30]

Johnson finally got the photograph he was looking for after leaving the White House. Taken at the ranch, it is filed at the Johnson Library under "John Wayne Photo." The photographer, Frank Wolfe, explains what Johnson liked about the photograph: the cowboy hat and shirt give an "earthy look," making him appear "tall and robust." Johnson was "deeply involved in ranch activities" after leaving the White House and "that's the image he took up." The photograph (Figure 15) is unposed.[31]

Unfortunately for President Johnson, hundreds of thousands of photographs, personal television addresses, telephone calls, press conferences, consultations with media experts, and advice from staff members failed to persuade Americans to think of him as a John Wayne hero. Instead the President was charged with a credibility gap, a catch-phrase used in the 1960s to indicate that a government official was not telling the truth. Historian Eric Goldman reports that shortly after Johnson made a major foreign-policy address at Johns Hopkins University in April 1965, a *New York Herald Tribune* reporter, David Wise, published a piece entitled "Credibility Gap." This May 23, 1965, article, Goldman believes, was "the first use of the phrase in print." He adds that the phrase received its "principal popularization" from a December 5, 1965, article Murray Marder wrote for the *Washington Post*.[32] The growing doubts concerned what had actually taken place in the Tonkin Gulf in August 1964, along with the administration's inability to prove that the

Figure 16. The "new" Johnson using his hands to sell Vietnam policies, November 17, 1967. He used a lavaliere microphone which enabled him to get away from "mother," the large podium where he kept his answer book. The boom mike in the background enabled reporters to ask questions. In spite of his success Johnson never again used such a microphone, fearing that it would make him an "actor" instead of a President. Robert Fleming says Johnson was offended by a *New York Times* story the next day which likened his "performance" to that of Kennedy (Fleming interview, November 8, 1979). Walt Rostow, *The Diffusion of Power: An Essay in Recent History* (New York, 1972), p. 532, recalls this conference as follows: "Using a lavaliere microphone, he strode about, speaking with vividness and force on a wide range of issues. The effect was electric. But he never did it again."

sending of U.S. Marines to the Dominican Republic in 1965 had actually been in response to a communist-directed attempted takeover. By the autumn of 1965 many no longer believed Johnson was telling the truth about foreign-policy matters.

The phrase did not lose its currency. George Reedy has an unusual explanation: "Many former White House members blame [Press Secretary Bill] Moyers for the credibility gap," he claims. "It was no accident that the President's popularity started to fall abruptly as soon as Bill took over."[33] Such a claim may say more about the relations between Reedy and Moyers than anything else, but the President's reputation for candor did not improve in 1967.

Staff members provided the President with many ideas about how to counter the criticism, but cosmetics did little good. Johnson was furious at Walter Lippmann's March 1967 series of articles on

Figure 17. The "Wise Men" meeting with Johnson. To his right are Dean Acheson and Henry Cabot Lodge. The group gave the President some somber advice: the country would support no further widening of the war.

the credibility gap. Max Frankel published a lead article in the *New York Times Magazine* on January 7, 1968, entitled "Why the Gap between L.B.J. and the Nation: Failure to Communicate?" The same year a small book on the subject appeared: *Lyndon Johnson's Credibility Gap.*[34]

Several White House staff members collected materials about the credibility gap in 1967–1968, in particular Fred Panzer, though his memoranda suggest a siege mentality rather than reasoned thought. In February 1968 Panzer finished a position paper explaining the psychology of the credibility gap and its proponents and blaming the phrase on "antiwar and anti-Johnson forces—an assortment of Republicans, Democrats, the old Left and the New Left"—focusing on the charge that "LBJ lied to the American people in the 1964 campaign, . . . in particular that he promised not to send American boys to fight an Asian war." Panzer included an appendix describing charges that Franklin Roosevelt had also promised not to send American soldiers to war and asserted "that this statement too is an out of context distortion."[35] Other Panzer memoranda of the period suggest that this adviser really believed the enemy was at the gate.

While such materials may be taken as evidence that Johnson insulated himself from critics by late 1967, they really prove only what staff members thought and not necessarily what Johnson thought. One document in the President's own hand (a rare thing) suggests that Johnson had not become so angry at his critics that he no longer listened. *Time* ran a story in the last week of December 1967 stating that a head of the American Forces Network in Europe had issued an order saying that a military broadcasting affiliate should perform as a band. "The band," *Time* added, "can't make a political comment, can't say a wrong thing unless some s.o.b. has his horn out of tune." On the margin Johnson scrawled, "This is disgraceful—come on now—where is this commander in chief I read about? Send this guy to the Antarctic."[36]

The most elaborate attempt at improving Johnson's credibility in the fall of 1967 was his televised press conference of November 17, 1967.[37] The President had called General William Westmoreland home from Vietnam to make a progress report. Westmoreland spoke about "light at the end of the tunnel," and Johnson elaborated on the encouraging signs of progress. He felt he had hard facts with which to disarm his critics, and he even experimented with a new type of microphone (see Figure 16).

No event proved more devastating to Johnson than the Tet Offensive, which in the first few days of February 1968 utterly destroyed administration credibility with the American people.[38] Coming hard on the heels of Westmoreland's optimistic reports, it seemed to make a mockery of administration claims to competence on the field of battle. The North Vietnamese massive assault on cities throughout Vietnam appeared in some of the most vivid newsfilm to come out of the war. A Herblock cartoon of February 1, 1968, captures the mood. A military flack grinds out optimistic press releases in Saigon, the office in ruins, enemy soldiers at the door. "Everything's Okay—They Never Reached the Mimeograph Machine," he reports over the phone. The moral was obvious: there was not a shred of truth in Johnson's claims about Vietnam; what appeared on television was reality.

Two pieces of television coverage from downtown Saigon had particular impact. On January 31 NBC showed footage of Vietcong sappers inside the supposedly bomb-proof American ambassador's compound. How, viewers asked, could there be a strategic hamlet program if the ambassador's own residence was not even secure? The visual image of disaster remained in the minds of viewers at home though the terrorists were quickly killed by American forces.

Two days later television destroyed every official pronouncement about the democratic quality of America's ally, South Vietnam. General Loan, chief of the South Vietnamese police, executed a Vietcong terrorist in front of two television camera crews and an AP photographer. The photograph appeared in newspapers all over the world; two networks ran the footage of the execution. Viewers simply could not reconcile this "rough justice on a Saigon street" with official pledges of a "democratic" government of South Vietnam.[39] The photograph became a weapon for those who opposed the war and proved indefensible by administration representatives. It did not matter that General Loan's action was justifiable, that the Vietcong who appeared so frail in his plaid shirt was a well-known terrorist leader who had just killed a large number of South Vietnamese civilians. Television captured the instant of death, and blood spurting from the head of the victim spoke of the brutal murder of a civilian, not justifiable action under martial law. Perhaps, as General Loan feels today, his blunder had to do with the management of news. He says his wife "gave him hell" for not confiscating the film.[40]

The 1968 Tet Offensive, though in retrospect clearly a military disaster for the North Vietnamese, at the time proved a psychological victory of overwhelming proportions. Taking the war into the cities for the first time was a risky venture that worked for the Vietcong. Visual reports of disaster gave tremendous impetus to the antiwar movement in America. After February 1968 Johnson no longer had a credibility gap—a mere problem with information management. The gap had become a chasm; skepticism had turned to massive disbelief. On March 26, 1968, the President met with the "Wise Men," a group of influential leaders, to discuss whether or not to escalate further the Vietnam war (Figure 17).[41] Five days later, Johnson, in a televised address, shocked the nation with his announcement that he would not seek reelection.

The Real Johnson

An often-noted concern of scholars working in the presidential libraries of recent Presidents is the scarcity of administrative material originating from the Presidents themselves. It often seems infinitely more difficult to discover the President's own views than those of his speech writers, opponents, and staff members. The Johnson Library is no exception: the more voluminous the records, the more the chief executive recedes from view. This situation gives special significance to audiovisual records, for here the thoughts, character, and methods of the real Johnson are revealed.

Like Richard Nixon, Johnson secretly recorded telephone conversations, though not in great quantity. Seven boxes of recordings are in the Johnson Library, closed to researchers until 2023.[42] A secretary in Johnson's outer office, after getting a signal from the President, would record the conversation. One telephone conversation with Kennedy aide Theodore Sorensen, dated June 3, 1963, has been recently opened. This conversation shows the real Johnson in action and explains why he was so extraordinarily persuasive in private. Vice-President Johnson was explaining to Sorensen the importance of passing a civil rights bill in Congress and of President Kennedy's taking his case to the public. Johnson insisted repeatedly that Kennedy go to the South:

> If he goes down there and looks them in the eye and states the moral issue and the Christian issue, and he does it face to face, these Southerners at least respect his courage. . . . The southern whites and the *Negroes* share one point of view that's identical. They're not certain that the government is on the side of the *Negroes.* The whites think we're just playing politics to carry New York. The *nigras* feel and they're suspicious that we're just doing what we got to do. . . . I don't think the *Negroes'* goals are going to be achieved through legislation and a little thing here on impact area or vote or something. I think the *nigger* leaders are aware of that. What *nigras* are really seeking is moral force.[43]

For nearly thirty minutes Johnson rushed on, making some points again and again, building an irresistible demand for action. The syntax was garbled, the Texas accent apparent in every syllable—the accent which plagued his attempts to convince the North about the sincerity of his racial convictions. In the heat of the moment, while promoting a point of view revealing great political acumen, Johnson slipped from "Negro" to "nigra" to "nigger leaders." Perhaps these potentially objectionable elements of Johnson's speech explain his fear of speaking spontaneously in televised addresses.

In the same conversation Johnson made some pointed remarks about Senator Hubert Humphrey and how to line up Senate support:

> [Kennedy] ought to get his own team in line about chairmen of committees. He got Humphrey. What the hell is Humphrey? He's a wonderful man, but we know he like Bob Taylor's goat, he's done voted. We've got to get some other folks in this thing to get that cloture. You got to get a good many of your western-

Figure 18. During the June 1967 Arab-Israeli War, a television set in the White House Situation Room was on during Ambassador Goldberg's speech. Policy makers talking directly with Moscow were able to watch the debate at the United Nations.

Figure 19. Clark Clifford, Richard Helms, Earle Wheeler, and the President watching Dean Rusk testify before the Senate Foreign Relations Commit- tee. Here television enabled a Cabinet member to speak to his peers. Dean Rusk once explained his frequent appearances on NBC's *Today Show* as "the only place where he could talk directly to his president, the Cabinet, and forty senators without any interruptions" (interview with Robert Fleming, November 8, 1979). Walt Rostow, it should be noted, is not seated where he can see the screen.

ers. You got to sit down with them, help them have a reason, let their people go to them from Wyoming, and Montana, and Idaho, and some of these other places.[44]

Johnson had a sharp sense of humor unknown to those who sat through his televised presidential addresses. The Johnson Library's sales desk has a cassette recording, "LBJ Humor," which can do a great deal to bring the real Johnson to life. The President loved to tell stories, many with a political point, often with details or entire incidents manufactured out of whole cloth. Rural Texas in the 1930s was a setting for some of the best stories, since eastern audiences could be counted on to believe almost any detail as at least possibly true. Try reading this example aloud:

> Ah was tryin' tuh build a simple rural 'lectric line out tuh the farmers that lived in mah hill country. The pahwer companies wouldn' let muh dew it. Ah didn' know ah needed their permission but ah found out ah did. And ah met with the president of the most pahwerful pahwer company in the state and he had one word, cwop-ration. He looked a good deal lak' a Methodist bishop. He was strikin'. He had long gray hair—mebbe' not as long as we wear today—some. He would say 'Ah want tew cwop-rate. Ah want tew cwop-rate.' And he jest cwop-rated meh out of evruh' meetin' ah ever got in. [laughter]
>
> And ah never did get the 'lectricity. Till finally one day in my youthful impetuosity ah jumped up and said 'well ah've tried to work with yew now for a yeah heah and we haven' got an ounce of 'lectricity and yew can take a runnin' jump and go straight to hell as far as ah'm concerned,' and that broke up the meetin' and all the crowd 'plauded jest lak' ah'd been talkin' 'bout cheap labor.
>
> And ah looked around for approval. . . . And ah looked at this old lawyer who had been my mentor for several years. Finally ah asked him what he thought of my speech. He said 'Come by my office,' and ah knew then what he thought 'bout it. [laughter] And he got meh in the room and he said 'Lyndon, now yer in public life. Ah want yew to go far. Ah'm glad yew have the courage to stand up and tell this representative of 'Lectric Bond and Share to go straight to hell. Ah'm glad yew've got the courage tuh dew that. But one thing ah want yew to learn now is tellin' a man tuh go to hell and makin' him go is two different propositions. [laughter and applause] He dudn't want tuh go. [laughter] He's been told it's hot down there. [laughter]

'It took meh nearly two years to get this conciliation—this mediation—to the point where we could meet together to try an' solve this thing—and reason together. And yew busted it up in two minutes and ah've got to start all over.'

Lincoln told stories as President, but Lyndon Johnson felt his presidential image did not allow him to do the same on television. Humor can be a risky business when one's audience includes millions of possibly humorless listeners, including Methodist bishops, widows of Methodist bishops, and presidents of power and light companies.

The Johnson Legacy

Before Johnson there was not much reason for a President to watch television news nightly or to urge his staff to do so—television news, still only fifteen minutes in the evening, had not come of age. In the 1960 campaign, to be sure, televised debates between Kennedy and Nixon helped some voters decide a close race, but daily television coverage in the campaign was central to neither candidate's campaign strategy. Kennedy proved adept in handling televised press conferences, but television as a medium matured technologically just as Johnson entered the White House, particularly in the around-the-clock coverage of the assassination, the shooting of Lee Harvey Oswald, and the Kennedy funeral. Network news went to thirty minutes in 1963.

Johnson believed in making full use of the television medium. For a time staff members prepared daily summaries of the evening news on each network, and a videotape playback machine recorded broadcasts for the President to see later. With three monitors in the Oval Office, the President's bedroom, the ranch, and the offices of selected staff members and a television broadcast facility in the White House for presidential addresses and press conferences, Johnson believed in using the medium for all it was worth.

But the more he saw, the less he liked—the image just did not seem right. So he ordered professional home movies to show friends at the ranch or aboard the presidential yacht. Each month from June 1966 through January 1969, the Naval Photographic Laboratory produced an elaborate sixteen-millimeter film, *The President*, in color, with sound and music, generally thirty minutes in length.[45] There is considerable footage of such events as the Tuesday luncheons of the National Security Council, Cabinet briefings, and trips. The monthly films are uncritical of the President, but the technical quality is superb.[46] A monument to personal vanity, to be sure, these films are also a boon to documentary film makers and will be immensely useful to all who teach the history of the 1960s.

A more subtle legacy to the office of the presidency was Johnson's insistence that staff members pay attention to television—in effect, that television be brought into the decision-making process. Those around Johnson, in particular some staff members with considerable influence, did not take kindly to the presidential assignment. Walt Rostow, for example, recalls how much he resisted Johnson's insistence that he watch television. "It is a minor comic affair of the administration," he says,

> because I did not regard it as my duty to follow the television news closely. President Johnson did and he called down saying "Did you see Senator Fulbright on the *Today Show* this morning?" I said, "No Sir, I've been busy with something else." Finally he installed in my office a small television set and he said, "Now, I don't want you ever again to tell me that if I call down here that you can't watch it or you're not watching—it's important that you do it." I must confess, that was one of the orders of the emperor I did disobey. . . . I didn't figure that was what the taxpayers were paying me for.[47]

The President also had more direct methods of making aides watch television. During the National Security Council Tuesday luncheon on March 12, 1968, Johnson had a television placed next to the table.

Other staff members turned to television news of their own accord, sometimes with significant results. Harry McPherson, for example, feels in retrospect that television coverage of the Tet crisis in 1968 told him something more truthful than what he could get from hourly intelligence bulletins in the White House Situation Room. "I suppose from a social scientist's point of view," he declares,

> it is particularly interesting that people like me, people who had some responsibility for expressing the presidential point of view, could be so affected by the media as everyone else was. While downstairs within fifty yards of my desk was that enormous panoply of intelligence-gathering devices—tickers, radios, messages coming in from the field. I assume the reason . . . I put aside my own interior access to confidential information and was more persuaded by what I saw on the tube and in the newspapers was that like everyone else who had been deep-

ly involved in explaining the policies of the war, . . . I was fed up with the light at the end of the tunnel stuff.[48]

Television images of disaster gave McPherson evidence enabling him to change his mind about supporting further American involvement in Vietnam. McPherson did not turn from hawk to dove solely because of television, but his example suggests that television images such as that of the Vietcong sappers inside the American ambassador's compound in Saigon and General Loan's execution of the Vietcong must have had definite impact on an administration aide already worried about the validity of American policy in Vietnam. For McPherson, certain television images proved more powerful than the immense amount of factual data coming to the White House through official channels. But something George Christian recently said about this television-inspired-conversion is also worth remembering: "Harry probably didn't see as much television as he thinks now that he saw."[49]

What conclusions can be drawn about Johnson and the media? Several points should be made.

1. Policy making in a fishbowl. Decision making in the Johnson years involved living in the presence of unremitting aural and visual publicity: 500,000 official photographs; television consoles in numerous offices; film camera crews recording Cabinet briefings, National Security Council luncheons, and even decisions made in the White House Situation Room at the height of the Tet crisis; televised press conferences; daily reminders from Johnson about radio, television, and newspaper commentary; and hordes of press photographers and television crews from all over the world. This emphasis on instant communication with the outside world, on news as technology, and on the aural and visual recording of events demands that the scholar be sensitive to the media as an irritant and a constant presence not to be ignored. The nervousness implicit in trying to keep up with such a deluge of information and publicity must be recognized in any retrospective account of decision making.

2. Johnson and his critics. Those who differed with Johnson in the 1960s frequently asserted that he was out of touch with the mood of the country, that he insulated himself and his staff from what critics were saying. The evidence does not substantiate this charge. Walt Rostow, a particular target for such criticism, notes that he "followed the press and TV commentators and knew well the views being articulated. . . . LBJ was quite right in insisting that his staff not insulate itself from public and elite opinion." Rostow insists that if Johnson "took a different path than his critics advocated, it was not because he had not heard or listened with sympathy to their views."[50] Johnson listened to more news, talked with more people, especially by long distance telephone, read more newspapers, and watched more television than any previous occupant of the White House, thanks in part to technological innovations. Records at the Johnson Library amply support the view that the President paid careful attention to what his critics were saying. Indeed, Johnson not only tried to know what every medium of communication was saying but also set up even more elaborate systems of information retrieval within the White House itself.

3. *Television as a tool for policy makers.* Television came of age during the Johnson years, as symbolized by the banks of three monitors.[51] Of more lasting significance is the emergence of television as a tool for policy making. Johnson watched the confrontation at Selma to get a feeling for the reality of the situation. He watched television to see what was really happening in Detroit during the riots. He made those present at a National Security Council luncheon watch Dean Rusk testify before the Senate Foreign Relations Committee. He ordered summaries of evening news broadcasts. He watched debate at the United Nations during the Arab-Israeli War. He watched the *Today Show* to learn what Cabinet officers or the Senate opposition thought. Johnson used television to gauge public sentiment on a variety of issues, to vivify confrontation elsewhere, and to try to sell his own policies. His image kept him from selling himself successfully, but his obsession with television news increased the salience of the medium for policy makers.

For scholars, there are a number of questions to be considered. Were decisions made more effectively because of the speed with which information came to the White House? Were policies arrived at more scientifically because of faster and more elaborate methods of gauging popular and elite opinion? Did media technology improve the functioning of democracy in this country? Or did the enormous flow of information actually impede decisions, as aides frantically struggled to assimilate the latest mountain of data. Perhaps the image of the sorcerer's apprentice trying to hold back floods of undigested opinion and information is more appropriate. The Johnson era seems more likely to be remembered for the amount of information received and given than for the effective use of that information in decision making. Media technology seems to have evolved more rapidly than presidential mechanisms for dealing with it.

4. *The necessity of audiovisual archives to the scholar.* The investigator writing about the Johnson years cannot do justice to the subject without using audiovisual records. The "real" Johnson is not found in his public speeches or in scattered check marks on memoranda. Even the best oral history interviews, of which there are many in the Johnson Library, present a picture of a President Johnson filtered through the biases of the interviewees. It is the audiovisual material that reveals the Johnson hidden in the pages of *The Vantage Point*, the Johnson who eluded those who watched his stiff television addresses. The real man emerges from the telephone conversation explaining to Sorensen how to get civil rights legislation through Congress; the tape of Johnson telling an audience how he learned the hard way about the dangers of "youthful impetuosity"; the photos of Johnson posing as John Wayne, dropping out of the sky in a helicopter, or presiding at a National Security Council luncheon with a television set turned on.

Audiovisual archives need not serve to burnish the President's image. They represent a central source of material for the scholar who seeks not to improve Johnson but to understand him and to explain him both to college students too young to remember his presidency, who never knew the man or felt anything about his policies, and to older Americans who never had a chance to observe Johnson's genius for privately manipulating individuals toward a particular goal.

Notes

Peter Rollins read an earlier version of this essay and made many helpful suggestions.

1. David Halberstam, *The Powers That Be* (New York, 1979), p. 6; Doris Kearns, *Lyndon Johnson and the American Dream* (New York, 1977), p. 7; telephone interview with George Christian, September 7, 1979. A transcript of this interview is now part of the Oral History Collection at the Johnson Library.

2. Harry McPherson Oral History Interview, tape 4, p. 27, Johnson Library; Kearns, *Johnson and the American Dream*, pp. 385–390; filmed interview with Harry McPherson, Baton Rouge, La., April 27, 1979.

3. George Reedy, *Twilight of the Presidency* (New York, 1970), p. 107. Robert Giles Swan, in charge of all television coverage for Truman and Stevenson in the 1952 campaign, wrote Johnson about the tinkering: "I have been astonished by the number of experiments attempted on your telecasts" (Swan to Johnson, July 3, 1966, box 22, General File 11, White House Central Files, Johnson Library).

4. Kearns, *Johnson and the American Dream*, p. 77.

5. Johnson's obsession with photography has led to an immense amount of material for the scholar. In the Johnson Library are over 500,000 photographs from the presidential years, of which approximately 100,000 are filed according to date, name, and subject. David Humphrey, of the library's audiovisual archives, helped me locate some of the photographs used in this essay. Researchers can request a two-page description, *Still Pictures*, summarizing the library's holdings.

6. Lady Bird Johnson to David Culbert, November 30, 1979; J. Evetts Haley, *A Texan Looks at Lyndon: A Study in Illegitimate Power* (Canyon, Tex., 1964), p. 65. Haley makes the purchase of the radio station sound sinister and dwells on the alleged impropriety of Johnson's television monopoly in Austin, dating from 1952.

7. Interview with Robert Fleming, Washington, D.C., November 8, 1979. A transcript of this interview is now part of the Oral History Collection at the Johnson Library.

8. Stanton and a CBS engineer installed the unit in the President's bedroom on August 5, 1964. Jack Valenti to Bill Moyers, August 4, 1964, filed Frank Stanton Name File, box 518, White House Central Files, Johnson Library.

9. David Garrow, *Protest at Selma: Martin Luther King, Jr., and the Voting Rights Act of 1965* (New Haven, Conn., 1978), pp. 84–85, 89.

10. Lyndon Johnson, *The Vantage Point: Perspectives of the Presidency, 1963–1969* (New York, 1971), p. 162.

11. Ibid., p. 171.

12. Dan Rather with Mickey Herskowitz, *The Camera Never Blinks: Adventures of a TV Journalist* (New York, 1978), p. 172. Kearns, *Johnson and the American Dream*, p. 8, also tells how Johnson called to scold offending reporters.

13. A significant exception is Frank Stanton.

14. Transcript, Earle Wheeler Oral History Interview, tape 1, p. 8, Johnson Library.

15. Telephone interview with Juanita Roberts, January 15, 1980. Two of Johnson's other secretaries, Yolanda Boozer and Dorothy Territo, both on the staff of the Johnson Library, confirmed the testimony of Roberts. We studied the White House telephone installations in the museum part of the Johnson Library as well.

16. Interview with Robert Fleming, November 8, 1979. The Appointment File, Diary Backup often shows Johnson meeting with people at the time the evening news was broadcast.

17. Interview with Fleming, November 8, 1979. For example see Fleming to Johnson, January 26, January 31, February 1, February 9, and February 13–14, 1968, all filed in CBS 1967 Name File, box 344, White House Central Files, Johnson Library. Fleming summarized the evening news for February 1 as follows: "All three evening shows opened with almost 15 minutes of film from Vietnam, most of it the first they've had on the Saigon fighting. The film was reasonably interesting, though not showing much of the scope

of the activity. All three used the still picture of the South Vietnamese police chief General Loan shooting the prisoner: CBS called it 'rough justice on the streets'; ABC quoted the police chief as saying his action was 'justified because he had killed many Americans and many of our people'; NBC said 'war was not all men hiding behind trees or in buildings.'" Another Fleming memorandum, dated March 11, 1968 cites a New York *Daily News* columnist as saying, "What possible point does Church have in asking Rusk, in open session, why we plan to defend Khe Sanh? Can a senator seriously believe Rusk should answer such questions on television?" (March 1, 1968 folder, box 361, PR 18, Executive File, White House Central Files, Johnson Library). The first Benchley memorandum, which summarizes a week's coverage, is found in George Christian to Johnson, August 14, 1967, Publicity 1967 folder, box 83, PR 18, Confidential File, White House Central Files, Johnson Library.

18. Peter Braestrup, *Big Story: How the American Press and Television Reported and Interpreted the Crisis of Tet 1968 in Vietnam and Washington* (Boulder, Colo., 1977), 1:158, 2:180–189.

19. Halberstam, *The Powers That Be*, p. 514.

20. For example, Alexander Kendrick, *Prime Time: The Life of Edward R. Murrow* (Boston, 1969), pp. 35–71.

21. *Public Papers of the Presidents: Lyndon B. Johnson, 1968–69* (Washington, D.C., 1970), 1:288–289, prints the President's remarks. A footnote says he spoke at 9:54 p.m., not 10:06.

22. Before December 1967 the President had to go to where the equipment was set up, as was the case when he looked at a videotape of his November 11, 1967 press conference (W. Marvin Watson to Johnson, December 3, 1967, box 22, General File 11, White House Central Files, Johnson Library).

23. Telephone interview with George Christian, September 17, 1979.

24. Filmed interview with Harry McPherson, April 27, 1979.

25. Haley, *A Texan Looks at Lyndon*, presents a great deal of detail about how Johnson supposedly stole the election.

26. Interview with Archer Mayor, Johnson Library, October 15, 1979. The library has a collection of cartoons in eight boxes located in the search room on the eighth floor. The collection is unrepresentative, with numerous examples by second-rate artists supporting the President but virtually none from the best-known cartoonists of the 1960s. The Lyndon B. Johnson Foundation has commissioned an anthology of selected cartoons to be published in 1981.

27. Address at White House, May 13, 1965, in *Public Papers: 1965* (Washington, D.C., 1966), 1:525.

28. The letters, most with the photograph as it appeared in American and British newspapers and magazines, can be found in box 8, Bill Moyers Files, Johnson Library. *Life* published the photograph under "Medicine" as a full-page spread. The *New York Times* ran a small copy on an inside page.

Some publications placed the photograph and the enlargement of the scar on page one.

29. By comparison Kennedy's official photographers took approximately 30,000 pictures, about one-seventeenth as many. Johnson's *Vantage Point* contains seventy-two pages of photographs. Liz Carpenter, ed., *LBJ: Images of a Vibrant Life* (Austin, 1973), contains fifty photographs, many in color.

30. Harry McPherson Oral History Interview, tape 4, p. 29, Johnson Library. The photograph has not been located.

31. Interview with Frank Wolfe, Johnson Library, October 19, 1979. The photograph was taken at the ranch on September 18, 1972.

32. Eric Goldman, *The Tragedy of Lyndon Johnson* (New York, 1969), p. 409.

33. George Reedy Oral History Interview, tape 4, pp. 11–14, Johnson Library. Reedy makes no such claims in his more dispassionate *Twilight of the Presidency.*

34. Max Frankel, "Why the Gap between L.B.J. and the Nation: Failure to Communicate?" *New York Times Magazine,* January 7, 1968, p. 7; J. Deakin, *Lyndon Johnson's Credibility Gap* (Washington, D.C., 1968); E. V. Wolfenstein, "The Two Wars of Lyndon Johnson," *Politics and Society* 4 (1974): 357–396, discusses the gap in terms of Vietnam and the War on Poverty. Also important is Philip G. Goulding, *Confirm or Deny: Informing the People on National Security* (New York, 1970). The various editions of *The Pentagon Papers* provide further evidence of the gap between promise and performance during the Johnson years.

35. Fred Panzer to Marvin Watson, George Christian, and Ernest Goldstein, filed February 21, 1968, FG 11-8-1/Panzer, Executive File, White House Central Files, Johnson Library. There are also folders relating to credibility and the credibility gap under the same file number for Christian, Goldstein, and Watson.

36. December 16, 1967 folder, box 361, PR 18, Executive File, White House Central Files, Johnson Library.

37. *Public Papers: 1967* (Washington, D.C., 1968), 2:1045–1055. The Johnson Library audiovisual archives have the entire press conference on videotape and audiotape, and there are numerous still photographs.

38. Braestrup, *Big Story,* covers in monumental detail the media coverage of Tet 1968. A recent summary may be found in George C. Herring, *America's Longest War: The United States and Vietnam, 1970–1975* (New York, 1979), pp. 183–216. Those interested in researching television news coverage of the war or of Johnson are hampered because the networks did not save complete nightly broadcasts on kinescope and the Vanderbilt Television News Archive in Nashville, Tennessee did not begin taping network news until August 5, 1968. Although the Chicago convention coverage, including everything shown by NBC during the night of greatest violence, is available from Vanderbilt on videotape, most of the Johnson presidency

television materials are a hit-or-miss affair. The National Archives in Washington, D.C. has a great deal of material on Vietnam beginning May 27, 1967, when the Department of Defense began videotaping network news to send to military officials in Saigon. These kinescopes are an invaluable source for the 1968 Tet Offensive, but network permission to reproduce is rarely given, though it is possible to get a copy for classroom use. For information about the location and use of these materials, see Fay C. Schreibman, "Television News Archives: A Guide to Major Collections," in *Television Network News: Issues in Content Research,* ed. William Adams and Fay Schreibman (Washington, D.C., 1978), pp. 89–110. The National Archives has Department of Defense summary sheets for the 1967 and 1969 broadcasts, including brief descriptions of each story, but not in the admirable detail of the monthly *Television News Index and Abstracts* published by the Vanderbilt Television News Archive. Most major university libraries have this finding aid, of which 1968 to 1972 is available only on microfilm.

39. For an analysis of the execution newsfilm and photograph see David Culbert, "Historians and the Visual Analysis of Television News," in *Television Network News,* ed. Adams and Schreibman, pp. 139–154; and George A. Bailey and Lawrence W. Lichty, "Rough Justice on a Saigon Street: A Gatekeeper Study of NBC's Tet Execution Film," *Journalism Quarterly* 44 (Summer 1972): 221–229, 238.

40. Interview with General Loan, Burke, Virginia, July 25, 1979. Peter Rollins and I are currently completing a documentary film, *Television's Vietnam: The Battle of Khe Sanh,* which discusses the impact of visual images on the way Americans made policy decisions during the 1968 Tet crisis.

41. Herbert Schandler, *The Unmaking of a President: Lyndon Johnson and Vietnam* (Princeton, N.J., 1977), pp. 256–265.

42. Six of the boxes are dictabelt recordings. A seventh box records conversation at cabinet meetings, mostly 1968 meetings relating to Vietnam. A "T" next to a White House card file telephone entry indicates that the conversation was recorded.

43. Italics added. Telephone conversation between Johnson and Theodore Sorensen, June 3, 1963, transcript, p. 4, SRT no. 9024, Johnson Library. The library's transcript does not indicate the varieties of pronunciation.

44. Ibid., p. 11. Johnson urged five things: (1) Screen the proposed legislation more carefully. (2) Give Negro leaders a sense of Kennedy's moral commitment to blacks. (3) Talk to Republican leaders, particularly members of Congress and Eisenhower. (4) "Get [Kennedy's] own team in line about chairmen of committees." (5) Speak openly about civil rights in the South.

45. One issue runs fifty-four minutes; all footage is in the public domain. The Johnson Library has the unedited outtakes as well as release prints. Estimated annual costs for these films ranged from $240,000 to $360,000. The army, navy, and air force estimated $20,000 to $22,000 per issue; commercial contractors estimated $30,000. The navy also said it

needed $95,000 for new equipment, seventeen new personnel, and an estimated $1,000 per month in overtime pay for civilian personnel. The navy got the contract (White House Communications Agency to Panzer, September 29, 1965, box 22, General File 11, White House Central Files, Johnson Library).

46. For classroom use this material can be purchased on ¾-inch videocassettes. Ten minutes costs $20; sixty minutes, $60. Philip Scott, head of the audiovisual archives at the Johnson Library, can answer questions about other prices, particularly if one wishes to use an Austin film laboratory for processing sixteen-millimeter footage in the public domain.

47. Filmed interview with Walt Rostow, Austin, July 20, 1979.

48. Filmed interview with Harry McPherson, April 27, 1979.

49. Telephone interview with George Christian, September 17, 1979.

50. Walt Rostow to David Culbert, December 19, 1979.

51. Students of media realize that network records are generally closed to researchers. The Johnson Library has much material on the functioning of Washington bureaus and is thus a most important source for those interested in network policy related to news gathering.

A Bibliographic Note

For published materials relating to Johnson and the media, see Fred I. Greenstein et al., *Evolution of the Modern Presidency: A Bibliographic Survey* (Washington, D.C., 1977). Entries 1078–1204 relate to Johnson and entries 1854–1890 to mass media; many are annotated. For the development of television news see Erik Barnouw's fine books, in particular *Tube of Plenty: The Evolution of American Television* (New York, 1975) and *The Sponsor: Notes on a Modern Potentate* (New York, 1978). The latter has a good deal to say about public broadcasting, which Johnson did much to develop.

Clearly the most important source of information for media coverage of the Vietnam War is Peter Braestrup, *Big Story: How the American Press and Television Reported and Interpreted the Crisis of Tet 1968 in Vietnam and Washington*, 2 vols. (Boulder, Colo., 1977). David Halberstam's *The Powers That Be* (New York, 1979) discusses Johnson and the media but is marred by sloppy research. Thomas Powers, *The War at Home* (New York, 1973) surveys those who opposed the war and claims that domestic protest forced the United States out of the war. John Mueller, *War, Presidents, and Public Opinion* (New York, 1973) is a valuable guide to the confusion surrounding poll responses relating to Vietnam. Arleen Keylin and Suri Boiangin, *Front Page Vietnam as Reported by the New York Times* (New York, 1979) reproduces over 175 front pages, mostly from the 1960s, and gives a useful overview of attitudes in official circles toward Johnson's policies.

Two of Johnson's press secretaries have published accounts of some interest: George Christian, *The President Steps Down: A Personal Memoir of the Transfer of Power* (New York, 1970); and George Reedy, *The Twilight of the Presidency* (New York, 1970). The various bibliographical articles in William Adams and Fay Schreibman, eds., *Television Network News: Issues in Content Research* (Washington, D.C., 1978) provide an up-to-date summary of research, particularly on the role of television in political campaigns. For data relating to audience attitudes in the Johnson years, see Robert T. Bower, *Television and the Public* (New York, 1973). Les Brown, *Television: The Business behind the Box* (New York, 1971) is a good survey of the business side of the medium. For a comprehensive critical bibliography of materials relating to film and television, see David Culbert, "Bibliographic Guide for Film and Video Studies," in *Scholars' Guide to Washington, D.C. Film and Video Collections*, ed. Bonnie G. Rowan (Washington, D.C.: Smithsonian Institution Press, 1980).

Every biography of Johnson has a good deal to say about his problems with his media critics. See in particular Doris Kearns, *Lyndon Johnson and the American Dream* (New York, 1977), and Eric Goldman, *The Tragedy of Lyndon Johnson* (New York, 1969). Merle Miller, *Lyndon* (New York, 1980) contains useful material about Johnson and his critics. David Garrow, *Protest at Selma: Martin Luther King, Jr., and the Voting Rights Act of 1965* (New Haven, 1978) is unusual for its serious attempt to relate Johnson's decision making to television coverage of violent confrontation. Walt Rostow, *The Diffusion of Power: An Essay in Recent History* (New York, 1972) contains an excellent analysis of Johnson and public opinion, a subject overlooked by critics when the book first appeared.

Certain primary sources will be of definite value. Johnson's memoir, *The Vantage Point: Perspectives of the Presidency, 1963–1969* (New York, 1971), includes a few fleeting references to media; the numerous photographs of record are sometimes illuminating. Liz Carpenter, ed., *LBJ: Images of a Vibrant Life* (Austin, 1973), has an unprepossessing title but contains excellent photographs and examples of Johnson's story telling which relate to media. *Public Papers of the Presidents, Lyndon B. Johnson*, 10 vols. (Washington, D.C., 1965–1970), includes transcripts of Johnson's televised press conferences, addresses to the nation, and speeches to groups professionally interested in media.

Appendix

Historical Materials in the Lyndon B. Johnson Library

This list of historical materials in the Lyndon B. Johnson Library represents an abbreviated version of the library's list of holdings which will be published in 1981. Quantity, restrictions on access, availability, and detailed descriptions have been omitted. Please contact the library for any information concerning these omissions.

Manuscripts and Archives: Papers of Lyndon B. Johnson

I. Precongressional Papers
  A. Family Correspondence

II. Prepresidential Papers

  A. House of Representatives Papers, 1937–1949
     Political Correspondence
     Correspondence
     Congressional Committees and Legislative Matters
     Project Files
     Case Files
     Office Files, 1940–1948
     Speech Files, 1937–1948
     Photographs
     Clippings, 1933–1948
     Case Files of W. Lee O'Daniel, 1946–1948
     Scrapbooks

  B. Senate Papers, 1949–1961
     Card Indexes of Correspondence, 1948–1953
     "Master Files," 1953–1960
     Legislative Files, 1949–1960
     Nomination Files, 1949–1957
     Committee Files
     Papers of the Democratic Leader, 1951–1960
     Political Files, 1949–1960
     General Correspondence Files, 1948–1961
     Subject Files, 1958–1960
     Case and Project Files

Academy Appointment Files, 1949–1960
Chronological Files, 1958–1961
Office Files, 1949–1961
Papers Relating to Scott and White Memorial Hospitals and
    Scott, Sherwood, and Brindley Foundation, 1950–1954
Christmas Cards, 1958, 1960
Newspaper Clippings, 1949–1960
Public Relations Files, 1948–1952
Speech File, 1951–1960

C. Vice Presidential Papers, 1961–1963
"Master Files," 1961–1963
Subject Files, 1961–1963
Academy Appointment Files, 1961–1963
Congressional Files, 1961–1963
Working Papers of the President's Committee on Equal
    Employment Opportunity, 1960–1963
Correspondence of the Vice President Elect, 1960–1961
Correspondence of the Vice President Elect Relating to
    Inaugural Festivities, 1960–1961
Case Files, 1961–1963
VP Travel (LBJA)
Vice Presidential Security File (Security Classified)

D. Lyndon Baines Johnson Archives, 1931–1968
The "LBJA Files" were created about 1958 to maintain items considered historically valuable and Johnson's correspondence with associates and national figures. The files are in four parts: LBJA Congressional File, LBJA Famous Names, LBJA Selected Names File, and LBJA Subject File.

E. White House Famous Names, 1937–1969
White House Famous Names includes Johnson correspondence with former presidents and their families, Hubert H. Humphrey, and others.
(For additional Prepresidential materials, see the files of Mildred Stegall, Willie Day Taylor, and Dorothy Territo.)

III. Presidential Papers, 1963–1969

A. White House Central Files (WHCF)
Central Files is a permanent White House Office. During the Johnson administration most nonclassified correspondence and memoranda were sent to Central Files, since President Johnson did not maintain a separate office file. WHCF consists of the following series:

1. *Subject Files:* contain memoranda, correspondence, and reports filed under sixty major subject headings. The subject files were maintained in two categories: "Executive" and "General." Executive material consists of correspondence, memoranda, and other papers of particular importance because of their source or nature. General material is that received from the public or handled at a lower level of government.

Agriculture	AG	Meetings-Conferences	MC
Arts	AR	Messages	ME
Atomic Energy	AT	National Security—Defense	ND
Business-Economics	BE	Natural Resources	NR
Civil Aviation	CA	Outer Space	OS
Commodities	CM	Parks-Monuments	PA
Countries	CO	Peace	PC
Disasters	DI	Personnel Management	PE
Education	ED	Political Affairs	PL
Federal Aid	FA	Postal Service	PO
Federal Government	FE	President	PP
Federal Government—		Procurement-Disposal	PQ
Organizations	FG	Public Relations	PR
Finance	FI	Publications	PU
Foreign Affairs	FO	Real Property	RA
Gifts	GI	Recreation-Sports	RE
Health	HE	Religious Matters	RM
Highways-Bridges	HI	Reports-Statistics	RS
Holidays	HO	Safety—Accident Prevention	SA
Housing	HS	Science	SC
Human Rights	HU	Social Affairs	SO
Immigration-Naturalization	IM	Speeches	SP
Indian Affairs	IN	States-Territories	ST
Insurance	IS	Tariffs	TA
International Organizations	IT	Transportation	TN
Invitations	IV	Trips	TR
Judicial—Legal Matters	JL	Utilities	UT
Labor Management		Veterans Affairs	VA
Relations	LA	Welfare	WE
Legislation	LE	White House	
Local Governments	LG	Administration	WH
Medals-Awards	MA		

2. *Name File:* serves as a name index to the Subject File. It includes copies of correspondence and memoranda, cross-reference sheets, copies of referrals of correspondence to federal agencies, and incoming correspondence not filed in the Subject File.

3. *Chronological File:* copies of letters signed by the President.

4. *Confidential File:* security classified or otherwise sensitive materials arranged in a subject, name, and agency file. (C.F.)

5. *Oversize Attachments:* individual items or files too large or bulky for a letter-size filing cabinet. Cross-references to these items are found in the WHCF and C.F. Name and Subject Files.

6. *Storage Files—White House Offices:*
   Records from the White House Telegraph Office: a chronological file of all telegrams sent to or received from the White House.
   Records from the White House Telephone Office: records of telephone calls made or received in the White House and kept by White House Operators. (Closed)
   Records from the White House Press Office: transcripts of presidential press conferences, the press secretary's news conferences; news conferences and briefings with the cabinet, military, and others; as well as briefings with the President and working papers of the press office.
   Records of the White House Gift Unit: lists and descriptions of all gifts received by the President and his family. (Closed)
   Records from the White House Records Office: reports to the President on enrolled legislation.
   Records from the White House Personnel Office: card files, personnel folders, applications, and other personnel-related records apparently turned over to Central Files for storage, 1961–1965. (Closed)
   Records from the White House Tour Office: requests for special tours, 1965–1967.

7. *Storage Files—White House Aides:* Presidential assistants kept working files in their offices. When no longer required these files were sent to Central Files. Folder title lists were used as cross-references in the Subject File. In

the case of a few aides, files were transferred to the library both from WHCF storage and the aides' offices. Had time permitted the latter material probably would have been sent to Central Files. The files of certain aides were rarely transferred to Central Files; these members of the White House staff are designated by asterisks.

* Ceil Bellinger, 1966–1969   (Research Assistant/ Speechwriter)

Peter B. Benchley, 1967–1968
Fred Bohen, 1966–1968
Horace Busby, 1963–1968
Joseph A. Califano, 1963–1969
Clifton C. Carter, 1963–1964
S. Douglass Cater, 1963–1968
George Christian, 1966–1968
Ervin Duggan, 1964–1969
Ralph A. Dungan, 1963–1964
* James Gaither, 1963–1969   (Staff Assistant/ Task Forces and LE)

E. Ernest Goldstein, 1967–1968
Richard N. Goodwin, 1961–1965
Robert L. Hardesty, 1967–1968
Brooks Hays, 1965–1966
Charles A. Horsky, 1963–1967
Hubert H. Humphrey, 1967
Walter W. Jenkins, 1963–1964
James Robert (Jim) Jones, 1966–1969
Robert E. Kintner, 1966–1967
Larry Levinson, 1966–1969
Frank M. McDermott, 1964
Harry C. McPherson, 1965–1969
* John Macy, 1961–1969   (Chairman, Civil Service Comm.)

Charles Maguire, 1965–1968
Mike Manatos, 1961–1968
Dean Markham, 1963, 1965
Harry J. Middleton, 1967–1969
Bill Moyers, 1960–1966
Charles Murphy, 1968
Richard Nelson, 1964
Matthew Nimetz, 1966–1968

Lawrence F. O'Brien, 1961–1968
Kenneth O'Donnell, 1961–1964
* Frederick Panzer, 1963–1968   (Staff Assistant for
                                             Reference Files)
DeVier Pierson, 1967–1969
Paul M. Popple, 1964–1966
George E. Reedy, 1962–1964
Juanita Roberts, 1967
John E. Robson and Stanford G. Ross, 1966–1968
                                             (Pricing Files)
Charles Roche, 1965–1968
Pierre Salinger, 1963–1964
Milton Semer, 1961–1966
Whitney Shoemaker, 1967
Ivan Sinclair, 1964–1965
William R. Sparks, 1966–1968
Irvine R. Sprague, 1966–1968
* Mildred Stegall, 1950–1975   (Staff Assistant)
* Willie Day Taylor, 1941–1969   (Staff Assistant)
Larry Temple, 1968–1969
* Dorothy P. Territo, 1959–1976   (Staff Assistant)
Bruce Thomas, 1963–1968
W. Marvin Watson, 1966–1968
Ben Wattenberg, 1966–1969
Lee C. White, 1963–1966
Henry H. Wilson, Jr., 1963–1967

8. *Storage Files—Miscellaneous:* public opinion mail; Congressional Records seen by the President; Congressional Favors File, 1961–1968; Democratic National Committee press releases; statistical mail summaries, Department of State transmittals; files from the Task Force on Education of Gifted Persons; material from the 1964 campaign; clippings and nongovernment press releases.

B. National Security File
The National Security File was the working file of President Johnson and his two successive special assistants for national security affairs, McGeorge Bundy and Walt W. Rostow. The file is arranged in several series. A portion of the documents were originated by Bundy or Rostow and their staffs, but most of the documents originated in the various executive departments and agencies, especially those having to do with foreign affairs and national defense, such as the State

Department, the Defense Department, and the Central Intelligence Agency. Most of the documents are therefore classified. Access to them requires declassification under the procedures of Executive Order 12065.

1. Country File
2. Head of State Correspondence File
3. International Meetings and Travel File
4. Speech File
5. Situation Room File
6. Subject File
7. Agency File
8. Committee File
9. Name File
10. Intelligence File
11. National Security Council File
12. Aides Files
13. National Security Council Histories

C. Diaries and Appointment Logs of Lyndon B. Johnson
The logs contain the following series: Desk Diaries, 1947–1963 (incomplete); Daily Diary sheets prepared by his secretaries, January 1, 1959–May 3, 1970; appointment log notebooks, November 22, 1963–January 19, 1965; diary index cards alphabetically arranged and keyed to the Daily Diary sheets, November 22, 1963–January 20, 1969; and a Diary backup file of schedules, correspondence, and memoranda for each day's appointments, 1962–January, 1973.

D. Statements of Lyndon B. Johnson
Chronologically arranged file of addresses, remarks, and speeches of Lyndon B. Johnson throughout his career, 1927–1972. Includes his early published writings as student editor of his college newspaper.

E. Administrative Histories
Agency-prepared narratives of their activities during the Johnson administration.

F. Scrapbooks
Oversize volumes of clippings from major eastern dailies, chronologically arranged, 1963–1969.

G. White House Social Files (not available)
1. Alphabetical File
2. Storage File

  3. Liz Carpenter's Subject Files
  4. Bess Abell's Subject Files
  5. Social Entertainment Office
  6. Beautification Files
H. Special Files
  1. Legislative Background
  2. Files Pertaining to Abe Fortas and Homer Thornberry, 1955–1968
  3. Reports on Pending Legislation
  4. Task Force Reports and Task Force Summaries
  5. Condolence Mail
  6. Cabinet Meetings
  7. Special File on the Assassination of John F. Kennedy
  8. Facsimile Copies of Public Laws

IV. Postpresidential Papers, 1969–1973 (not available)
A. Postpresidential Files
  1. Name File
  2. Subject File
  3. Chronological File
  4. Storage File
B. Correspondence and Files Sections
C. Willie Day Taylor Files
D. Files from Ranch Office

Manuscripts and Archives: Collections of Personal and Organizational Papers

I. Collections of Personal and Organizational Papers
The Johnson Library's efforts to acquire personal papers of friends and associates of Lyndon Johnson began while President Johnson was in office; it is now a continuous program. Most of the personal papers in the library have not been processed and are not available for research. Some of these papers are on deposit at the library. (Donors of books have been omitted from the list.)

Mrs. Bess Abell
Gardner Ackley
Dorothy Plyler Palmie Alford
Robert Allnutt
Harry R. Anderson
David W. Angevine

Robert N. Anthony
Miss Grace Arledge
Brent Ashabranner
Dr. Kenneth H. Ashworth
Charles F. Baird
John A. Baker

Arthur Barber
Delbert Barney
Joseph W. Barr
Fraser Barron
Joe Bastien
Gerold F. Baumann
Leo C. Beebe
Frederick C. Belen
B. A. Bennett, Sr.
Sgt. and Mrs. B. J. Bennett
William Berger
Beatrice Berler
W. Sherman Birdwell, Jr.
William M. Blackburn
Mrs. Billie Blackstock
Joseph L. Block
Mrs. Paul Bolton
Bernard L. Boutin
Charles A. Bowsher
Alan S. Boyd
Walter E. Boyd
Dolph Briscoe
Robert A. Brooks
Harold Brown
Philip N. Brownstein
McGeorge Bundy
John E. Byrne
Dr. James C. Cain
Stanley A. Cain
William J. Campbell
Edward M. Cape
Mrs. E. M. Cape
William D. Carey
Elizabeth S. Carpenter
Leslie Carpenter
Warren Christopher
Ramsey Clark
Mrs. Wallace Clarke
Cyril Clemens
Clark Clifford
James L. Cochrane
John D. Cofer

Wilbur Cohen
Richard W. Conklin
Mrs. Ellen Taylor Cooper
Alfred H. Corbett
Mrs. Pauline W. Cordell
Dean W. Coston
Howard R. Cottam
Mike Cox
Dave W. Crenshaw
Thomas E. Cronin
Robert K. Crook
John H. Crooker, Jr.
Brig. General James U. Cross
Dr. George Curtis
Ross D. Davis
Willard Deason
Paul G. Dembling
Democratic National
    Committee
Thomas R. Donahue
Jean Dugat
H. G. Dulaney
Richard F. Dungar
Virginia F. Durr
India Edwards
Newton W. Edwards
Winant S. Ellmore
Alain C. Enthoven
Luther H. Evans
George J. Feldman
Alfred B. Fitt
Alexander H. Flax
Robert J. Fleming, Jr.
Mr. and Mrs. Sam Fore, Jr.
Henry H. Fowler
Harry W. Frantz
Frankie M. Freeman
Orville L. Freeman
Mrs. Gordon Fulcher
Helen Fuller
Francis J. Galbraith
John Gardner

Ralph W. Gardner
James J. Gehrig
E. Ernest Goldstein
Lee John Govatos
Katharine Graham
Ms. Mary Green
Samuel W. Halperin
D. B. Hardeman
Mary Hardesty (Mrs. Robert)
Bertrand M. Harding
Louis Harris and Associates
John S. Hayes
Kathryn G. Heath
W. W. Heath
General Lewis B. Hershey
Luther H. Hodges
Luther Holcomb
John Holton
Kenneth Holum
Roy Hoopes
Welly K. Hopkins
Donald F. Hornig
Mr. and Mrs. J. N. Houck
Harold Howe, II
James O. Hubbard
Everett Hutchison
Robert M. Jackson
Harold Jenks
Lyndon B. Johnson Memorial
    Grove
Rebekah Baines Johnson
U. Alexis Johnson
Billy Mac Jones
John Wesley Jones
Luther E. Jones, Jr.
William J. Jorden
Kansas City Star
Ted Kaufman
Carroll Keach
Val M. Keating
Konrad Kelley
Larry Kellogg

James F. Kelly
Master Sgt. O. H. Kennedy
Robert W. Komer
Eugene B. Konecci
Marcia E. Krafsur
Leo M. Langlois
Gene Latimer
Charles Lee
John Lehman
Gould Lincoln
Clarence B. Lindquist
Charles P. Little
Henry Cabot Lodge
Marcus L. Loftis
Mrs. Bob (Betty) Long
Lower Colorado River
    Authority (LCRA)
Diana T. MacArthur
George C. McGhee
William Hunter McLean
William M. McMillan
Robert S. McNamara
John W. (Jack) McNulty
Harry C. McPherson, Jr.
Lawrence C. McQuade
Roy L. McWilliams
Mrs. John C. Mackey
John W. Macy, Jr.
Leonard H. Marks
Leonard Marks, Jr.
Charles E. Marsh
Mrs. George Marshall (Cecille
    Harrison)
W. Wortham Maxwell
Mike Minor
Mrs. A. P. Mitchell
Booth Mooney
J. Cordell Moore
George A. Morgan
Richard J. Murphy
A. F. Nahas
Dorothy Nichols

Ralph W. Nicholson
Thomas H. Nielson
L. A. Nixon
Walter D. Noelke
Don Oberdorfer
Will Odom
Frank Ogden
Tony Ojeda
Arthur M. Okun
Covey T. Oliver
John L. O'Marra
Cora M. Oneal (Mrs. Ben G.)
Gary Orfield
Leo S. Packer
Dorothy Palmie (see Alford)
Fred Panzer
Mollie Parnis
Loyd Parton
Wright Patman
Bradley Patterson
James Cato Pattillo
Drew Pearson
J. W. Pearson
Ann Cooper Penning
Robert Perrin
Arthur C. Perry
W. M. Peterson
Edward J. Pfeiffer
Robert L. Phinney
J. J. (Jake) Pickle
Clarence S. Pittard
Rutherford M. Poats
Paul Porter
Daniel J. Quill
Laura Ramsay
Paul J. Randolph
Harry H. Ransom
Mary Rather
Edward D. Re
Douglas D. Richards
Gary Boyd Roberts
Ray Roberts

John P. Roche
Franklin D. Roosevelt Library
Walt W. Rostow
C. Fenner Roth
William M. Roth
James J. Rowley
Dean Rusk
Robert J. Ryan
Lee Salzberger
Harold Barefoot Sanders, Jr.
Steven Scher
Mrs. A. W. Schlesinger
M. B. Schnapper
Ruth Schumm
Robert C. Seamans, Jr.
Ann T. Shalicky
Louis E. Shecter
Ted Shiftlett
Sargent Shriver
Donald F. Simpson
Kurt Singer
Byron Skelton
Elliott P. Skinner
Hazel Smith (Mrs. R. O.)
Hugh H. Smythe
Anthony M. Solomon
Southwestern Meat Packers
    Association
Southwest Texas State
    University (SWTSU)
William R. Sparks
Stephen J. Spingarn
Mrs. Ed Stallman
Max Starcke
John Lawrence Steele
William H. Stewart
William H. Sullivan
Marshall E. Surratt
Sutton Family
Helen Tackett
T. J. Taylor, III
Winston Taylor

Edward A. Tenenbaum
Texas State Democratic
    Committee
Mrs. Lucile P. Thomas
Norman C. Thomas
Paul J. Tierney
S. F. Tillman
Walter Torbriner
Edmunds Travis
General Arthur G. Trudeau
Ray Tucker
Donald F. Turner
Joe W. Tyson
University of Texas at Austin
Mrs. Lester H. Wand
W. Marvin Watson

Ben Wattenberg
James E. Webb
Edward C. Welsh
Mrs. Robert L. White
Franklin H. Williams
Lee Wilson
Melvin Winters
Alvin J. Wirtz
Robert C. Wood
Sam Wood
Warren Woodward
Mrs. Ewell Woodyard (Nettie
    Mason Pattillo)
Eugene Worley
Nannie Young
Mrs. William A. Zachry

Manuscripts and Archives: Records from Government Agencies

The Johnson Library is the official repository for the records of its own operation; for a small body of Department of Treasury records; and for the records of seventeen temporary federal commissions, committees, and conferences which met partially or entirely during Lyndon Johnson's presidency. The library also holds copies of selected records from government agencies covering mainly the period of Lyndon Johnson's presidency and vice-presidency. Most of these records are on microfilm, but also included are photocopies on paper, carbon copies, and printed materials. The majority of the agency records are open for research, but some are security classified and some commission records have not yet been processed.

I. Original Agency Records

Commission on Marine Science, Engineering, and Resources, 1967–1969

Commission on Obscenity and Pornography, 1968–1970

Department of State, U.S.-Mexico Commission for Border Development and Friendship, 1967–1968

Department of the Treasury, United States Secret Service, 1963–1969

General Services Administration, Lyndon Baines Johnson Library, 1969–1975

National Advisory Commission on Civil Disorders, including

the President's National Advisory Panel on Insurance in
Riot-Affected Areas, 1967–1968
National Advisory Commission on Food and Fiber, 1965–1967
National Advisory Commission on Libraries, 1966–1968
National Advisory Commission on Rural Poverty, 1966–1967
National Commission on the Causes and Prevention of
Violence, 1968–1969
President's Advisory Committee on Supersonic Transport,
1964–1968
President's Commission on Heart Disease, Cancer, and Stroke,
1964–1965
President's Commission on Law Enforcement and the
Administration of Justice, 1965–1967
President's Committee on Consumer Interests; Consumer
Advisory Council, 1962–1969
President's Committee on Equal Opportunity in Housing,
1962–1968
President's Committee on Traffic Safety, 1954–1967
President's Committee on Urban Housing, 1967–1968
Temporary Alaska Claims Commission, 1960–1964
White House Conference "To Fulfill These Rights," 1965–1966

II. Copies of Agency Records

Bureau of the Budget, 1963–1969
Central Intelligence Agency, 1963–1969
Civil Aeronautics Board, 1963–1968
Commission of Fine Arts, 1910–1967
Council of Economic Advisors, 1961–1968
Department of Agriculture, 1961–1968
Department of Commerce, 1963–1968
Department of Defense, 1963–1969
Department of Health, Education, and Welfare, 1962–1969
Department of Housing and Urban Development, 1963–1968
Department of the Interior, 1963–1969
Department of Justice, 1961–1968
Department of Labor, 1962–1968
Department of State, 1946–1969
Department of Transportation, 1953–1969
Department of the Treasury, 1962–1969
Federal Power Commission, 1963–1968
Federal Trade Commission, 1964–1968
General Services Administration, 1961–1968

National Aeronautics and Space Administration, 1961–1968
National Aeronautics and Space Council, 1961–1968
National Council for Marine Resources and Engineering
    Development, 1966–1969
National Foundation on the Arts and Humanities, 1965–1968
National Science Foundation, 1963–1968
National Youth Administration, 1935–1937
Office of Economic Opportunity, 1964–1968
Office of Emergency Planning, 1951–1968
Office of Science and Technology, 1957–1968
Post Office Department, 1963–1968
President's Committee on Consumer Interests; Consumer
    Advisory Council, 1963–1969
Small Business Administration, 1960–1968
Smithsonian Institution, 1961–1968
Tennessee Valley Authority, 1963–1968
United States Arms Control and Disarmament Agency,
    1964–1968
United States Information Agency, 1956–1968
Veterans Administration, 1963–1968

Audiovisual Materials

I. Motion Pictures

Films Produced by Government Departments and Agencies
Films from Television Networks
Films from the Democratic National Committee
Films from Foreign Governments
Films from Columnist Drew Pearson
Films Given to President Johnson and to the Library by Diverse
    Individuals and Organizations
Films Produced by or Commissioned for the Library

II. Sound Recording Tapes

Addresses and Remarks of President Johnson
Selected Speeches and Remarks of Lyndon B. Johnson,
    1936–1963
Selected Speeches and Remarks by Mrs. Lyndon B. Johnson,
    1964–1969
Selected Speeches and Remarks by Lyndon B. Johnson,
    1969–1973, and Mrs. Johnson, 1969–
Administration Tapes, 1965–1968

Congressional Briefings, 1965–1968
Addresses and Remarks of President Kennedy,
    1/20/61–11/22/63
Government Departments, Agencies, and Commissions
Tapes Received from the Democratic National Committee and
    Related Organizations

III. Videotape Recordings

WHCA One-inch Series
LBJ Library Series

IV. Still Pictures

The Johnson Library has three major collections of still
pictures and nine smaller collections.

Prepresidential Collection, 1908–1963
Presidential Collection, 1963–1969
Postpresidential Collection, 1969–

Abbie Rowe Collection, 1963–1968
Art Kowert Collection, 1952–1963
Austin *American-Statesman* Collection, 1937–1953
Autographed Print Collection, 1933–1969
Frank Muto Collection, 1957–1965
Harry Ransom Collection, 1948–1966
International Association of Machinists and Aerospace
    Workers Collection, 1948–1972
Johnson City Collection, 1875–1951
Johnson Family Collection, ca. 1870–1969

Oral History Collection

The oral history collection at the Johnson Library contains interviews with over eight hundred people. Since many of these individuals were interviewed more than once, the number of transcripts
exceeds twelve hundred. Researchers may obtain a list of the interviewees and information about the availability of transcripts from
the library.

Index

Meier, August, 125 n. 75
Memphis, Tenn., 106
Meranto, Philip, 160, 174
Mexico, 63–64, 68, 78
Mexico City, 83
Miller, Merle, 3
Miller, Paul, 181 n. 45
Mills, Wilbur, 181 n. 38
Miroff, Bruce, 94, 111
Mississippi: civil rights unrest in, 102; hunger among blacks in, 140
Mitchell, Clarence, 95, 104
Model Cities Program, 146 n. 4
Montgomery, Ala., 103
Mooney, Booth, 4, 6, 15
Morey, Roy, 160–161, 174–175
Morrill Acts (1862, 1890), 155
Morse, Wayne, 30, 161–162, 181 n. 38
Mosher, Edith Kern, 160–161, 167, 171, 174–175
Moyers, Bill, 10, 183 n. 55; and civil rights, 117; and credibility gap, 193, 209 n. 28, 231; and education, 162; and Latin America, 66, 83; as member of White House staff, 189–190, 192–195, 198–199, 209–212 passim; and task forces, 158, 164–165, 178 n. 18; and War on Poverty, 136, 139
Moyers, James, 211 n. 45
Moynihan, Daniel Patrick, 134–135, 137, 149 n. 27
Moynihan Report, 110, 123 n. 60
Moynihan Report and the Politics of Controversy, The, 110–111
Murrow, Edward R., 224
My Brother Lyndon, 9–10

National Association for the Advancement of Colored People (NAACP), 107–108
National Council of Churches, 163
National Defense Education Act (NDEA), 156
National Science Foundation Act (1950), 156
National Urban Coalition, 171

National Welfare Rights Organization, 152 n. 53
National Youth Administration: LBJ and, 96, 224 (Fig. 10), 228
Nennen, Henry, 192
Newark, N.J., 107
New Deal, 4, 17, 20, 128, 132, 224 (Fig. 10)
New Frontier, 98, 128
New Hampshire Primary (1968), 201, 203–205
Nimetz, Matthew, 164, 169–170
Nixon, Richard M., 4, 134; and education, 168; and election of 1968, 199, 206–207; and OEO, 138, 143; and television, 238; and Vietnam War, 29, 35; and White House taping, 235
No Hail, No Farewell, 15
North Vietnam: and peace negotiations, 47–48, 53; and Tet offensive, 49–51, 53, 233; and Vietnam War, 27–28, 35–36, 38; and will to win, 43, 46, 48. See also South Vietnam; Tet offensive; Vietcong; Vietnam War
Northwest Ordinance (1787), 155
Novak, Robert, 12–13, 120 n. 23, 131, 200

OAS, 67–69, 73, 78, 84
Oberdorfer, Don, 52
O'Brien, Lawrence, 169, 200, 202–203, 211 n. 45
O'Donnell, Kenneth, 190, 201
Office of Economic Opportunity (OEO), 127, 131; criticism of, 136–137; as coordinator of War on Poverty, 137–140; and ghetto riots, 151 n. 49; and negative income tax, 143. See also Community Action Program; Great Society; War on Poverty
Office of Education, 167, 170–171, 180 n. 29, 181 n. 48. See also Education; Education legislation
Oliver, Covey, 64, 66, 83
Onganía, Juan Carlos, 78–79